Thomas Dick

The Philosophy of a future State

Thomas Dick

The Philosophy of a future State

ISBN/EAN: 9783743336278

Manufactured in Europe, USA, Canada, Australia, Japa

Cover: Foto ©Thomas Meinert / pixelio.de

Manufactured and distributed by brebook publishing software (www.brebook.com)

Thomas Dick

The Philosophy of a future State

Collins's Select Library.

THE
PHILOSOPHY
OF A
FUTURE STATE.

BY

THOMAS DICK, LL.D.

AUTHOR OF "THE CHRISTIAN PHILOSOPHER," "THE PHILOSOPHY OF RELIGION,"
"DIFFUSION OF KNOWLEDGE," "MORAL IMPROVEMENT,"
"CELESTIAL SCENERY," ETC.

NEW EDITION.

GLASGOW AND LONDON:
WILLIAM COLLINS, SONS, & COMPANY.
1869.

TO

THOMAS CHALMERS, D.D. AND LL.D.

Sir,

In Dedicating to you this Volume, which has for its object to exhibit a popular view of the Philosophy of a Future State, as deduced from the light of science and revelation,—a consideration of a far higher nature than the formal and customary honour of addressing a man of literary and scientific attainments induced me to shelter it under your patronage.

In the several vocations in which Providence has called you to officiate, you have proved yourself the warm and disinterested patron of all that is benevolent and good, of every thing that concerns the present and eternal welfare of mankind: and your praises have been re-echoed from one corner of the land to another as the champion of the Christian religion, the doctrines of which, your voice and your pen have done so much to illustrate.

Your writings furnish ample testimony to the world of your earnest, active, and unwearied solicitude for the moral and religious improvement of mankind; a solicitude which is not abated by any minor differences of opinion in those with whom you co-operate, where the great object is, to diffuse knowledge and happiness over the face of the earth.

Your kind indulgence to me, on the slight acquaintance I have of you personally, and your approbation of some of my labours, in endeavouring to connect Science with Religion, induced me to hope, that, if the views taken of the present subject in any measure correspond with your own, you will countenance my humble attempts to dispel the prejudices which many well-meaning Christians may entertain, as to the beneficial tendency of exhibiting the sciences of a *present*, as applicable to the circumstances and relations of a *future* world.

That you may long be spared as the advocate of vital Christianity, as a blessing and an ornament to your country, and as a zealous instructor of those who are destined to promote its best interests; and that you may enjoy, without interruption, the pleasures arising from a consciousness of the esteem and approbation of the wise and the pious, is the sincere prayer of,

SIR,

Your much obliged,

and humble Servant,

THOMAS DICK.

Broughty Ferry, near Dundee,
Dec. 28, 1827.

PREFACE.

THE reasonings and illustrations contained in the following pages, are intended to direct the intelligent Christian in some of those trains of thought which he ought to prosecute, when looking forward to the scene of his future destination. The Author was induced to engage in the discussion of this subject from a consideration, that many vague and erroneous conceptions are still entertained among Christians in regard to the nature of heavenly felicity and the employments of the future world. In elucidating the train of thought which is here prosecuted, he has brought forward, without hesitation, the discoveries of modern science, particularly those which relate to the scenery of the heavens; convinced, that all the manifestations of himself which the Creator has permitted us to contemplate, are intended to throw light on the plan of his moral government in relation both to our present and our future destiny. He has carefully avoided every thing that might appear like vague or extravagant conjecture; and he trusts, that the opinions he has broached, and the conclusions he has deduced, will generally be found accordant with the analogies of Nature and the dictates of Revelation. He is aware, that he has many prejudices to encounter, arising from the vague and indefinite manner in which such subjects have been hitherto treated, and from the want of those expansive views of the Divine operations which the professors of Christianity should endeavour to attain; but he feels confident, that those who are best qualified to appreciate his sentiments, will treat with candour an attempt to elucidate a subject hitherto overlooked, and in which every individual of the human race is deeply interested.

It was originally intended to publish what is contained in Parts II and III without any dissertation on the evidences of a future state as deduced from the light of nature, taking the immortality of man for granted on the authority of Revelation. But, on second thought, it was judged expedient, for the sake of general readers, to exhibit a condensed view of those arguments which even the light of reason can produce in favour of the immortality of man.

In this department of the volume, the Author has brought forward several arguments, which he is not aware have been taken notice of by ethical writers, when treating on this subject. He has endeavoured to illustrate these and the other arguments here adduced, in minute detail, and in a popular manner, so as to be level to the comprehension of every reader; and he trusts, that the force of the whole combined will be found to amount to as high a degree of moral demonstration as can be expected in relation to objects which are not cognizable by the eye of sense.

The greater portion of what is contained in Part III having been written a number of years ago, several *apparent* repetitions of facts alluded to in the preceding Parts, may perhaps be noticed by the critical reader; but, in general, it will be found, that, where the same facts are repeated, they are either exhibited in a new aspect, or brought forward to elucidate another subject.

The practical reflections and remarks embodied in the last Part of this Work, will not, the Author is persuaded, be considered by any of his readers, as either **unnecessary**, or inappropriate to the subjects treated of in the preceding Parts of this volume. It is of the utmost importance that every individual be convinced, that he cannot be supposed a candidate for a blessed immortality, unless the train of his affections, and the general tenor of his conduct, in some measure correspond to the tempers and dispositions, and the moral purity, which prevail in the heavenly state.

The favourable reception which the public have given to the volumes he has formerly published, induces the Author to indulge the hope, that the present volume may not be altogether unworthy of their attention. That it may tend to convince the sceptical of the reality of an immortal existence; to expand the believer's conceptions of the attributes of the Divinity, and of the glory of " that inheritance which is reserved in heaven" for the faithful; and to excite in the mind of every reader, an ardent desire to cultivate those dispositions and virtues which will prepare him for the enjoyment of celestial bliss, is the Author's most sincere and ardent wish, as it was the great object he had in view when engaged in its composition.

CONTENTS

PART I.

INTRODUCTION.—Importance of the question which relates to the **reality** of a future world: folly of the indifference which prevails in relation to this point, 13—17.

CHAPTER I.

PROOFS OF A FUTURE STATE FROM THE LIGHT OF NATURE.

SECT. I.—*On the universal belief which the doctrine of Immortality has obtained in all ages*, 19.

Opinions of the Greeks, Romans, Egyptians, Scythians, etc. Doctrines of Zoroaster, 19. Of Socrates, 20. Allusions of the ancient Poets, 21. Opinions of the inhabitants of the *Society* and the *Friendly Islands*, of the *New Zealanders*, the *Samoiedians*, the *Kalmuc Tartars*, the *Birmans*, the *Japanese*, the *Africans*, the *American Indians*, etc. 22—24. Force of the argument in favour of Immortality derived from these opinions, 24—27.

SECT. II.—*On the desire of future existence implanted in the human mind*, 28.

This fact illustrated by various examples, 28. Desire of posthumous fame, 30. Desire of immortality most ardent in cultivated minds, 31. Force of the argument derived from these facts, 32. Fears and apprehensions in regard to futurity, 33. Doctrine of immortality renders the Creator's conduct consistent with itself, 34.

SECT. III.—*On the intellectual faculties of man, and the strong desire of knowledge implanted in the human mind*, 35.

Desire of knowledge natural to every rational being, 35. Reasons why it is not more ardent, 36—38. Sublimity and energy of the intellectual faculties, 41. *Memory*, its **utility, 42, 43. Instances** of the improvement of which it is susceptible, 43. Argument in favour of **a future state** founded on these considerations, 44—46.

Sect. IV.—*On the perpetual progress of the mind towards perfection*, 47.

No limits to the excursions of the intellect, 47. Extract from Addison, 47.

Sect. V.—*On the unlimited range of view which is opened to the human faculties throughout the immensity of space and of duration*, 50.

Immensity of the universe, 51. Intention of the Deity in directing the human mind in the path **of** discovery, 52. Desires excited by the boundless views **which the** universe unfolds, 52. Inquiries **suggested** respecting other **worlds**, 52, 53. Man endowed **with capacities for acquir**ing an indefinite extent of knowledge respecting the wonders of creation, 54. Limited nature of his present knowledge, **55.** Universe intended to display the Divine perfections, and to afford gratification to intellec**tual** beings, 56. The desires of the human soul will not be disappointed, **57.** Conclusion from these premises, 58.

Sect. VI.—*On the moral powers of man*, 59.

Sublimity of these powers exemplified: Regulus, Phocion, Cyrus, **Sci**pio, *Aristides*, 60. *Paul, Howard*, Sharpe, etc., 61—63. Argument founded on the moral faculties, 63. A system of benevolence going **on** throughout the universe, in **the** agency of intelligent beings, 65, **66.** Summary of **the** arguments derived **from** the moral and intellectual powers, 67—69.

Sect. VII.—*On the apprehensions and forebodings* **of the** *mind, when under the influence of remorse*, 69.

Examples of remorse: Belshazzar, Tiberius, Antiochus, Charles IX, Richard III, Bessus, Hobbes, etc., 70—74. Conclusion deduced from such facts, 75.

Sect. VIII.—*On the disordered state of* **the** *moral world, when contrasted with the regular and systematic order of* **the** *material*, 75.

Harmony and order of nature; in the heavens; the earth; **the** animal system, etc., 75—77. Disorders in the moral world; Ravages of Alexander, Alaric, **Tamerlane**, Jenghiz Khan, etc., 78, 79—of the Goths, Vandals, Huns, etc., 79. Scenes of carnage and devastation, 79, 80. Present state of the moral and political world, in Asia, Africa, Europe, and America, 81. Argument founded on these disorders, 85.

SECT. IX.—*On the unequal distribution of rewards and punishments in the present state,* **87.**

Examples of unequal distribution of rewards, etc. 88. The Waldenses, **French** Protestants, in the reign of Louis XIV, persecutions in England and Netherlands, Irish Massacre, Ali Pacha, etc., 89, 90. Force of the argument derived from this source, 91—93. Moral perceptions implanted in man, 94.

SECT. X.—*On the absurdity of supposing that the thinking principle in man will ever be annihilated.* 95.

Changes in the material system, but no instance of **annihilation**, 95. Transformation of insects, 96. **Considerations which prove the duration** of *mind*, 97. Conclusions from this subject, 99

SECT. XI.—*On the gloomy considerations and absurd consequences involved in the denial of a future state,* 100.

The denial of a future state **involves in** impenetrable mystery the nature of **man** and the end **of his** existence; the scenes of **nature**; the moral government of God; the sufferings to which man **is subjected**; the attributes of the Creator; and damps the mind **in its researches after** truth, 100—107. Argument for a future state **founded on such** considerations, 109, 110.

Summary of arguments, 110. Their force when **combined, 110.** Principles of Atheism do not necessarily exclude **the** possibility **of a future** state, 111. Impression which the arguments **adduced** ought to make **on** every mind, 112, 113. Why the Author has set aside **the** argument founded on the *immateriality* of the soul, 114—116.

CHAPTER II.

PROOFS OF A FUTURE STATE FROM DIVINE REVELATION.

A future state revealed to the Jews, 118—120. Why it is not more frequently adverted to in the Old Testament, 121. Proofs from the writings of the New Testament, 121—124. Resurrection: qualities of the resurrection body, 125.

On the practical influence which the doctrine of a future state ought to have upon our affections and conduct, 126—133.

PART II.

ON THE CONNECTION OF SCIENCE WITH A FUTURE STATE.

Prejudices which exist in relation to this subject, 134—136. *Object of scientific investigation*, 137. Objects on which the faculties of celestial intelligences will be employed, 140. Inquiry into the *extent* of the general conflagration, 141. Explanation of Scriptural allusions to this subject, 142—146. Permanency and perpetuity of the material universe, 146. Figments of poets in regard to this subject, 148. Predicted changes in the system of Nature, 149—153. General relations of the universe, 154.

Sciences which will be prosecuted in a future state, 155. *Arithmetic*, its objects: utility of numbers and their combinations: illustrations from Scripture, 158, 159. *Mathematical* sciences, their utility: angels recognise the principles of these sciences: the Creator has laid the foundation of these sciences in his works, 160—162. *Astronomy*, its objects: presents an immense field of contemplation, 163. The heavens constitute the principal part of the Divine empire: illustrations from Scripture, 165. Limited extent of our present knowledge on this subject, 166. Communications of superior beings in relation to the universe, 167. This subject can never be exhausted, 168. *Natural Philosophy*, its objects and discoveries, 169: unvails the Divine attributes, 171. Abundant *scope* for its prosecution in the future world, 172. Chemistry, 174. *Anatomy and Physiology*, their objects: wonders of the human frame: resurrection body, etc., 174—176. *History*: contains a record of the ways of Providence: our ignorance of many important facts in history: history of angels and other intelligences, 177—179. Connection of the different branches of science, 180.

Locality of heaven, 180. Different opinions which may be formed on this point, 181. Sciences applicable in every supposed case, 182. Arts and sciences which will *not* be cultivated, 183. Intellectual energy of the inhabitants of heaven, 184. Sublimity of the mental powers in several human beings: Pascal, Martianus Capella, Crichton, Gassendi, Horrox, Grotius, Newton, Baratier, 184—186. Our knowledge in heaven will not be diminished, 187. Distinctions, in point of knowledge, among the inhabitants of heaven, "degrees of glory," 188. General remarks, 191. Objection obviated, 193.

PART III.

ON THE AIDS WHICH THE DISCOVERIES OF SCIENCE AFFORD FOR ENABLING US TO FORM A CONCEPTION OF THE PERPETUAL IMPROVEMENT OF THE CELESTIAL INHABITANTS IN KNOWLEDGE AND FELICITY.

Vague and distorted conceptions in regard to the employments of heaven, 195. Whether the subject of human redemption will occupy the whole attention of redeemed men, 197. Its mysteries: analysis of its leading facts, 197—199. Glorified humanity of Christ, 200. Objects of contemplation in heaven, 202. Planetary and starry systems, 202—205. Number of worlds in the *visible* universe, 206. **Analysis of the objects and scenes which the universe presents**, 207. *Material* structures, 207. *Infinite diversity of scenery*, 208: may be produced from a few general laws, 208. **Variety in the** animal, vegetable, and mineral kingdoms, 209, and in the solar system, 210. Organized and intelligent beings: *gradation* of intellect: powers of the highest order of intelligences, 211—213. Perfections of angels, 214. Vehicles of celestial beings: material vehicles of angels, etc., 215—217. Variety of senses, 218—221. Leading transactions in the history of other worlds, their *moral* economy etc., 222—223: will unfold the *moral* character of Deity, 223—225. Illustrations from Scripture, 225. Manner in which information may be communicated on such subjects, 225: The REDEEMER: Lectures on the moral history of other worlds: Examples in reference to two different worlds, 227—232. Extract from Dr. Watts, (Note,) 233.

Worlds belonging to the solar system: their peculiarities: changes, diversity of scenery, etc., 234—236. Universe extends far beyond the limits of human vision, 237, 238. The empire of the Almighty boundless to the view of finite beings: new creations, 239, 240. THRONE OF GOD, 241. Capital of the universe, 242. Astronomical observations which illustrate this subject, 243, 244. Nothing less than the most sublime conceptions of the *extent* of the universe, comport with the idea of an infinite Being, 245. Preceding views corroborated by Revelation, 246: open an interesting train of thought in relation to the Deity, and the scenes of futurity, 247. Subjects of study in the heavenly world, 249—250. One constituent part of the *misery of the wicked* in the future world, 251, 252. Their *moral state* in that world, 253. Sources of misery, 253. Boundless nature of Divine love, 253. Summary of topics Illustrated, 254. Harmony of science and Revelation, 254. Value of the human soul, 255. Importance of **man's** eternal **destiny**, and the folly of overlooking it, 255—258.

PART IV.

ON THE MORAL QUALIFICATIONS REQUISITE **TO THE ENJOYMENT OF** THE FELICITY OF THE FUTURE WORLD.

Fallacious views in relation to this point, 259. Requisites in order to the enjoyment of happiness, 260. Infatuation of the bulk of mankind in reference to their eternal interests, 261. Foundation of future felicity, 262. Love to God, its foundation, reasonableness, and properties, 262—264. Love to man, its foundation and obligation, 265. Love to angels, 266, 267. *Humility*, its reasonableness, and conformity to the condition of man, 268: forms a trait in the character of angels, **270**—271. Folly of pride, 272, 273. Active beneficence, 274—276. Ministry of angels, 276. Effects of malignity, 277. Society of heaven, 278—281. Examples of malignity: Antiochus Epiphanes, 282, the Turks, 284, the Norman barons and chevaliers, 286. Examples of depravity; Buonaparte, 287—289. Lord Byron, 290. Example from Cochrane's Travels, 291. Misery resulting from the association of malignant characters, 292. Punishment of the wicked, 293, 294. Concluding remarks, 295, 296.

APPENDIX.

Mr. Sheppard's **Letter to Lord Byron**, 297. **His** Lordship's reply; his last sentiments in reference to religion and eternity, 299—302. Buonaparte's opinion of the morality of the New Testament, etc., 302, 303.

THE PHILOSOPHY OF A FUTURE STATE.

PART I.

PROOFS OF A FUTURE STATE.

INTRODUCTION.

THE sketches contained in **Parts II** and III of this Work being chiefly intended to illustrate the connection of science with the scenes of a future world, and the aids which its discoveries afford, for enabling us to form some conception of the *perpetual improvement* of its inhabitants in knowledge and felicity; I shall endeavour, in this First Part, to exhibit a condensed view of some of those *evidences* which prove the immortality of the soul, and the eternal destination of man.

This is an inquiry far more interesting and important, to every individual of mankind, than any other which comes within the range of the human mind. Next to the Being of a God, the doctrine of the immortality of man lies at the foundation of all religion, and of all the animating prospects which can cheer us in the land of our pilgrimage. Remove from the mind the belief of a future existence, and the hope of immortality, and religion becomes a shadow, life a dream, and the approach of death a scene of darkness and despair. Upon this short question, "*Is man immortal, or is he not?*" depends all that is valuable in science, in morals, and in theology; and all that is most interesting to man as a social being, and as a rational and accountable intelligence. If he is destined to an eternal existence, an immense importance must attach to all his present affections, actions, and pursuits! and it must be a matter of infinite moment, that they be directed in such a channel, as will tend to carry him forward, in safety, to the felicities of a future world. But if his whole existence be circumscribed within the circle of a few fleeting years, man appears an enigma, an inexplicable phenomenon in the universe, human life a mystery, the world a scene of confusion, virtue a mere phantom, the Creator a capricious Being, and his plans and arrangements an inextricable maze.

There is too much reason to believe, that the indifference to religion which so generally prevails, especially among those who are raised a little above the vulgar throng, and the unhallowed propensities and vicious practices to which it gives rise, are owing in a considerable degree, to the want of a *full conviction* of the reality of a future existence, or to some **doubts** which hover about the mind, in relation to this important point. There is no man, however insensible to the obligations of religion, that can fully satisfy his own mind, or the minds of others, that the idea of a future world is a mere chimera. On the contrary, the possibility, and even the probability, of the truth of man's eternal destiny, will, at certain seasons, force themselves upon the minds even of the most careless and profane. Yet it is amazing to consider, with what ease and indifference multitudes of this description can glide down the stream of time, under the awful uncertainty whether it will land them in the shades of annihilation, the realms of bliss, or the regions of endless woe. "Between us and these three periods or states," says a celebrated French writer, "no barrier is interposed but life, the most brittle thing in all nature; and the happiness of heaven being certainly not designed for those who doubt whether they have an immortal part to enjoy it, such persons have nothing left, but the miserable chance of annihilation, or of hell. There is not any reflection which can have more reality than this, as there is none which has greater terror. Let us set the bravest face on our condition, and play the heroes as artfully as we can, yet see here the issue which attends the goodliest life upon earth! It is in vain for men to turn aside their thoughts from this eternity which awaits them, as if they were able to destroy it, by denying it a place in their imagination. It subsists *in spite of them;* it advances unobserved; and death, which is to draw the curtain from it, will, in a short time, infallibly reduce them to the dreadful necessity of being for ever nothing, or for ever miserable."

To treat a subject, so interesting and momentous, with levity or indifference; to exert all the energies of the soul in the pursuit of objects, which a few years at most will snatch for ever from their embrace, and never to spend one serious hour in reflecting on what may possibly succeed the present scene of existence, or in endeavouring to find some light, to clear up the doubts that may hang over this important inquiry, and to treat with derision and scorn those who would direct them in this serious investigation, is not only foolish and preposterous, but the height of infatuation and of madness. It is contrary to every principle on which reasonable men act, in relation to the affairs of the present world. To retain the profits of a lucrative business, or to prevent the loss of fortune, or of honour, a man will sometimes strain every nerve, stretch every faculty, deprive himself of sleep, submit to numerous privations, encounter the raging elements, and brave the dangers of the ocean. Nay, he will often be overwhelmed with despondency at the slightest inconveniences, and will pass whole weeks and months in sullenness and chagrin, for an imaginary affront, or for the loss of a few pounds, while, at the same time, he remains perfectly indifferent, and without the least emotion, in regard to the unknown scenes of the eternal world, and the danger of endless misery to which he is exposed. Such a conduct, and such dispositions, which are too frequently realized in the case of thousands who occasionally mingle in our religious assemblies, are obviously inconsistent with the dictates of prudence and of common sense, and with every thing that ought to characterize a rational and an accountable creature.

When we look back into the inexplorable abyss of that eternity which is already past, when we look forward to the immeasurable extent, and the unfathomable depths, of eternity to come; when we behold *Time*, and all its circling years, appearing only like a point on the surface of that vast and boundless ocean; when we consider the immense spaces of the universe with which we are surrounded, and the innumerable worlds which lie dispersed in every direction throughout the immeasurable tracts of creation; when we consider, that our existence, as thinking beings, may run parallel with interminable ages; and that, in the revolutions of eternity, we may exist in regions of space immeasurably distant from our present habitation, associate with other orders of intelligent beings, and pass through new scenes and changes in distant worlds; and when we consider that **our** relation to time may be dissolved, and our connection with eternity commence, within the space of a few months or years, or even before the sun shall have described another circuit around the earth; no inquiry can appear so momentous and interesting, as that **which leads to** the determination of our future and eternal destiny, and of **those** realities which await us beyond the tomb. To remain insensible to the importance of such an inquiry, and unaffected at the prospect of the result to which it may lead, while we are feelingly alive **to all the** paltry concerns and little ills of life, would argue the most unaccountable stupidity, inconsistency, and infatuation.

The man whose heart pants after substantial knowledge and felicity, whose affections centre on the Author of his existence, and who delights to contemplate his character and perfections, **will** enter with pleasure on every investigation, which has a tendency to throw a light on the scene of his future destination. He will weigh with impartiality, every consideration, and **will** seize, with delight, upon every argument, by which a full conviction of his immortal destiny may be indelibly riveted upon his mind; and he will endeavour to **cheer** his soul amidst the sorrows of mortality, with the consideration, that "when the earthly house of his tabernacle is dissolved, he has a building of God, an house not made with hands, eternal in the heavens."

In illustrating the evidences of a future state, I shall, *in the first place*, state some of those proofs which Reason, or the light of nature furnishes of man's eternal destination; and *secondly*, those which are derived from the system of Revelation.

CHAPTER I.

PROOFS OF A FUTURE STATE FROM THE LIGHT OF NATURE.

The evidences of a future state which the light of reason affords, though not so clear and decisive as those which are derived from Divine Revelation, are worthy of the serious consideration of every one in whose mind the least doubt remains on this important subject. The conviction they are calculated to produce when attentively weighed, is sufficient to leave every one without excuse who trifles with the concerns of his future destiny, and overlooks his relation to the eternal world. Though the Deity is invisible to mortal eyes, yet his existence and perfections are clearly demonstrated by his visible operations, and he has not left himself without a witness to his beneficence, in any age, "in his giving rain from heaven, and fruitful seasons, and filling our hearts with food and gladness." In like manner, though the realities of a future world are not presented directly to the eye of sense, yet the faculties with which man is endowed, when properly exercised on all the physical and moral scenes which the universe displays, are sufficient to evince the high degree of probability, if not absolute certainty, that his duration and his sphere of action are not confined to the narrow limits of the present world, but have a relation to a future and an immortal existence. In illustrating this topic, I shall waive the consideration of several of those metaphysical arguments which have been adduced by Philosophers and Divines, founded on the immateriality of the human soul, and confine myself chiefly to those popular considerations, which are level to every capacity, and perhaps, more convincing than the subtile and refined disquisitions of metaphysical minds.

SECTION I.

ON THE UNIVERSAL BELIEF WHICH THE DOCTRINE OF IMMORTALITY HAS OBTAINED IN ALL AGES.

It forms a presumptive proof of the immortality of man, that this doctrine has obtained universal belief among all nations, and in every period of time.

That the thinking principle in man is of an immortal nature, was believed by the ancient Egyptians, the Persians, the Phenicians, the Scythians, the Celts, the Druids, the Assyrians, by the wisest and most celebrated characters among the Greeks and Romans, and by almost every other ancient nation and tribe whose records have reached our times. The notions, indeed, which many of them entertained of the scenes of futurity were very obscure and imperfect; but they all embraced the idea, that death is not the destruction of the rational soul, but only its introduction to a new and unknown state of existence. The ancient Scythians believed that death was only a change of habitation; and the Magian sect, which prevailed in Babylonia, Media, Assyria, and Persia, admitted the doctrine of eternal rewards and punishments. The doctrines taught by the second Zoroaster, who lived in the time of Darius, were, "That there is one Supreme Being, independent and self-existent from all eternity; that under him there are two angels, one the angel of light, who is the author of all good; and the other the angel of darkness, who is the author of all evil: that they are in a perpetual struggle with each other; that where the angel of light prevails, there good reigns; and that where the angel of darkness prevails, there evil takes place; that this struggle shall continue to the end of the world; that then there shall be a general resurrection and a day of judgment, wherein all shall receive a just retribution according to their works. After which, the angel of darkness and his disciples shall go into a world of their own, where they shall suffer, in everlasting darkness, the punishment of their evil deeds; and the angel of light and his disciples shall also go into a world of their own, where they shall receive, in everlasting light, the reward due to their good deeds; that after this they shall remain separated for ever, and light and darkness be no more mixed to all eternity."[1] The remains of this sect, which are scattered over Persia and India, still hold the same doctrine, without any variation, even at this day.

It is well known that Plato, Socrates, and other Greek philosophers, held the doctrine of the soul's immortality. In his admirable dialogue, entitled, "The Phædon," Plato represents Socrates, a little before his death, encompassed with a circle of philosophers, and discoursing with them on the arguments which prove the eternal destiny of man. "When the dead," says he, "are arrived at the rendezvous of departed souls, whither their angel conducts them, they are all judged. Those who have passed their lives in a manner neither entirely criminal, nor absolutely innocent, are sent into a place where they suffer pains proportioned to their faults, till, being purged and cleansed of their guilt, and afterwards restored to liberty, they receive the reward of the good actions they have done in the body. Those who are judged to be incurable, on account of the greatness of their crimes, the fatal Destiny that passes judgment upon them, hurls them into Tartarus, whence they never depart. Those who are found guilty of crimes, great indeed, but worthy of pardon, who have committed violences, in the transports of rage, against their father and mother, or have killed some one in a like emotion, and afterwards repented, suffer the same punishment with the last, but for a time only, till, by prayers and supplications, they have obtained pardon from those they have injured. But those who have passed through life with peculiar sanctity of manners, are received on high into a pure region, where they live without their bodies to all eternity, in a series of joys and delights which cannot be described." From such considerations, Socrates concludes, "If the soul be immortal, it requires to be cultivated with attention, not only for what we call the time of life, but for that which is to follow, I mean eternity; and the least neglect in this point may be attended with endless consequences. If death were the final dissolution of being, the wicked would be great gainers by it, by being delivered at once

[1] Rollin's Ancient History, vol. ii.

from their bodies, their souls, and their vices; but as the soul is immortal, it has no other means of being freed from its evils, nor any safety for it, but in becoming very good and very wise; for it carries nothing with it, but its good or bad deeds, its virtues and vices, which are commonly the consequences of the education it has received, and the causes of eternal happiness or misery." Having held such discourses with his friends, he kept silence for some time, and then drank off the whole of the poisonous draught which had been put into his hand, with amazing tranquillity, and an inexpressible serenity of aspect, as one who was about to exchange a **short and wretched life, for a blessed and eternal existence.**

The descriptions and allusions contained in the writings of the ancient Poets are a convincing proof, that the notion of the soul's immortality was a universal opinion in the times in which they wrote, and among the nations to whom their writings were addressed. Homer's account of the descent of Ulysses into hell, and his description of Minos in the shades below, distributing justice to the dead assembled in troops around his tribunal, and pronouncing irrevocable judgments, which decide their everlasting fate, demonstrate that they entertained the belief, that virtues are rewarded, and that crimes are punished, in another state of existence. The poems of Ovid and Virgil contain a variety of descriptions, in which the same opinions are involved. Their notions of future punishment are set forth in the descriptions they give of *Ixion*, who was fastened to a wheel, and whirled about continually with a swift and rapid motion; of *Tantalus*, who, for the loathsome banquet he made for the gods, was set in water up to the chin, with apples hanging to his very lips, yet had no power either to stoop to the one to quench his raging thirst, or to reach to the other to satisfy his craving appetite; of the *fifty Daughters of Danaus*, who, for the barbarous massacre of their husbands in one night, were condemned in hell to fill a barrel full of holes with water, which ran out again as fast as it was filled; of *Sisgphus*, who, for his robberies, was set to roll a great stone up a steep hill, which, when it was just at the top, suddenly fell down again, and so renewed his labour; and of *Tityus*, who was adjudged to have a vulture to feed upon his liver and entrails, which still grew and increased as they were devoured. Their notions of future happiness are embodied in the descriptions they have given of the Hesperian gardens, and the Elysian fields, where the souls of the virtuous rest secure from every danger, and enjoy perpetual and uninterrupted bliss.

And as the nations of antiquity recognised the doctrine of a future state of existence, so there is scarcely a nation or tribe of mankind presently existing, however barbarous and untutored, in which the same opinion does not prevail. The natives of the *Society Isles* believe, that after death, there is not only a state of conscious existence, but degrees of eminence and felicity, according as men have been more or less pleasing to the *Eatooa*, or Deity, while upon earth. The chiefs of the *Friendly Islands* believe in the immortality of their soul, which, at death, they say, is immediately conveyed in a fast sailing canoe, to a distant country, called Doobludha, which they describe as resembling the Mahometan paradise; that those who are conveyed thither are no more subject to death, but feast on all the favourite productions of their native soil, with which this blissful abode is plentifully furnished. The *New Zealanders* believe, that the third day after the interment of a man, the heart separates itself from the corpse, and that this separation is announced by a general breeze of wind, which gives warning of its approach, by an inferior divinity that hovers over the grave, and who carries it to the clouds. They believe that the soul of the man whose flesh is devoured by the enemy, is doomed to a perpetual fire, while the soul of the man whose body has been rescued from those that killed him, and the souls of all who die a natural death, ascend to the habitations of the gods. The inhabitants of the *Pelew Islands*, according to the account of Captain Wilson, although they have few religious rites and ceremonies, believe in one Supreme Being, and in a future state of rewards and punishments. In the religion of the *Kalmuc Tartars*, the doctrine of a future state holds a conspicuous place. They believe that hell is situated in the middle region, between heaven and earth, and their devils are represented with all sorts of frightful forms, of a black and hideous aspect, with the heads of goats, lions, and unicorns. Their holy Lamas, who have obtained a victory over all their passions, are supposed to pass immediately into heaven, where they enjoy perfect rest, and exercise themselves in divine service. The *Samoiedians* of Northern Tartary believe, that there is one Supreme Being, that he is our all-merciful and common Parent, and that he will reward with a happy state hereafter, those who live virtuously in this world. The *Birmans* believe in the transmigration of souls, after which, they maintain, that the radically bad will be sentenced to lasting punishment, while the good will enjoy eternal happiness on a mountain called Meru.

The various tribes which inhabit the continent of Africa, in so far as we are acquainted with their religious opinions, appear to recognise the doctrine of a future state. "I was lately discoursing on this subject," says Mr. Addison, in one of his Spectators, "with a learned person, who has been very much conversant among the inhabitants of the most western parts of Africa. Upon his conversing with several in that country, he tells me, that their notion of heaven, or of a future state of happiness, is this: that every thing we there wish for will immediately present itself to us. We find, say they, that our souls are of such a nature that they require variety, and are not capable of being always delighted with the same objects. The Supreme Being, therefore, in compliance with this taste of happiness which he has implanted in the soul of man, will raise up, from time to time, say they, every gratification which it is in the human nature to be pleased with. If we wish to be in groves or bowers, among running streams or falls of water, we shall immediately find ourselves in the midst of such a scene as we desire. If we would be entertained with music, and the melody of sounds, the concert arises upon our wish, and the whole region about us is filled with harmony. In short, every desire will be followed by fruition; and whatever a man's inclination directs him to will be present with him." The Negroes and other inhabitants of the interior of Africa, according to the account of Mr. Park, believe in one Supreme Ruler, and expect hereafter to enter into a state of misery or felicity. The Gallas of Abyssinia, though they reject the doctrine of future punishment, admit the reality of a future state. The Mandingoes, the Jaloffs, the Feloops, the Foulahs, the Moors, and all the other tribes who have embraced the Mahometan faith, recognise the doctrine of the immortality of the soul, and of future rewards in a celestial paradise. The natives of Dahomy entertain the same belief; and hence, it is a common practice with the sovereign of that country, to send an account to his forefathers of any remarkable event, by delivering a message to whoever may happen to be near him at the time, and then ordering his head to be chopped off immediately, that he may serve as a courier, to convey intelligence to the world of spirits.[1]

The Persians are said to leave one part of their graves open, from a belief, that the dead will be reanimated, and visited by angels, who will appoint to them their appropriate **abodes** in a future state. From a similar belief, thousands **of Hindoo** widows annually sacrifice themselves on the funeral piles of their deceased husbands, in the hope of enjoying with them the felicities of eternal life. The Japanese believe that the souls of men and beasts are alike immortal; that a just distribution of rewards and punishments takes place after death; that there are different degrees of happiness, as well as of punishment, **and** that the souls of the wicked transmigrate, after death, into the bodies of animals, and at last, in case of amendment, are translated back again into the human form.[2] From a conviction of the reality of a future world, the Wahabee Arabs regard it as impious to mourn for the dead, who, they say, are enjoying felicity with Mahomet **in** paradise; and the Javanese make several feasts, on the decease **of** their friends and relations, to commemorate their entrance into a world of bliss. The North American Indians believe that, beyond the most distant mountains of their country, there is a wide river; beyond that river a great country; on the other side of that country a world of water; in that water are a thousand islands, full of **trees** and streams of water, and that a thousand buffaloes, and **ten** thousand deer, graze on the hills, or ruminate in **the** valleys. When they die, they are persuaded that the Great **Spirit** will conduct them to this land of souls.

Thus it appears, that not only **the** philosophers of antiquity, and the most civilized nations presently existing on the globe, have recognised the doctrine of the immortality of man, but

M'Leod's Voyage to Africa, 1820, p. 64.   [2] Thunberg's Travels.

that even the most savage and untutored tribes fortify their minds in the prospect of death, with the hope of a happiness commensurate to their desires, in the regions beyond the **grave**.

> "Even the poor Indian, whose untutored mind
> Sees God in clouds, or hears him in the wind,
> Whose soul proud Science never taught to stray
> Far as the solar walk or milky way;
> Yet simple nature to his hope has given,
> Behind the cloud-topt hill, an humbler heaven;
> Some safer world in depth of woods embraced,
> Some happier island in the watery waste,
> Where slaves once more their native land behold,
> No fiends torment, no Christians thirst for gold;
> And thinks, admitted to yon equal sky,
> His faithful dog shall bear him company."—POPE.

Among the numerous and diversified tribes that are scattered over the different regions of the earth, that agree in scarcely any other sentiment or article of religious belief, we here find the most perfect harmony in their recognition of a Supreme Intelligence, and in their belief that the soul survives the dissolution of its mortal frame. And, as Cicero long since observed, "In every thing the consent of all nations is to be accounted the law of nature, and to resist it is to resist the voice of God." For we can scarcely suppose, in consistency with the Divine perfections, that an error, on a subject of so vast importance to mankind, should obtain the universal belief of all nations and ages; and that God himself would suffer a world of rational beings, throughout every generation, to be carried away by a delusion, and to be tantalized by a hope which has no foundation in nature, and which is contrary to the plan of his moral government. It is true, indeed, that several of the opinions to which I have now adverted, and many others which prevail among the uncivilized tribes of mankind, in regard to the *condition* of disembodied spirits, and the *nature* of future happiness, are very erroneous and imperfect; but they all recognise this grand and important truth, that death is not the destruction of the rational soul, and that man is destined to an immortal existence. Their erroneous conceptions in respect to the rewards and punishments of the future world may be easily accounted for, from a consideration of the imperfect conceptions they have formed of the Divine Being and of the principles of his moral government; from their ignorance of those leading principles and moral laws, by which the Almighty regulates the intelligent universe; from the false ideas they have been led to entertain respecting the nature of substantial happiness; from the cruel and absurd practices connected with the system of Pagan superstition; from the intellectual darkness which has brooded over the human race ever since the fall of man; and from the universal prevalence of those depraved dispositions and affections which characterise the untutored tribes on whom the light of Revelation has never shone.

To whatever cause this universal belief of a future existence is to be traced—whether to a universal tradition derived from the first parents of the human race; to an innate sentiment originally impressed on the soul of man; to a Divine revelation disseminated and handed down from one generation to another, or to the deductions of human reason—it forms a strong presumption, and a powerful argument, in favour of the position we are now endeavouring to support. If it is to be traced back to the original progenitors of mankind, it must be regarded as one of those truths which were recognised by man in a state of innocence, when his affections were pure, and his understanding fortified against delusion and error. If it be a sentiment which was originally impressed on the human soul by the hand of its Creator, we do violence to the law of our nature when we disregard its intimations, or attempt to resist the force of its evidence. If it ought to be considered as originally derived from Revelation, then it is corroborative of the truth of the Sacred Records, in which "life and immortality" are clearly exhibited. And if it be regarded as likewise one of the deductions of natural reason, we are left without excuse, if we attempt to obscure its evidence, or to overlook the important consequences which it involves. As the consent of all nations has been generally considered as a powerful argument for the existence of a Deity, so the universal belief of mankind in the doctrine of a future state ought to be viewed as a strong presumption, that it is founded upon truth. The human mind is so constituted, that, when left to its native unbiassed energies, it necessarily infers the existence of a Supreme Intelligence, from the existence of matter and the economy of the material world; and, from the nature of the human faculties, and the moral attributes of God, it is almost as infallibly led to conclude, that a future existence is necessary, in order to gratify the boundless desires of the human soul, and to vindicate the wisdom and rectitude of the moral Governor of the world. These two grand truths, which constitute the foundation of all religion, and of every thing that is interesting to man as an intelligent agent, are interwoven with the theological creed of all nations; and, in almost every instance, where the one is called in question, the other is undermined or denied: so that the doctrine of the immortality of man may be considered as resting on the same foundation as the existence of a Supreme Intelligence.

It must indeed be admitted, that individuals have appeared, in every age, who have endeavoured to call in question, or to deny, this fundamental truth. But this circumstance forms no valid objection to the force of the argument to which I have now adverted. For the number of such persons has been extremely small, when compared with the mass of mankind; and their opinions on this subject have generally originated either from wilful ignorance; from an affectation of singularity and of appearing superior to vulgar fears; or from indulging in a course of wickedness and impiety, which has led them to wish, and if possible to believe, that there are neither punishments nor rewards beyond the grave. If it appear strange and unnatural that any man should wish his soul to be mortal, Hierocles assigns the true reason of it: " A wicked man," says he, "is afraid of his Judge, and therefore wishes his soul and body may perish together by death, rather than it should appear before the tribunal of God." If a number of fools should think fit to put out their own eyes, to prevent them from feeling the effects of light, as Democritus, the ancient philosopher, was said to have done, it would form no argument to prove that all the rest of the world was blind. And, if a few sceptics and profligates endeavour to blind the eyes of their understanding by sophistry and licentiousness, it cannot prevent the light of reason, which unvails the realities of a future world, from shining on the rest of mankind, nor constitute the slightest argument to prove the fallacy of the doctrine they deny.

SECTION II.

ON THE DESIRE OF FUTURE EXISTENCE IMPLANTED IN THE HUMAN MIND.

Those strong and restless desires after future existence and enjoyment, which are implanted in the soul of man, are a strong presumptive proof that he is possessed of an immortal nature.

There is no human being who feels **full** satisfaction in his present enjoyments. The mind is for ever **on the** wing in the pursuit of new acquirements, of new objects, and, if possible, of higher degrees **of** felicity, than the present moment can afford. However exquisite any particular enjoyment **may** sometimes be found, it soon begins to lose its relish, and to pall the intellectual appetite. Hence the voracious desire, apparent among all ranks, for variety of amusements, both of a sensitive and of an intellectual nature. Hence the keen desire for novelty, for tales of wonder, for beautiful and splendid exhibitions, and for intelligence respecting the passing occurences of the day. Hence the eagerness with which the daily newspapers are read by all ranks who have it in their power to procure them. However novel or interesting the events which are detailed to-day, an appetite for fresh intelligence is excited before to-morrow. Amidst the numerous objects which are daily soliciting attention, amidst the variety of intelligence which newsmongers have carefully selected for the gratification of every taste, and amidst the fictitious scenes depicted by the Novelist and the Poet, "the eye is not satisfied with seeing, nor the ear with hearing." Hence, too, the insatiable desires of the miser in accumulating riches, and the unremitting career of ambition, in its pursuits of honour and of fame. And hence the ardour with which the philosopher prosecutes one discovery after another, without ever arriving at a resting-point, or sitting down contented with his present attainments. When Archimedes discovered the mode of determining the relative quantities of gold and silver in Hiero's crown, did he rest satisfied with this new acquirement? No. The ecstacy he felt at the discovery, when he leaped from the bath, and ran naked through the streets of Syracuse, crying, " I have found it, I have found it," soon subsided into indifference, and his mind pushed forward in quest of new discoveries. When Newton ascertained the law of universal gravitation, and Franklin discovered the identity of lightning and the electric fluid, and felt the transports which such discoveries must have excited, did they slacken their pace in the road of scientific discovery, or sit down contented with their past researches? No. One discovery gave a stimulus to the pursuit of another, and their career of improvement only terminated with their lives. After Alexander had led his victorious armies over Persia, Babylonia, Syria, Egypt, and India, and had conquered the greater part of the known world, did he sit down in peace, and enjoy the fruit of his conquests? No. His desires after new projects and new expeditions remained insatiable; his ambition rose even to madness; and when the philosopher Anaxarchus told him that there was an infinite number of worlds, he wept at the thought that his conquests were confined to one.

These restless and unbounded desires are to be found agitating the breasts of men of all nations, of all ranks and conditions of life. If we ascend the thrones of princes, if we enter the palaces of the great, if we walk through the mansions of courtiers and statesmen, if we pry into the abodes of poverty and indigence, if we mingle with poets or philosophers, with manufacturers, merchants, mechanics, peasants, or beggars; if we survey the busy, bustling scene of a large city, the sequestered village, or the cot which stands in the lonely desert; we shall find, in every situation, and among every class, beings animated with desires of happiness which no present enjoyment can gratify, and which no object within the limits of time can fully satiate. Whether we choose to indulge in ignorance, or to prosecute the path of knowledge; to loiter in indolence, or to exert our active powers with unremitting energy; to mingle with social beings, or to flee to the haunts of solitude, we feel a vacuum in the mind, which nothing around us can fill up; a longing after new objects and enjoyments, which nothing earthly can fully satisfy. Regardless of the past, and unsatisfied with the present, the soul of man feasts itself on the hope of enjoyments which it has never yet possessed.

> "Hope springs eternal in the human breast;
> Man never *is* but always *to be* blest:
> The soul, uneasy and confined from home,
> Rests and expatiates in a life to come."

That the desire of immortality is common, and natural to all men, appears from a variety of actions, which can scarcely be accounted for on any other principle, and which prove that the mind feels conscious of its immortal destiny. Why otherwise, should men be anxious about their reputation, and solicitous to secure their names from oblivion, and to perpetuate their fame, after they have descended into the grave? To accomplish such objects, and to gratify such desires, Poets, Orators, and Historians, have been flattered and rewarded to celebrate their actions; monuments of marble and of brass have been erected to represent their persons, and inscriptions engraved in the solid rock, to convey to future generations a record of the exploits they had achieved. Lofty columns, triumphal arches, towering pyramids, magnificent temples, palaces, and mausoleums, have been reared, to eternize their fame and to make them live, as it were, in the eyes of their successors, through all the future ages of time. But, if the soul be destined to destruction at the hour of death, why should man be anxious about what shall happen, or what shall not happen, hereafter, when he is reduced to a mere nonentity, and banished for ever from the universe of God? He can have no interest in any events that may befall the living world, when he is cancelled from the face of creation, and when the spark of intelligence he possessed is quenched in everlasting night. If any man be fully convinced that the grave puts a final period to his existence, the only *consistent* action he can perform, when he finds his earthly wishes and expectations frustrated, is to rush into the arms of death, and rid himself at once of all the evils connected with his being. But we find the great majority of mankind, notwithstanding the numerous ills to which they are subjected, still clinging with eagerness to their mortal existence, and looking forward, with a certain degree of hope to a termination of their sorrows.

"They rather choose to bear those ills they have
Than fly to others that they know not of."

There is, I presume, no individual in a sound state of mind, who can entirely throw aside all concern about his posthumous reputation, and about the events that may happen in the world after his decease. And if so it clearly demonstrates, not only that he does not *wish*, but that he does not even *suppose*, that his existence will be for ever extinguished at death. The idea of the shame of being exposed naked after their death, produced such a powerful effect upon the minds of the Milesian virgins, that it deterred them from putting an end to their lives, after all other arguments had been tried in vain.[1] The desire of existence, and of existence, too, which has no termination, appears to be the foundation of all our desires, and of all the plans we form in life. Annihilation cannot be an object of desire to any rational being. We desire something that is *real*, something that is connected with *happiness or enjoyment*, but non-existence has no object nor concern whatever belonging to it. When a wicked man, under a consciousness of guilt, indulges a wish for annihilation after death, it is not because non-existence *is in itself an object of desire*, but he would choose it as the least of two evils; he would rather be be blotted out of creation than suffer the punishment due to his sins in the eternal world.

It may also be remarked, that the desire of immortality, however vigorous it may be in ordinary minds, becomes still more glowing and ardent in proportion as the intellect is cultivated and expanded, and in proportion as the soul rises to higher and higher degrees of virtue and moral excellence. It forms a powerful stimulus to the performance of actions which are noble, generous, public-spirited, benevolent, and humane, and which have a tendency to promote the intellectual improvement and the happiness of future generations. Hence the most

---

[1] " I beseech men for God's sake, (says Hale,) that if at any time there arise in them a desire or a wish that others should speak well of their death, then at that time they would seriously consider, whether these motions are not from some spirit to continue a spirit, after it leaves its earthly habitation, rather than from an earthly spirit, a vapour which cannot act, or imagine, or desire, or fear things beyond its continuance."

illustrious characters of the heathen world, the poets, the orators, the moralists, and philosophers of antiquity, had their minds fired with the idea of immortality, and many of them were enabled to brave death without dismay, under the conviction that it was the messenger which was to waft their spirits to the realms of endless bliss. When Demosthenes had fled for shelter to an asylum from the resentment of Antipater, who had sent Archias to bring him by force, and when Archias promised upon his honour that he should not lose his life if he would voluntarily make his personal appearance, "God forbid," said he, "that after I have heard Xenocrates and Plato discourse so divinely on the immortality of the soul, I should prefer a life of infamy and disgrace to an honourable death." Even those who were not fully convinced of the doctrine of immortality, amidst all their doubts and perplexities on this point, *earnestly wished that it might prove true*, and few if any of them absolutely denied it. Hence, too, the noble and disinterested actions which Christian heroes have performed, under the influence of unseen and everlasting things. They have faced dangers and persecutions in every shape; they have endured " cruel mockings, scourgings, bonds, and imprisonments;" they have triumphed under the torments of the rack, and amidst the raging flames; they have surmounted every obstacle in their benevolent exertions to communicate blessings to their fellow-men; they have braved the fury of the raging elements, traversed sea and land, and pushed their way to distant barbarous climes, in order to point out to their benighted inhabitants the path that leads to eternal life. Nor do they think it too dear to sacrifice their lives in such services, since "they *desire* a better country," and feel assured that death will introduce them to " an exceeding great and an eternal weight of glory."

Since then it appears that the desire of immortality is common to mankind, that the soul is incessantly looking forward to the enjoyment of some future good, and that this desire has been the spring of actions the most beneficent and heroic, on what principle is it to be accounted for?

> " Whence springs this pleasing hope, this fond desire,
> This longing after immortality?

> Or, whence this secret dread, and inward horror,
> Of falling into nought? Why shrinks the soul
> Back on herself, and startles at destruction?"—ADDISON.

Whence proceeds the want we feel amidst the variety of objects which surround us? Whence arises the disgust that so quickly succeeds every enjoyment? Wherefore can we never cease from wishing for something more exquisite than we have ever yet possessed? No satisfactory answer can be given to such questions, if our duration be circumscribed within the limits of time, and if we shall be blotted out of creation when our earthly tabernacles are laid in the dust. The desires to which I now refer appear to be an essential part of the human constitution, and, consequently, were implanted in our nature by the hand of the Creator; and, therefore, we must suppose, either that the desire of immortality will be gratified, or that the Creator takes delight in tantalizing his creatures with hopes and expectations which will end in eternal disappointment. To admit the latter supposition would be inconsistent with every rational idea we can form of the moral attributes of the Divinity. It would be inconsistent with his *veracity;* for, to encourage hopes and desires which are never intended to be gratified, is the characteristic of a deceiver, and therefore contrary to every conception we can form of the conduct of " a God of truth." It would be inconsistent with his *rectitude;* for every such deception implies an act of injustice towards the individual who is thus tantalized. It would be inconsistent with his *wisdom;* for it would imply that he has no other means of governing the intelligent creation than those which have a tendency to produce fallacious hopes and fears in the minds of his rational offspring. It would be inconsistent with his *benevolence;* for as " the desire accomplished is sweet to the soul," so disappointed hopes uniformly tend to produce misery. Yet the benevolence of the Deity, in every other point of view, is most strikingly displayed in all his arrangements in the material universe, and towards every species of sensitive existence.

What has been now stated in relation to desire and hope will equally apply to those *fears* and apprehensions which frequently arise in the mind in reference to the punishments of a future world. A Being possessed of perfect benevolence cannot be supposed to harass his intelligent creatures, and to render their lives bitter with alarming apprehensions, **for** which there is not the slightest foundation. But if there **is no** state either of punishment or reward beyond **the** grave, those desires of immortal duration, which seem at first view to elevate man above the other inhabitants of this globe, actually place him below the level of the beasts, which bound through the forests and lawns, and find their chief enjoyment in browsing on the grass. They are alive to present enjoyment, but appear to have no anticipations of the future; they feel present pain, but there is no reason to believe that they are ever tormented with fears or forebodings of future punishment. They are contented with the organs with which Nature has furnished them; they appear fully satisfied with ranging the fields and feasting **on** the herbage; their desires need no restraint, and their wishes are completely gratified; and what pleased them yesterday will likewise give them pleasure to-morrow, without being harassed with insatiable desires after novelty and variety. They live divested of those innumerable cares and anxieties which harass and perplex the children of men, and they never wish to go beyond the boundary which nature prescribes. "The ingenious bee constructs commodious cells, but never dreams of rearing triumphal arches or obelisks to decorate her waxen city." Through ignorance of the future, they pass from life to death, with as much indifference as from watching to sleep, or from labour to repose. But man, amidst all the enjoyments and prospects which surround him, feels uneasy and unsatisfied, because he pants after happiness infinite in duration. His hopes and desires overstep the bounds of time and of every period we can affix to duration, and move onward through a boundless eternity. And if he is to be for ever cut off from existence when his body drops into the grave, how **dismal** the continued apprehension of an everlasting **period** being put to all his enjoyments after a prospect of immortality has been opened to his view!

How then shall we account for these anomalies? how shall **we** reconcile these apparent inconsistencies? In what light shall we exhibit **the** conduct of the Creator so as to render it consistent with itself? There is but one conclusion we can form, in consistency with the moral attributes of God, which will completely unravel the mystery of man being animated with unbounded desires, and yet confined to a short and limited duration in the present world; and that is, that this world is not the place of our final destination, but introductory to a more glorious and permanent state of existence, where the desires of virtuous minds will be completely gratified, and their hopes fully realised. I do not now see how any other conclusion can be drawn, without denying both the *moral character*, and even the *very existence*, of the Deity.

SECTION III.

ON THE INTELLECTUAL FACULTIES OF MAN, AND THE STRONG DESIRE OF KNOWLEDGE WHICH IS IMPLANTED IN THE HUMAN MIND.

The principle of curiosity, or the strong desire of knowledge, which is implanted in the mind of man, and the noble intellectual faculties for acquiring it with which he is endowed, are evidences and proofs of his immortal destination.

Though this argument may be considered, by some, as only a branch of the preceding, it may not be inexpedient, for the sake of impression, to consider it separately, as it will admit of reasonings and illustrations distinct from those which have now been brought forward.

The desire of knowledge is natural to every rational being, and appears to be a fundamental part of the constitution of the human mind. It is perceptible even in the first stage of its progress, and has a powerful influence over the movements and enjoyments of the young. Present to a child a beautiful landscape, as exhibited through an optical machine, and it will be highly delighted with the exhibition. Present a second and a third of a different description, in succession, and its delight will be increased; it will anxiously desire exhibitions of new and varied objects, and its curiosity will never be satisfied but with a constant succession of **scenes** and objects which tend to widen the circle of its knowledge, and enlarge the capacity of its mind. **Hence** the keen desires of the young for shows, spectacles, processions, and public exhibitions of every description, and the delight which they feel in making excursions from **one scene to** another. Hence the delight with which travellers traverse the Alpine scenes of nature, cross seas and oceans, descend into the gloomy subterraneous cavern, or climb to the summit of the flaming volcano, notwithstanding the fatigues and perils to which they are exposed.

> "For such the bounteous providence of Heaven,
> In every breast implanting the desire
> Of objects new and strange, to urge us on
> With unremitted labour to pursue
> Those sacred stores that wait the ripening soul,
> In truth's **exhaustless bosom.**———
> ——————— For this the daring youth
> Breaks from his weeping mother's anxious arms,
> In foreign climes to rove; the pensive sage,
> Heedless of sleep, or midnight's harmful damp,
> Hangs o'er the sickly taper; and untired
> The virgin follows with enchanted step
> The mazes of some wild and wondrous tale,
> From morn to eve."———
>
> AKENSIDE.

If the desire of knowledge appears, in many instances, to be less ardent in after life, it is owing in a great measure to the methods of our education, and the false principles on which we attempt to convey instruction to the youthful mind. Our initiatory instructions, hitherto, present the young with little more than the *key* of knowledge, instead of *knowledge itself.* We lead them to the threshold of the temple of science without attempting to unfold its treasures. We deem it sufficient that they be taught to pronounce like a number of puppets, a multitude of *sounds* and terms to which they **attach** no distinct conceptions, while we decline to communicate clear and well-defined *ideas.* We load their memories with technical phrases and propositions which they do not understand, while the objects of substantial science are carefully concealed both from the eye of sense and from the eyes of their understandings.

Instead of leading them by gentle steps, in the first stage of their progress, over the grand and beautiful and variegated scenery of Nature and Revelation, where almost every object is calculated to arrest their attention, and to excite admiration, we confound them with an unintelligible jargon of grammar rules, of metaphysical subtilties, and of dead languages, associated with stripes, confinement, and painful recollections, which frequently produce a disgust at every thing which has acquired the name of learning, before they are made acquainted with that in which true knowledge consists. Yet, notwithstanding the injudicious methods by which we attempt to train the youthful intellect, it is impossible to eradicate the desire of knowledge from the human mind. When substantial knowledge is presented to the mind, in a judicious and alluring manner, it will not only be relished, but prosecuted with ardour, by every one whose faculties are not altogether immersed in the mire of sensuality. Let a man, however ignorant and untutored, be made acquainted with some of the interesting details of geography, with the wonders of the ocean, and the numerous rivers continually rolling into its abyss with the lofty ranges of mountains which stretch along the continents, and project their summits beyond the clouds, with the volcanoes, the tornadoes, the water-spouts, and the sublime and beautiful landscapes which diversify the different climates of the earth, with the numerous tribes of animated beings which people its surface, and the manners and customs of its human inhabitants, he will feel an eager desire to know every thing else that appertains to this subject, and will posecute his inquiries with avidity, in so far as his means and opportunities permit. Acquaint him with some of the most striking facts in ancient and modern history, and he will feel a desire to know every thing of importance that has occurred in the annals of the world since the commencement of time. Unfold to him some of the discoveries which have been made in relation to the constitution of the atmosphere, the electric, magnetic, and galvanic fluids, and the chemical changes and operations that are constantly going on in the animal, vegetable, and mineral kingdoms, and his curiosity will be strongly excited to penetrate still farther into the mysteries of nature. Direct his views to the concave of the firmament, and tell him of the vast magnitude of the **sun,** and the planetary globes, the amazing velocity with which they run their destined rounds, and of the immense number and distances of the stars; and he will eagerly pant after **more** minute information respecting the great bodies of the **universe,** and feel delighted at hearing of new discoveries being **made in** the unexplored regions of creation.

I never knew an instance in which knowledge **of this** description was communicated *in a rational, distinct,* **and** *alluring manner,* where it was not received with **a certain degree** of pleasure, and with an **ardent** desire to make **further investigations** into the wonders of creating Wisdom **and Power.** Such appears to be the original constitution **of the human mind that** it is necessarily gratified with every thing **that gives scope to** the exercise of its faculties, and which has **a** tendency **to extend** the range of their action. It is **true,** indeed, that, **in some** men, the desire of knowledge appears **to be** blunted and almost annihilated, so that they appear to be **little** superior in their views to the **lower orders** of sensitive **existence.** But this happens only in those cases where the intellectual faculties are benumbed and stupified by *indolence* and *sensuality.* Such persons do all they can to *counteract* the original propensities of their nature; **and** yet, even in **the** worst cases of this **kind** that can occur, the original desire is never altogether extirpated, so long as the senses are qualified to perform their functions. For the most brutish man is never found entirely divested of the principle of curiosity, when any striking or extraordinary object is presented to his view. On such an occasion, the original principles of his constitution will be roused into action, and he will feel a certain degree **of** wonder and delight **in** common with other rational minds.

And, as man has a natural desire after knowledge, and a delight in it, so he is furnished *with noble faculties and vast capacities of intellect* for enabling him to acquire and to treasure it up. He is furnished with *senses* calculated to convey ideas of the forms, qualities, and relations of the various objects which surround him. His sense of vision, in particular, appears to take in a wider range of objects than that of any other sensitive being. While some of the lower animals have the vision circumscribed within a circle of a few yards or inches in diameter, the eye of man can survey, at one glance, an extensive landscape, and penetrate even to the regions of distant worlds. To this sense we are indebted for our knowledge of the sublimest objects which can occupy the mind, and for the ideas we have acquired of the boundless range of creation. And, while it is fitted to trace the motions of mighty worlds, which roll at the distance of a thousand millions of miles, it is also so constructed as to enable him, with the assistance of art, to survey the myriads of living beings which people a drop of water. All his other senses are likewise calculated to extend the range of his knowledge, to enable him to communicate his ideas to others, and to facilitate the mutual interchanges of thought and sentiment between rational minds of a similar construction with his own.

His understanding is capable of taking in a vast variety of sentiments and ideas in relation to the immense multiplicity of objects which are perceived by his external senses. Hence the various sciences he has cultivated, the sublime discoveries he has made, and the noble inventions he has brought to light. By the powers of his understanding he has surveyed the terraqueous globe, in all its varieties of land and water, continents, islands, and oceans; determined its magnitude, its weight, its figure, and motions; explored its interior recesses, descended into the bottom of its seas, arranged and classified the infinite variety of vegetables, minerals, and animals, which it contains; analysed the invisible atmosphere with which it is surrounded, and determined the elementary principles of which it is composed, discovered the nature of thunder, and arrested the rapid lightnings in their course; ascertained the laws by which the planets are directed in their courses, weighed the masses of distant worlds, determined their size and distances, and explored regions of the universe invisible to the unassisted eye, whose distance exceeds all human calculation and comprehension. The sublime sciences of Geometry, Trigonometry, Conic Sections, Fluxions, Algebra, and other branches of Mathematics, evince the acuteness and perspicacity of his intellect; and **their** application to the purposes of Navigation and Geography, and to the determination of the laws of the celestial motions, the periods of their revolutions, their eclipses, and the distances at which they are placed from our sublunary mansion, demonstrate the vigour and comprehension of those reasoning faculties with which he is endowed.

By means of the instruments and contrivances which his inventive faculty has enabled him to form and construct, he can **transport** ponderous masses across **the** ocean, determine the exact position in which he is **at any time** placed upon its surface, direct his course along pathless deserts and through the billows of the mighty deep;—transform a portion of *steam* into **a** mechanical power for impelling waggons along roads, and large vessels, with great velocity, against wind and tide; and can even transport himself through the yielding air beyond **the** region of the clouds. He can explore the invisible worlds which are contained in a putrid lake, and bring to view their numerous and diversified inhabitants; and the next moment he can penetrate to regions of the universe immeasurably distant, and contemplate the mountains **and the** vales, the rocks and the plains, which diversify **the scenery of** distant surrounding worlds. He can extract an invisible substance from a piece of coal, by which he can produce, almost in a moment, the most splendid illumination throughout every part of a large and populous city; he can detach the element of fire from the invisible air, and cause the hardest stones and the heaviest metals to melt like wax under its powerful agency; and he can direct the lightnings of heaven to accomplish his purposes, in splitting immense stones into **a** multitude of fragments. He can cause a splendid city, adorned with lofty columns, palaces, and temples, to arise in a spot where nothing was formerly beheld but a vast desert, or a putrid marsh; and can make "the wilderness and the solitary place to be glad, **and the** desert to bud and blossom as the rose." He can communicate his thoughts and sentiments, in a few hours, **to** ten hundred thousands of his fellow-men; in a few weeks to the whole civilized world; and after his decease, he can diffuse important instructions among mankind, throughout succeeding generations. In short, he can look back and trace the most memorable events which have happened in the world since time began, he can survey the present aspect of the moral world among all nations: He can penetrate beyond the limits of all that is visible in the immense canopy of heaven, and range amidst the infinity of unknown systems and worlds dispersed throughout the boundless regions of Creation, and he can overleap the bounds of time, and expatiate amidst future scenes of beauty and sublimity, which "eye hath not seen," throughout the countless ages of eternity.

What an immense multitude of ideas, in relation to such subjects, must the mind of such a person as Lord BACON have contained, whose mental eye surveyed the whole circle of human science, and who pointed out the path by which every branch of knowledge may be carried towards perfection! How sublime and diversified must have been the range of thought pursued by the immortal NEWTON, whose capacious intellect seemed to grasp the vast system of universal Nature, who weighed the ponderous masses of the planetary globes, and unfolded the laws by which their diversified phenomena are produced, and their motions directed!

> " He, while on this dim spot, where mortals toil,
> Clouded in dust, from Motion's simple laws
> Could trace the secret hand of Providence,
> Wide-working through this universal frame.
> —All-intellectual eye, our solar round
> First gazing through, he, by the blended power
> Of Gravitation and Projection, saw
> The whole in silent harmony revolve.
> —Then breaking hence, he took his ardent flight
> Through the blue infinite, and every star
> Which the clear concave of a winter's night
> Pours on the eye or astronomic tube,—
> ———————————— at his approach
> Blazed into suns, the living centre each
> Of an harmonious system."———

Such minds as those of Socrates, Plato, Archimedes, Locke, Boyle, La Place, and similar illustrious characters, likewise demonstrate the vast capacity of the human intellect, the extensive range of thought it is capable of prosecuting, and the immense number of ideas it is capable of acquiring. And every man, whose faculties are in a sound state, is endowed with similar powers of thought, and is capable of being trained to similar degrees of intellectual excellence.

And as man is endued with capacious intellectual powers for the *acquisition* of knowledge, so he is furnished with a noble faculty, by which he is enabled *to retain* and *to treasure up* in his intellect the knowledge he acquires. He is endowed with the faculty of *Memory*, by which the mind retains the ideas of past objects and perceptions, accompanied with a persuasion, **that** the objects or things remembered were formerly real **and** present. Without this faculty we could never advance a single step in the path of mental improvement. If the information we originally derive through the medium of the senses were to vanish the moment the objects are removed from our immediate perception, we should be left as devoid of knowledge as if we had never existed. But, by the power of memory, we can treasure up, as in a storehouse, the greater part, if not the whole, of the ideas, notions, reasonings, and perceptions, which we formerly acquired, and render them subservient to our future progress in intellectual attainments. **And** it is probable, that **even a human spirit, in** the vigorous exercise of the faculties **with** which it **is now furnished,** may go forward, through an interminable duration, making continual accessions to its stores of knowledge, without losing one leading idea, or portion of information, which it had previously acquired.

The power of memory in retaining past impressions, and **its** susceptibility of improvement, are vastly **greater** than **is** generally imagined. In many individuals, both in ancient **and in modern** times, it has been found in such a state of perfection **as to** excite astonishment, and almost to transcend belief. **It is reported** of Seneca, that he could repeat two thousand **verses** at **once, in** their order, and then begin at the end and rehearse them backwards, without missing a single syllable. Cyrus is said **to have been able to** call every individual **of his** numerous army by his own name. Cyneas, who was sent **by** Pyrrhus to the senate at Rome, on an expedition, the very next day after his arrival, both knew and saluted by their names all the Senate, and the whole order of the gentlemen in Rome. Mithridates, who governed twenty-three nations, all of different languages, could converse with every one of them in their own language.[1] An ancient author mentions one Oritus, a Corsican boy, to

[1] Senec. Controvers. lib. 1.   Pliny's Nat. Hist., etc.

whom he dictated a great number of words, both sense and nonsense, and finding he could rehearse a considerable number without missing one, and in the same order in which he dictated them, increased them to the number of forty thousand, and found, to his astonishment, that he could repeat them all from beginning to end, or from the end backwards to the beginning, in the order in which they were dictated.

In modern times, there have likewise been many instances of extraordinary powers of retention. Dr. Wallis, in a paper in the Philosophical Transactions, informs us that he extracted the cube root of the number *three*, even to thirty places of decimals, by the help of his memory alone. Maglia Bethi, an Italian, had read all the books that were published in his lifetime, and most of those which were published before, and could not only give an account of what was contained in each author, but could likewise, from memory, quote the chapter, section, and page of any book he had read, and repeat the author's own words, in reference to any particular topic. A gentleman, in order to try his memory, lent him a long manuscript he was about to publish, and after it had been returned, called upon him soon afterwards, pretending he had lost it, and desired him to write as much of it as he could remember; when, to his surprise, he wrote it over accurately word for word, the same as in the manuscript he had lent him. M. Euler, a late celebrated mathematician and philosopher, who died in 1783, having lost his sight by too intense application to study, afterwards composed his "Elements of Algebra," and a work "On the inequalities of the Planetary motions," that required immense and complicated calculations, which he performed by his memory alone, to the admiration and astonishment even of the philosophic world. His memory seemed to retain every idea that was conveyed to it, either from reading or from meditation, and his powers of reasoning and of discrimination were equally acute and capacious. He was also an excellent classical scholar, and could repeat the Æneid of Virgil from the beginning to the end, and indicate the first and last line of every page of the edition he used.[1] I have conversed with an individual, who was born blind, and who could repeat the whole of the Old and the New

[1] Encyclopedia Britan. Art. *Euler*.

Testaments from beginning to end; and not only so, but could repeat any particular chapter or *verse* that might be proposed to him, the moment after it was specified.

Thus it appears, that man is not only possessed of an ardent desire after knowledge, but is endued with the most penetrating and capacious powers of intellect, both for acquiring and for treasuring it up in his mind; powers which appear susceptible of indefinite improvement in this world: and the legitimate inference that may be drawn from this is, that they will continue to be exerted with uninterrupted activity, throughout an unceasing duration. And is it possible to suppose, in consistency with the moral attributes of the Deity, that the exercise of such powers is intended to be confined within the narrow limits of time, and to the contracted sphere of the terraqueous globe?

> ———————" Say, can a soul possessed
> Of such extensive, deep, tremendous powers,
> Enlarging still, be but a finer breath
> Of spirits dancing through their tubes a while,
> And then for ever lost in vacant air?"

Such a conclusion never can be admitted while we recognise the Divinity as possessed of boundless goodness and unerring wisdom. It is the province of Goodness to gratify those pure and ardent desires which it hath implanted in the soul; and it is the part of Wisdom to proportionate means to ends. But if the whole existence of human beings had been intended to be confined to a mere point in duration, is it rational to suppose, that Infinite Wisdom would have endowed the human soul with powers and capacities so marvellous and sublime, and made so many great preparations and arrangements for promoting its physical and moral perfection? To acquiesce in such a supposition would be to degrade the Divine wisdom and intelligence below the level of the wisdom of man, and to impute imperfection and folly to Him who is the only wise God." For, in the conduct of human beings, we uniformly regard it as an evidence of folly, when they construct a complicated and an extravagant machine, which either accomplishes no end, or no end worthy of the expence and labour bestowed on its construction. And, therefore, if we would not ascribe imbecility or want of design to the adorable Creator of the universe, we must admit, that he has not formed the soul of man for this terrestrial scene *alone*, but has destined it to a stage of progressive improvement, and of endless duration.

This conclusion will appear still more evident, if we consider the endless round of business and care, and the numerous hardships, to which the bulk of mankind are subjected in the present state, which prevent the full and vigorous exercise of the intellectual powers on those objects which are congenial to the ardent desires and the noble faculties of the human soul. The greater part of mankind, in the present circumstances of their terrestrial existence, have their time and attention almost wholly absorbed in counteracting the evils incident to their present condition, and in making provision for the wants of their animal natures; and consequently, the full gratification of the appetite for knowledge, is an absolute impossibility, amidst the pursuits and the turmoils connected with the present scene of things. If we likewise consider the difficulty of directing the mind in the pursuit of substantial knowledge, and the numerous obstructions which occur in our researches after truth, amidst the contradictory opinions, the jarring interests, and the wayward passions of men; if we consider the imperfections of our senses, and the fallacies to which they are exposed, the prejudices and the passions which seduce us into error; how readily we embrace a glittering phantom for a substantial truth, and how soon our spirits faint under the pressure of intense application to mental pursuits, we shall be convinced, that, in this sublunary sphere, there is no scope for the full exercise of the intellectual powers, and that the present world must be only a *preparatory* scene to a higher state of existence. Besides, even in those cases where every requisite for the acquisition of knowledge is possessed; where leisure, wealth, education, books, instruments, and all the assistances derived from learned associations, are conjoined with the most splendid intellectual endowments, how feeble are the efforts of the most penetrating and energetic mind, and how narrow the boundary within which its views are confined! The brightest genius, standing on the highest eminence to which science can transport him, contemplates a boundless prospect of objects and events, the knowledge of which he can never hope to attain, while he is chained down to the limits of this terrestrial ball. His mental eye beholds an unbounded and diversified scene of objects, operations, relations, changes, and revolutions, beyond the limits of all that is visible to the eye of sense: he catches an occasional glimpse of objects and of scenes which were previously involved in obscurity, he strains his mental sight, stretches forward with eagerness to grasp at new discoveries, descries some openings which direct his view into the regions of infinity and eternity, is still restless and unsatisfied, perceives all his knowledge to be mere shreds and patches, or like a few dim tapers amidst the surrounding gloom, is convinced that his present faculties are too weak and limited, and that he must be raised to a sublimer station, before he can fully grasp the magnificent objects which lie hid in the unexplored regions of immensity. All his present views and prospects are confined within the circle of a few miles, and all beyond, in the universal system, which extends through the immeasurable tracts of infinite space, is darkness and uncertainty.

Can it, then, be supposed, that a soul furnished with such noble powers and capacities, capable of traversing the realm of creation, of opening new prospects into the unbounded regions of truth that lie before it, and of appreciating the perfections of the Sovereign of the universe; a soul fired with ardent desires after knowledge, panting after new discoveries of truth and of the grandeur of the Divinity, unsatisfied with all its past attainments, and contemplating a boundless unexplored prospect before it, should be cast off from existence, and sink into eternal annihilation, at the moment when its capacities were just beginning to expand, when its desires were most ardent, and when the scenes of immensity and eternity were just opening to its view? If such a supposition could be admitted, man would be the most inexplicable phenomenon in the universe; his existence an unfathomable mystery; and there could be no conceivable mode of reconciling his condition and destination with the wisdom, the rectitude, and the benevolence of his Creator.[1]

---

[1] Such considerations as those which I have now adduced seem to have

SECTION IV.

ON THE PERPETUAL PROGRESS OF THE MIND TOWARDS PERFECTION.

As a supplement to the preceding argument, it may be stated that the soul of man appears to be capable of making a perpetual progress towards intellectual and moral perfection, and of enjoying felicity in every stage of its career, without the possibility of ever arriving at a boundary to its excursions. In the present state we perceive no limits to the excursions of the intellect, but those which arise from its connection with an unwieldy corporeal frame, which is chained down, as it were, to a mere point, in the immensity of creation. Up to the latest period of its connection with time, it is capable of acquiring new accessions of knowledge, higher attainments in virtue, and more ardent desires after moral perfection; and the infinity of the Creator, and the immensity of that universe over which he presides, present a field in which it may for ever expatiate, and an assemblage of objects on which its powers may be incessantly exercised, without the most distant prospect of ever arriving at a boundary to interrupt its intellectual career.

As I cannot illustrate this topic in more beautiful and forcible language than has been already done by a celebrated Essayist, I shall take the liberty of quoting his words: "How can it enter into the thoughts of man," says this elegant writer, "that the soul, which is capable of such immense perfections, and of receiving new improvements to all eternity,

made a powerful impression upon the minds of the philosophers of antiquity. "When I consider," says Cicero, "the wonderful activity of the mind, so great a memory of what is past, and such a capacity of penetrating into the future; when I behold such a number of arts and sciences and such a multitude of discoveries thence arising, I believe, and am firmly persuaded, that a nature which contains so many things within itself cannot be mortal." Cicero, *de Senectute*, cap. 21. And if this argument appeared strong even in Cicero's time, it has received a vast accession of strength from the numerous arts, sciences, inventions, and discoveries, which are peculiar to the age in which we live.

shall fall away into nothing almost as soon as it is created? Are such abilities made for no purpose? A brute arrives at a point of perfection which he can never pass. In a few years he has all the endowments he is capable of; and, were he to live ten thousand more, would be the same thing he is at present. Were a human soul thus at a stand in her accomplishments, were her faculties to be full blown, and incapable of further enlargements, I could imagine it might fall away insensibly, and drop at once into a state of annihilation. But can we believe a thinking being, that is in a perpetual progress of improvements, and travelling on from perfection to perfection, after having just looked abroad into the works of the Creator, and made a few discoveries of his infinite goodness, wisdom, and power, must perish in her first setting out, and in the very beginning of her inquiries?

"A man, considered in his present state, seems only sent into the world to propagate his kind. He provides himself with a successor, and immediately quits his post to make room for him:

> Heir urges on his predecessor heir,
> Like wave impelling wave.

He does not seem born to enjoy life, but to deliver it down to others. This is not surprising to consider in animals, which are formed for our use, and can finish their business in a short life. The silk-worm, after having spun her task, lays her eggs and dies. But a man can never have taken in his full measure of knowledge, has not time to subdue his passions, establish his soul in virtue, and come up to the perfection of his nature, before he is hurried off the stage. Would an infinitely wise Being make such glorious creatures for so mean a purpose? Can he delight in the production of such abortive intelligences, such short-lived reasonable beings? Would he give us talents that are not to be exerted, capacities that are never to be gratified? How can we find that Wisdom, which shines through all his works in the formation of man, without looking on this world as a nursery for the next, and believing that the several generations of rational creatures, which rise up and disappear in such quick successions, are only to receive their first rudiments of existence here, and afterwards to be transplanted into a more friendly climate, where they may spread and flourish to all eternity?

"There is not, in my opinion, a more pleasing and triumphant consideration in religion than this, of the perpetual progress which the soul makes towards the perfection of its nature, without ever arriving at a period in it. To look upon the soul as going on from strength to strength; to consider that she is to shine for ever with new accessions of glory, and brighten to all eternity; that she will be still adding virtue to virtue, and knowledge to knowledge, carries in it something wonderfully agreeable to that ambition which is natural to the mind of man. Nay, it must be a prospect pleasing to God himself to see his creation for ever beautifying in his eyes, and drawing nearer to him by greater degrees of resemblance.

"Methinks this single consideration, of the progress of a finite spirit to perfection, will be sufficient to extinguish all envy in inferior natures, and all contempt in superior. That cherub, who now appears as a god to a human soul, knows very well that the period will come about in eternity when the human soul shall be as perfect as he himself now is: nay, when she shall look down upon that degree of perfection as much as she now falls short of it. It is true the higher nature still advances, and by that means preserves his distance and superiority in the scale of being; but he knows how high soever the station is, of which he stands possessed at present, the inferior nature will at length mount up to it, and shine forth in the same degree of glory.

"With what astonishment and veneration may we look into our own souls, where there are such hidden stores of virtue and knowledge, such inexhausted sources of perfection! We know not yet what we shall be, nor will it ever enter into the heart of man to conceive the glory that will be always in reserve for him. The soul considered with its Creator, is like one of those mathematical lines that may draw nearer to another for all eternity without a possibility of touching it: and can there be a thought so transporting as to consider ourselves in these perpetual approaches to Him who is not only the standard of perfection but of happiness!"[1]

SECTION V.

ON THE UNLIMITED RANGE OF VIEW WHICH IS OPENED TO THE HUMAN FACULTIES THROUGHOUT THE IMMENSITY OF SPACE AND OF DURATION.

The unlimited range of view which is opened to the human imagination throughout the immensity of space and of duration, and the knowledge we are capable of acquiring respecting the distant regions of the universe, are strong presumptions and evidences of the eternal destination of man.

If the universe consisted solely of the globe on which we dwell, with its appendages, and were the spaces with which it is surrounded nothing more than an immense void, it would not appear surprising were the existence of man to terminate in the tomb. After having traversed this earthly ball for eighty or a hundred years, and surveyed all the varieties on its surface; after having experienced many of the physical and moral evils connected with its present constitution, and felt that "all is vanity and vexation of spirit," and that no higher prospect, and that no further scope for the exercise of his faculties, were presented to view, he would be ready to exclaim with Job, "I loathe it, I would not live alway; let me alone, for my days are vanity: my soul chooseth strangling and death rather than my life." To run the same tiresome round of giddy pleasures, and to gaze perpetually on the same unvaried objects, from one century to another, without the hope of future enjoyment, would afford no gratification commensurate with the desires and capacities of the human mind. Its powers would languish, its energies would be destroyed, its progress to perfection would be for ever interrupted, and it would roam

[1] Spectator, vol. ii.

in vain amidst the surrounding void in quest of objects to stimulate its activity.

But, beyond the precincts of this earthly scene, "a wide and unbounded prospect lies before us;" and the increasing light of modern science has enabled us to penetrate into its distant regions, and to contemplate some of its sublime and glorious objects. Within the limits of the solar system, of which our world forms a part, there have been discovered twenty-nine planetary bodies, which contain a mass of matter more than two thousand five hundred times greater than the earth, besides the numerous comets, which are traversing the planetary regions in all directions, and the immense globe of the *Sun*, which is like a universe in itself, and which is five hundred times larger than the earth and all the planets and comets taken together. These bodies differ from each other in their magnitude, distances, and motions, and in the scenery with which their surfaces are diversified; and some of them are encircled with objects the most splendid and sublime. They appear to be furnished with every thing requisite for the accommodation of intellectual beings, are capable of containing a population many thousands of times greater than that of our world, and are doubtless replenished with myriads of rational inhabitants. Within the limits of this system the soul of man would find full scope for the exertion of all its powers, capacities, and activities, during a series of ages.

Our views of the universe, however, are not confined to the system with which we are more immediately connected. Every star which twinkles in the canopy of heaven is, on good grounds, concluded to be a *sun*, and the centre of a magnificent system similar to our own; and perhaps surrounded with worlds more spacious and splendid than any of the planetary globes which we are permitted to contemplate. Nearly a thousand of these systems are visible to every observer, when he directs his eye in a clear winter night to the vault of heaven. Beyond all that is visible to the unassisted eye, a common telescope enables us to discern several thousands more. With higher degrees of magnifying power, ten thousands more, which lie scattered at immeasurable distances beyond the former, may still be descried. With the best instruments which art has hitherto constructed, many *millions* have been detected in the different regions of the sky, leaving us no room to doubt that hundreds of millions more, which no human eye will ever discern in the present state, are dispersed throughout the illimitable tracts of creation. So that no limits appear to the scene of Creating Power, and to that vast empire over which the moral government of the Almighty extends. Amidst this boundless scene of Divine Wisdom and Omnipotence, it is evident, that the soul might expatiate in the full exercise of its energies, during ages numerous as the drops of the ocean, without ever arriving at a boundary to interrupt its excursions.

Now, it ought to be carefully remarked, in the first place, that God endowed the mind of man with those faculties with which he has been enabled to compute the bulk of the earth, to determine the size and distance of the planets, and to make all the other discoveries to which I now allude. In the course of his providence he led the human mind into that train of thought, and paved the way for those inventions, by means of which the grandeur and extent of his operations in the distant regions of space have been opened to our view. It therefore appears to have been his *will and intention*, that the glories of his empire, in the remote spaces of creation, should be, in some measure, unvailed to the inhabitants of our world.

Again, when the soul has once got a glimpse of the magnificence and immensity of creation, it feels the most *ardent desire* to have the vail which now interposes between us and the remote regions of the universe withdrawn, and to contemplate at a nearer distance the splendours of those worlds whose suns we behold twinkling from afar. A thousand conjectures and enquiries are suggested to the mind, in relation to the systems and worlds which are dispersed through the immensity of space. Are all those vast globes peopled with inhabitants? are they connected together, under the government of God, as parts of one vast moral system? are their inhabitants pure moral intelligences, or are they exposed to the inroads of physical and moral evil? What are the gradations of rank or of intellect which exist among them? What correspondence do they carry on with other provinces of the Divine empire? What discoveries have they made of the perfections of the Deity, of the plan of his government, and of the extent of his dominions? With what species of corporeal vehicles do they hold a correspondence with the material world? With what organs of perception, and with what powers of intellect, are they furnished? What faculties and organs different from those of man do they possess, and by what laws are their social intercourses regulated? Do benignity and love for ever beam from their countenances, and does ecstatic joy perpetually enrapture their hearts? What capacities for rapid movement do they possess? Are they confined within the limits of a single globe like ours, or can they fly from one world to another, on the wings of a seraph? What magnificent landscapes adorn the places of their residence? What celestial glories are hung out for their contemplation in the canopy of heaven? What visible displays of the presence and agency of their Creator are presented to their view? By what means are they carried forward in their progress towards intellectual and moral perfection? What sciences do they cultivate? what objects engage their chief attention? in what solemn and sublime forms of worship and adoration do they join? What changes or revolutions have taken place among them? What transactions does their history record? What scenes of glory or of terror have been displayed towards any particular system or province of this immense empire? Are sin, disease, and death, altogether unknown, and do their inhabitants bask for ever in the regions of immortality? What knowledge do they possess of the character and condition of the inhabitants of our globe, and of the system of which it forms a part? What *variety* of sensitive and intellectual beings is to be found in the different systems of the universe? What *diversity* of external scenery, superior to all that the eye of man has seen, or his imagination can conceive, is displayed throughout the numerous worlds which compose this vast empire? What systems exist, and what scenes of creating power are displayed in that boundless region which lies beyond the limits of human vision? At what period in duration did this mighty fabric of the universe first arise into existence? What successive creations have taken place since the first material world was launched into existence by the Omnipotent Creator? What new worlds and beings are still emerging into existence from the voids of space? Is this mighty expanse of creation to endure for ever, and to receive new accessions to its population and grandeur, while eternity rolls on? What are the grand and ultimate designs to be accomplished by this immense assemblage of material and intellectual beings, and is man never to behold this wondrous scene a little more unfolded?

Inquiries of this description, to which no satisfactory answers can be expected in the present state, might be multiplied to an indefinite extent. The soul of man is astonished, overwhelmed, and bewildered at the immensity of the scene which is opened before it, and at once perceives, that, in order to acquire a comprehensive knowledge of the character and attributes of the Divinity, to penetrate into the depths of his plans and operations, and to contemplate the full glory of his empire, ages numerous as the stars of heaven are requisite, and that, if no future existence awaits it beyond the grave, its ardent desires after progressive improvement and felicity, and its hopes of becoming more fully acquainted with the universe and its Author, must end in eternal disappointment.

Again, the mind of man is not only animated with ardent desires after a more full disclosure of the wonders of this boundless scene, but is endowed with capacities for acquiring an indefinite extent of knowledge respecting the distant regions of the universe and the perfections of its Author. Those who have taken the most extensive excursions through the field of science, still find that they are capable of receiving an addition to all the knowledge they have hitherto acquired on every subject, and of prosecuting inquiries beyond the range of the visible system, provided the means of investigation were placed within their reach. Were a human soul transported to a distant world, for example, to the regions of the planet *Saturn;* were it permitted to contemplate at leisure the sublime movement of its rings, and the various phenomena of its moons; the variety of landscapes which diversify its surface, and the celestial scenery which its firmament displays; were it to mingle with its inhabitants, to learn the laws by which their social intercourse is directed, the sciences which they cultivate, the worship in which they engage, and the leading transactions and events which their history records; it would find no more difficulty in acquiring and treasuring up such information than it now does in acquiring, from the narrative of a traveller, a knowledge of the customs and manners of an unknown tribe of mankind, and of the nature of the geographical territory it possesses. Were angelic messengers, from a thousand worlds, to be despatched at successive intervals, to our globe, to describe the natural and moral scenery, and to narrate the train of Divine dispensations peculiar to each world, there would be ample room in the human mind for treasuring up such intelligence, notwithstanding all the stores of science which it may have previously acquired. Such information would neither annihilate the knowledge we had formerly attained, nor prevent our further progress in intellectual acquisition. On the contrary, it would enlarge the capacity of the mind, invigorate its faculties, and add a new stimulus to its powers and energies. On the basis of such information the soul could trace new aspects, and new displays of Divine wisdom, intelligence, and rectitude, and acquire more comprehensive views of the character of God; just as it does, in the mean time, from a contemplation of those objects and dispensations which lie within its grasp. To such researches, investigations, and intellectual progressions, no boundary can be assigned, if the soul be destined to survive the dissolution of its mortal frame. It only requires to be placed in a situation where its powers will be permitted to expatiate at large, and where the physical and moral obstructions which impede their exercise shall be completely removed.

It may be further remarked, on the ground of what has been now stated, that all the knowledge which can be attained in the present state is but as a drop to the ocean when compared with "the treasures of wisdom and knowledge" that may be acquired in the eternal world. The proportion between the one and the other may bear a certain analogy to the bulk of the terraqueous globe, when compared with the immensity of the worlds and systems which compose the universe. If an *infinite variety* of designs, of objects, and of scenery, exist in the distant provinces of creation, as we have reason to believe, from the variety which abounds in our terrestrial system; if every world be peopled with inhabitants of a different species from those of another, if its physical constitution and external scenery be peculiar to itself, if the dispensations of the **Creator** towards its inhabitants be such as have not been displayed to any other world ; if "the manifold wisdom of God," in the arrangement of its destinies, be displayed in a manner in which it has never been displayed to any other class of intelligences; and, in short, if every province of creation exhibit a *peculiar manifestation* of the Deity,—we may conclude, that all the knowledge of God, of his works and dispensations, which can be attained in the present life, is but as the faint glimmering of a taper when contrasted with the effulgence of the meridian sun. Those who have made the most extensive and profound investigations into the wonders of nature, are the most deeply convinced of their own ignorance, and of the boundless fields of knowledge which remain unexplored. Sir Isaac Newton had employed the greater part of his life in some of the sublimest investigations which can engage the attention of the human mind, and yet he declared, a little before his death, " I do not know what I may appear to the world, but to myself I seem to have been only like a boy playing on the sea-shore, and diverting myself in now and then finding a pebble or a prettier shell than ordinary, while the great ocean of truth lay all undiscovered before me." And is it reasonable to believe, that after a glimpse of the boundless treasures of Divine science has flashed upon the mind, it is to pass only a few months or years in anxious desire and suspense, and then be extinguished for ever?

It may be further observed, in connection with the preceding remarks, that the creation of such a vast universe must have been chiefly intended to display the perfections of the Deity, and to afford gratification and felicity to the intellectual beings he has formed. The Creator stands in no need of innumerable assemblages of worlds and of inferior ranks of intelligences, in order to secure or to augment his felicity. Innumerable ages before the universe was created, he existed *alone*, independent of every other being, and infinitely happy in the contemplation of his own eternal excellences. No other reason, therefore, can be assigned for the production of the universe, but the gratification of his rational offspring, and that he might give a display of the infinite glories of his nature to innumerable orders of intelligent creatures. Ten thousand times ten thousand suns, distributed throughout the regions of immensity, with all their splendid apparatus of planets, comets, moons, and rings, can afford no spectacle of novelty to expand and entertain the Eternal Mind; since they all existed, in their prototypes, in the plans and conceptions of the Deity, during the countless ages of a past eternity. Nor did he produce these works for the improvement and information of *no being*. This amazing structure of the universe then, with all the sensitive and intellectual enjoyments connected with it, must have been chiefly designed for the instruction and entertainment of subordinate intelligences, and to serve as a magnificent theatre on which the energies of Divine power and wisdom, and the emanations of Divine benevolence might be illustriously displayed. And can we suppose that the material universe will exist, while intelligent minds, for whose improvement it was reared, are suffered to sink into annihilation?

Again, it cannot be admitted, in consistency with the attributes of God, that he will finally disappoint the rational hopes and desires of the human soul, which he himself has implanted and cherished. If he had no ultimate design of gratifying rational beings with a more extensive display of the immensity and grandeur of his works, it is not conceivable, that he would have permitted them to make those discoveries they have already brought to light, respecting the extent and the glory of his empire. Such discoveries could not have been made without his permission and direction, or without those faculties and means which he himself had imparted. And, therefore, in permitting the inhabitants of our world to take a distant glimpse of the boundless scene of his operations, he must have intended to excite those ardent desires which will be gratified in a future world, and to commence those trains of thought which will be prosecuted with increasing ardour, through eternity, till we shall be able to perceive and comprehend the contrivance and skill, the riches of Divine munificence, the vast designs, and the miracles of Power and Intelligence which are displayed throughout every part of the universal system. To suppose that the Creator would unfold a partial and imperfect view of the wonders of creation, and enkindle a rational longing and desire, merely for the **purpose** of mocking and tantalizing our expectations, would be to represent the moral character of the Deity as below the level of that of a depraved mortal. It would argue a species of deceit, of envy, and of malignity, which is altogether repugnant to the character of a Being of infinite benevolence. As his goodness was the principal motive which induced him to bring us into existence, his conduct must be infinitely removed from every thing that approaches to envy, malignity, or a desire to mock or disappoint the rational hopes of his creatures. His general character, as displayed in all his works, leads us to conclude that, so far from tantalizing the rational beings he has formed, he is both able and willing " to do to and for them exceeding abundantly above all that they can ask or think." If he had intended merely to confine our desires to sensitive enjoyments and to the present life, the habitation of man would have required no more contrivance or decoration than what are requisite for the lion's den and the retreats of the tiger, and no further display of the grandeur of his empire would have been unfolded to view.

Since, therefore, it appears that the universe is replenished with innumerable systems, and is vast and unlimited in its extent; since God endued the mind of man with those faculties by which he has explored a portion of its distant regions; since the soul feels an ardent desire to obtain a more full disclosure of its grandeur and magnificence; since it is endued with faculties capable of receiving an indefinite increase of knowledge on this subject; since all the knowledge it can acquire in the present state, respecting the operations and the government of God, is as nothing when compared with the prospects which eternity may unfold; since the universe and its material glories are chiefly intended for the gratification of intelligent minds; and since it is obviously inconsistent with the moral character of the Deity, to cherish desires and expectations which he will finally frustrate and disappoint, the conclusion appears to be unavoidable, *that man is destined to an immortal existence.* During the progress of that existence, his faculties will arrive at their full expansion, and there will be ample scope for their exercise on myriads of objects and events which are just now vailed in darkness and mystery. He will be enabled to penetrate more fully into the plans and operations of the Divinity, to perceive new aspects of the Eternal Mind, new evolutions of infinite Wisdom and design, new displays of Omnipotence, Goodness, and Intelligence, and to acquire a more minute and comprehensive view of all the attributes of the Deity, and of the connections, relations, and dependences, of that vast physical and moral system over which his government extends.

SECTION VI.

ON THE MORAL POWERS OF MAN.

The moral powers with which man is endued form a strong presumptive proof of his immortal destiny.

Man is formed for *action* as well as for contemplation. For this purpose there are interwoven in his constitution, powers, principles, instincts, feelings and affections, which have a reference to his improvement in virtue, and which excite him to promote the happiness of others. These powers and active principles, like the intellectual, are susceptible of vast improvement, by attention, by exercise, by trials and difficulties, and by an expansion of the intellectual views. Such are filial and fraternal affection, fortitude, temperance, justice, gratitude, generosity, love of friends and country, philanthropy, and general benevolence. Degenerate as our world has always been, many striking examples of such virtues have been displayed both in ancient and modern times, which demonstrate the vigour, expansion, and sublimity of the moral powers of man.

When we behold men animated by noble sentiments, exhibiting sublime virtues, and performing illustrious actions, displaying generosity and beneficence in seasons of calamity, and tranquillity and fortitude in the midst of difficulties and dangers; desiring riches only for the sake of distributing them; estimating places of power and honour only for the sake of suppressing vice, rewarding virtue, and promoting the prosperity of their country; enduring poverty and distress with a noble heroism; suffering injuries and affronts with patience and serenity; stifling resentment when they have it in their power to inflict vengeance; displaying kindness and generosity towards enemies and slanderers; vanquishing irascible passions and licentious desires in the midst of the strongest temptations; submitting to pain and disgrace in order to promote the prosperity of friends and relatives; and sacrificing repose, honour, wealth, and even life itself, for the good of their country, or for promoting the best interests of the human race: we perceive in such examples features of the human mind, which mark its dignity and grandeur, and indicate its destination to a higher scene of action and enjoyment.

Even in the annals of the Pagan world, we find many examples of such illustrious virtues. There we read of *Regulus* exposing himself to the most cruel torments, and to death itself, rather than suffer his veracity to be impeached, or his fidelity to his country to be called in question; of *Phocion*, who exposed himself to the fury of an enraged assembly, by inveighing against the vices, and endeavouring to promote the best interests of his countrymen, and gave it as his last command to his son when he was going to execution, "that he should forget how ill the Athenians had treated his father;" of *Cyrus*, who was possessed of wisdom, moderation, courage, magnanimity, and noble sentiments, and who employed them all to promote the happiness of his people; of *Scipio*, in whose actions the virtues of generosity and liberality, goodness, gentleness, justice, magnanimity, and chastity, shone with distinguished lustre; and of *Damon* and *Pythias*, who were knit together in the bonds of a friendship which all the terrors of an ignominious death could not dissolve. But of all the characters of the heathen world, illustrious for virtue, *Aristides* appears to stand in the foremost rank. An extraordinary greatness of soul (say Rollin) made him superior to every passion. Interest, pleasure, ambition, resentment, jealousy, were extinguished in him by the love of virtue and his country.

The merit of others, instead of offending him, became his own by the approbation he gave it. He rendered the government of the Athenians amiable to their allies, by his mildness, goodness, humanity, and justice. The disinterestedness he showed in the management of the public treasure, and the love of poverty, which he carried almost to an excess, are virtues so far superior to the practice of our age, that they scarcely seem credible to us. His conduct and principles were always uniform, steadfast in the pursuit of whatever he thought just, and incapable of the least falsehood, or shadow of flattery, disguise, or fraud, even in jest. He had such a control over his passions, that he uniformly sacrificed his private interests, and his private resentments, to the good of the public. *Themistocles* was one of the principle actors who procured his banishment from Athens; but, after being recalled, he assisted him on every occasion with his advice and credit, joyfully taking pains to promote the glory of his greatest enemy, through the motive of advancing the public good. And when afterwards the disgrace of Themistocles gave him a proper opportunity for revenge, instead of resenting the ill treatment he had received from him, he constantly refused to join with his enemies, being as far from secretly rejoicing over the misfortune of his adversary, as he had been before from being afflicted at his good success. Such virtues reflect a dignity and grandeur on every mind in which they reside, which appear incompatible with the idea, that it is destined to retire for ever from the scene of action at the hour of death.

But the noblest examples of exalted virtue are to be found among those who have enlisted themselves in the cause of Christianity. The apostle Paul was an illustrious example of every thing that is noble, heroic, generous, and benevolent in human conduct. His soul was inspired with a holy ardour in promoting the best interests of mankind. To accomplish this object, he parted with friends and relatives, relinquished his native country, and every thing that was dear to him either as a Jew or as a Roman citizen, and exposed himself to persecutions and dangers of every description. During the prosecution of his benevolent career, he was " in journeyings often, in perils of waters, in perils of robbers, in perils by his own countrymen, in perils by the heathen, in perils in the city, in perils in the wilderness, in perils in the sea, in perils among false brethren; in weariness and painfulness, in watchings often, in hunger and thirst, in fastings often, in stripes above measure, in cold and nakedness." Yet none of these things moved him, nor did he count his life dear to him, provided he might finish his course with joy, and be instrumental in accomplishing the present and eternal happiness of his fellow-men. In every period of the Christian era, similar characters have arisen to demonstrate the power of virtue and to bless mankind. Our own age and country have produced numerous philanthropic characters, who have shone as lights in the moral world, and have acted as benefactors to the human race. The names of Alfred, Penn, Barnard, Raikes, Neilde, Clarkson, Sharpe, Buxton, Wilberforce, Venning, and many others, are familiar to every one who is in the least acquainted with the annals of benevolence. The exertions which some of these individuals have made in the cause of liberty, in promoting the education of the young, in alleviating the distresses of the poor, in ameliorating the condition of the prisoner, and in counteracting the abominable traffic in slaves, will be felt as blessings conferred on mankind throughout succeeding generations, and will, doubtless, be held in everlasting remembrance.

But among all the philanthropic characters of the past or present age, the labours of John Howard stand pre-eminent. This illustrious man, from a principle of pure benevolence, devoted the greater part of his life to active beneficence, and to the alleviation of human wretchedness, in every country where he travelled; diving into the depth of dungeons, and exposing himself to the infected atmospheres of hospitals and jails, in order to meliorate the condition of the unfortunate, and to allay the sufferings of the mournful prisoner. In prosecuting this labour of love, he travelled three times through France, four times through Germany, five times through Holland, twice through Italy, once through Spain and Portugal, and also through Denmark, Sweden, Russia, Poland, and part of the Turkish empire, surveying the haunts of misery, and distributing benefits to mankind wherever he appeared.

  "From realm to realm, with cross or crescent crowned,
Where'er mankind and misery are found,
O'er burning sands, deep waves, or wilds of snow,
Mild HOWARD, journeying, seeks the house of woe.
Down many a winding step to dungeons dank,
Where Anguish wails aloud and fetters clank,
To caves bestrewed with many a mouldering bone,
And cells whose echoes only learn to groan;
Where no kind bars a whispering friend disclose,
No sunbeam enters, and no zephyr blows;
He treads, inemulous of fame or wealth,
Profuse of toil and prodigal of health;
Leads stern-eyed Justice to the dark domains,
If not to sever to *relax* the chains,
Gives to her babes the self-devoted wife,
To her fond husband liberty and life.
Onward he moves! disease and death retire;
And murmuring demons hate him and admire!"

DARWIN.

  Such characters afford powerful demonstrations of the sublimity of virtue, of the activity of the human mind, and of its capacity for contributing to the happiness of fellow-intelligences to an unlimited extent. We have also in our times, a class of men who have parted from their friends and native land, and who have gone to the "uttermost ends of the earth," to distant barbarous climes, exposing themselves to the frosts of Labrador and Greenland, to the scorching heats of Africa, and to the hostile attacks of savage tribes, in order to publish the salvation of God, and to promote the happiness of men of all languages and climates. Some of these have felt their minds inspired with such a noble ardour in the cause of universal benevolence that nothing but insurmountable physical obstructions prevented them from making the tour of the world, and imparting benefits to men of all nations, kindreds, and tongues.

  Can we then imagine, that such active powers as those to which I have now alluded, powers which qualify their possessors for diffusing happiness to an indefinite extent among surrounding intelligences, will be for ever extinguished by the stroke of death, and that, after a few feeble efforts during the present transitory scene, they will never again exert their energies through all eternity? This will appear in the highest degree improbable, if we consider, 1. The limited sphere of action to which the generality of mankind are confined in the present state. Most men are confined to laborious employments, and have their attention almost entirely absorbed in providing for their families, and in anxious solicitude for their animal subsistence and success in life, so that they find no scope for their moral powers beyond the circle of the family mansion, and of their own immediate neighbourhood. 2. The period within which the most energetic powers can be exerted is extremely limited. It is not before man has arrived near the meridian of life that his moral powers begin to be fully expanded; and it frequently happens, in the case of ardent benevolent characters, that, at the moment when their philanthropic schemes are matured, and they have just commenced their career of beneficence, death interposes, and puts a period to all their labours and designs. 3. In the present state of the world, numerous physical obstructions interpose to prevent the exertion of the moral powers, even in the most ardent philanthropic minds. The want of wealth and influence; the diseases and infirmities of an enfeebled corporeal frame; the impediments thrown in the way by malice and envy, and the political arrangements of States; the difficulty of penetrating into every region of the globe where human beings reside; and many other obstructions, prevent the full exercise of that moral energy which resides in benevolent and heroic minds, and confine its operations within a narrow span. But can we ever suppose, in consistency with Divine Wisdom and Benevolence, that God has implanted in the human constitution benevolent active powers, which are never to be fully expanded; and that those god-like characters that have occasionally appeared on the theatre of our world, are never to re-appear on the field of action, to expatiate, in the full exercise of their moral powers, in the ample career of immortality? To admit such a supposition would be in effect to call in question his Wisdom and Intelligence. It is the part of Wisdom to proportionate *means* to *ends*, and to adapt the faculties of any being to the scene in which it is to operate. But here we behold a system of powers which can never be brought into full operation in the present state; and therefore, if death is to put a final termination to the activity of man, the mighty powers and energies with which he is endowed have been bestowed in vain; and we are led to conceive of the Divine Being as deficient in Wisdom and Intelligence in his government of the intellectual beings he has formed.

This will, perhaps, appear still more obvious, if we attend to the following considerations: Throughout the universe we perceive traces of a system of universal benevolence. This is distinctly perceptible in relation to our own globe, in the revolution of day and night; in the constitution of the atmosphere; in the beautiful and sublime scenes presented to the eye in every country; in the agencies of light and heat, and of the electrical and galvanic fluids; in the splendour of the sun, and the glories of the midnight sky; in the organisation of the body of man, and the different senses with which he is endowed; in the general adaptation of the mineral and vegetable kingdoms, and of every element around us, to the wants of man and other sensitive beings; and in the abundant supply of food and drink which is annually distributed to every rank of animated existence. We perceive traces of the same benevolent agency in the arrangements connected with distant worlds, in the rotation of the planetary globes around their axes, in the assemblages of rings and moons with which they are environed, and in the diversified apparatus by which light and heat are distributed in due proportion to the several bodies which compose the solar system. And in other systems, in the distant regions of space, we perceive, that it is one great end of the Creator, to diffuse light and splendour throughout all the provinces of his immense empire, in order to unvail his glorious works to the eyes of unnumbered intelligences. But, although a system of benevolence is abundantly manifest in the mechanical fabric of the universe, yet it does not appear that happiness can be fully enjoyed *without the benevolent agency of intelligent beings.* We have abundant proofs of this position in the world in which we dwell. For although the goodness of the Creator is displayed throughout all its regions, yet the greater part of the human race is in a state of comparative misery, not owing to any deficiency in the Divine bounty, but to the selfishness, ambition, and malevolence of men. With the blessings which

Heaven provides from year to year, the whole population of our globe, and a thousand millions more, would be amply supplied, and happiness extensively diffused, were *benevolence* a prominent and universal trait in the character of mankind. Even in those places where **only a** few energetic **and** benevolent individuals bestir themselves in the cause of general philanthropy, a wonderful change is rapidly produced in the condition of society. Disease, and misery, and want, fly away at their approach, **the poor are** supplied, the wretched relieved, the prisoner released, the orphan provided for, and the widow's heart made to sing for joy.

Now, we have every reason to conclude, that *moral action* extends over the whole empire of God, that Benevolence exerts its noblest energies among the inhabitants of distant worlds, and that it is chiefly through the medium of reciprocal kindness and affection that ecstatic joy pervades the hearts of celestial intelligences. For we cannot conceive happiness to exist in any region of space, or among any class of intellectual beings, where love to the Creator, and to one another, is not a prominent and permanent affection.

It is, therefore, reasonable to believe, that those virtuous benevolent characters which have appeared in our world, have been only in the act of training for a short period, preparatory to their being transported to a nobler scene of action, and that their moral powers which could not be brought into full exercise in this terrestrial sphere, were intended to qualify them for mingling with more exalted intelligences, and co-operating with them in carrying forward that vast system of universal benevolence, to which all the arrangements of the Creator evidently tend.

Whether then, it may be asked, does it appear most consistent with the moral powers of man, and with the wisdom and goodness of God, to suppose that such illustrious characters as Penn, G. Sharpe, Clarkson, Venning, Howard, and the apostle Paul, are now for ever banished from creation, or that they are expatiating in a higher scene of action and enjoyment, where all their benevolent energies find ample scope, and where every blossom of virtue is fully expanded? If there is a God, and if Wisdom, Benevolence, and Rectitude, form an essential part of his character, we cannot doubt for a moment that such characters are still in existence, and shall reappear on a more splendid theatre of action in the future scenes of eternity.

I shall conclude my illustrations of the preceding arguments with the following extract from a judicious and elegant writer:

"In tracing the nature and *destination* of any being, we form the surest judgment from his *powers of action*, and the scope and *limits* of these compared with his *state* or that field in which they are exercised. If this being passes through different states or fields of action, and we find a *succession* of powers adapted to the different periods of his progress, we conclude, that he was destined for those successive states, and reckon his nature *progressive*. If, besides the immediate set of powers which fit him for action in his present state, we observe another set which appear superfluous if he were to be confined to it, and which point to another or higher one, we naturally conclude that he is not designed to remain in his present state, but to advance to that for which those supernumerary powers are adapted. Thus, we argue, that the *insect* which has wings forming or formed, and all the apparatus proper for flight, is not destined always to creep on the ground, or to continue in the torpid state of adhering to a wall, but is designed in its season to take its flight in the air. Without this further destination, the admirable mechanism of wings and the other apparatus, would be useless and absurd.

"The same kind of reasoning may be applied to man, while he lives only a sort of vegetative life in the womb. He is furnished even there with a beautiful apparatus of organs, eyes, ears, and other delicate senses, which derive nourishment indeed, but are in a manner folded up, and have no proper exercise or use in their present confinement. Let us suppose some intelligent spectator, who never had any connection with man, nor the least acquaintance with human affairs, to see this odd phenomenon, a creature formed after such a manner, and placed in a situation apparently unsuitable to such various machinery, must he not be strangely puzzled about the use of his complicated structure, and reckon such a profusion of art and admirable workmanship lost on the subject; or reason by way of anticipation, that a creature endured with **such various yet** unexerted capacities, was destined for a more enlarged sphere of action, in which those latent capacities shall have full play? The vast **variety, and yet** beautiful symmetry and proportions, of the several parts and organs with which the creature is endued, and their apt cohesion with and dependence on the curious receptacle of their life and nourishment, would forbid his concluding the whole to be the birth of chance, or the bungling effort of an unskilful artist; at least, **would** make him demur a while at so harsh a sentence. But if, **while** he is in this state of uncertainty, we suppose him **to see the babe,** after a few successful struggles, throwing of his fetters, breaking loose from his little dark prison, and emerging **into open day,** then unfolding his recluse and dormant powers, breathing **in air,** gazing at light, admiring colours, sounds, and all **the** *fair variety* of nature; immediately his doubts clear up, the propriety and excellence of the workmanship dawn upon him with full lustre, and the whole mystery of the first period is unraveled by the opening of this new scene. Though in his *second* period the creature lives chiefly a kind of *animal* life, that is, of *sense* and *appetite,* yet by various trials and observations he gains experience, and by the gradual evolution of the powers of the *imagination* he ripens apace for a *higher* life, for exercising the arts of *design* and *imitation,* and of those in which strength or dexterity are more requisite than acuteness or reach of judgment. In the succeeding *rational* or *intellectual* period, his *understanding*, which formerly crept in **a lower,** mounts into a higher sphere, canvasses the natures, judges of the relation of things, forms schemes, deduces consequences from what is past, and from present **as well as past** collects future events. By this succession of **states,** and of correspondent culture, he grows up at length into **a** *moral,* a *social,* and a *political* creature. This is **the last** period at which we perceive him to arrive in this **his** mortal career. Each period is introductory to the next succeeding one; each life is a field of exercise and improvement for the next higher one; the life of the *fœtus* for **that** of the *infant,* the life of the *infant* for that of the *child,* and all the lower for the highest **and best.**

"But is this the last period of nature's progression? Is this the utmost extent of her plot, where she winds up the drama, and dismisses the actor into eternal oblivion? Or does he appear to be invested with supernumerary powers, which have not full exercise and scope even in the last scene, and reach not that maturity or perfection of which they are capable, and therefore point to some higher scene, where he is to sustain another and more important character than he has yet sustained? If any such there are, may we not conclude from analogy, or in the same way of anticipation as before, that he is destined for that after part, and is to be produced upon a more august and solemn stage, where his sublimer powers shall have proportionate action, and his nature attain its completion."[1]

In illustrating the preceding arguments, I have shown that man is possessed of desires which cannot be fully gratified, and of moral and intellectual powers which cannot be fully exercised in the present world, and consequently, we have the same reason to conclude, that he is destined to a higher scene of existence, as we would have from beholding the rudiments of eyes and ears in the embryo in the womb, that it is destined to burst its confinement, and to enter into a world where sounds and light, and colours, will afford ample scope for the exercise of these organs.

SECTION VII.

ON THE APPREHENSIONS AND FOREBODINGS OF THE MIND, WHEN UNDER THE INFLUENCE OF REMORSE.

The apprehensions of the mind, and its fearful forebodings of futurity, when under the influence of remorse, may be considered as intimations of a state of retribution in another world.

As the boundless desires of the human mind, the vast com-

---

[1] Fordyce.

prehension of its intellectual faculties, and the virtuous exercise of its moral powers, are indications of a future state of more enlarged enjoyment, so those horrors of conscience which frequently torment the minds of the wicked, may be considered as the forebodings of future misery and woe. For it appears as reasonable to believe, that atrocious deeds will meet with deserved opprobrium and punishment in a future state, as that virtuous actions will be approved of and rewarded; and consequently, we find, that all nations who have believed in a future state of happiness for the righteous, have also admitted that there are future punishments in reserve for the workers of iniquity. Every man has interwoven in his constitution a moral sense which secretly condemns him when he has committed an atrocious action, even when the perpretration of the crime is unknown to his fellow-men, and when he is placed in circumstances which raise him above the fear of human punishment. There have been numerous individuals, both in the higher and the lower ranks of life, who, without any external cause, or apprehension of punishment from men, have been seized with inward terrors, and have writhed under the agonies of an accusing conscience, which neither the charms of music, nor all the other delights of the sons of men, had the least power to assuage. Of the truth of this position, the annals of history furnish us with many impressive examples. The following may suffice as specimens:

While *Belshazzar* was carousing at an impious banquet, with his wives and concubines and a thousand of his nobles, the appearance of the fingers of a man's hand, and of a writing on an opposite wall, threw him into such consternation, that his thoughts terrified him, the girdles of his loins were loosed, and his knees smote one against another. His terror, in such circumstances, cannot be supposed to have proceeded from a fear of man; for he was surrounded by his guards and his princes, and all the delights of music and of a splendid entertainment. Nor did it arise from the sentence of condemnation written on the wall; for he was then ignorant both of the writing and of its meaning. But he was conscious of the wickedness of which he had been guilty, and of the sacrilegious impiety, in which he was then indulging, and therefore, the extraordinary appearance on the wall was considered as an awful foreboding of punishment from that **Almighty and Invisible Being whom he had offended.** *Tiberius*, one of the Roman emperors, was a gloomy, treacherous, and cruel tyrant. The lives of his people became the sport of his savage disposition. Barely to take them away was not sufficient, if their death was not tormenting and atrocious. He ordered, on one occasion, a general massacre of all who were detained in prison, on account of the conspiracy of Sejanus his minister, and heaps of carcases were piled up in the public places. His private vices and debaucheries were also incessant, and revolting to every principle of decency and virtue. Yet this tyrant, while acting in the plenitude of his power, and imagining himself beyond the control of every law, had his mind tormented with dreadful apprehensions. We are informed by *Tacitus*, that, in a letter to the Senate, he opened the inward wounds of his breast, with such words of despair as might have moved pity in those who were under the continual fear of his tyranny.[1] Neither the splendour of his situation as an emperor, nor the solitary retreats to which he retired, could shield him from the accusations of his conscience, but he himself was forced to confess the mental agonies he endured as a punishment for his crimes. *Antiochus Epiphanes* was another tyrant remarkable for his cruelty and impiety. He laid siege to the city of Jerusalem, exercised the most horrid cruelties upon its inhabitants, slaughtered forty thousand of them in three days, and polluted, in the most impious manner, the temple and the worship of the God of Israel. Some time afterwards, when he was breathing out curses against the Jews for having restored their ancient worship, and threatening to destroy the whole nation, and to make Jerusalem the common place of sepulture to all the Jews, he was seized with a grievous torment in his inward parts, and excessive pangs of the cholic, accompanied with such terrors as no remedies could assuage. " Worms crawled from every part of him; his flesh fell away piecemeal, and the stench was so great, that it became intolerable to the whole army; and he thus finished an impious life,

---

[1] Tiberium non fortuna, non solitudines protegebant, quin tormenta pectoris suasque pœnas ipse fateretur, etc.—*Tacitus*.

by a miserable death."[1] During this disorder, says Polybius, he was troubled with a perpetual delirium, imagining that spectres stood before him, reproaching him with his crimes. Similar relations are given by historians, of *Herod*, who slaughtered the infants at Bethlehem; of Galerius Maximianus, the author of the tenth persecution against the Christians; of the infamous Philip II of Spain; and of many others whose names stand conspicuous on the rolls of impiety and crime.

It is related of Charles IX of France, who ordered the horrible Bartholomew massacre, and assisted in this bloody tragedy, that, ever after, he had a fierceness in his looks, and a colour in his cheeks, which he never had before,—that he slept little and never sound; and waked frequently in great agonies, requiring soft music to compose him to rest; and at length died of a lingering disorder, after having undergone the most exquisite torments both of body and mind. D'Aubigné informs us that Henry IV frequently told, among his most intimate friends, that eight days after the massacre of St. Bartholomew, he saw a vast number of ravens perch and croak on the pavilion of the Louvre; that the same night Charles IX, after he had been two hours in bed, started up, roused his grooms of the chamber, and sent them out to listen to a great noise of groans in the air, and among others, some furious and threatening voices, the whole resembling what was heard on the night of the massacre; that all these various cries were so striking, so remarkable, and so articulate, that Charles believing that the enemies of the Montmorencies and of their partizans had surprised and attacked them, sent a detachment of his guards to prevent this new massacre. It is scarcely necessary to add, that the intelligence brought from Paris proved these apprehensions to be groundless, and that the noises heard, must have been the fanciful creations of the guilty conscience of the king, countenanced by the vivid remembrance of those around him, of the horrors of St. Bartholomew's day.

King Richard III, after he had murdered his innocent royal nephews, was so tormented in conscience, as Sir Thomas More reports from the gentlemen of his bedchamber, that he had no peace or quiet in himself; but always carried it as if some

[1] Rollin's Ancient History

imminent danger was near him. His eyes were always whirling about on this side, and on that side; he wore a shirt of mail, and was always laying his hand upon his dagger, looking as furiously as if he was ready to strike. He had no quiet in his mind by day, nor could take any rest by night, but, molested with terrifying dreams, would start out of his bed, and run like a distracted man about the chamber.[1]

This state of mind, in reference to another case, is admirably described in the following lines of Dryden:

> "Amidst your train this unseen judge will wait,
> Examine how you came by all your state;
> Upbraid your impious pomp, and in your ear
> Will halloo, rebel! traitor! murderer!
> Your ill-got power wan looks and care shall bring;
> Known but by discontent to be a king.
> Of crowds afraid, yet anxious when alone,
> You'll sit and brood your sorrows on a throne."

Bessus the Pæonian, being reproached with ill nature for pulling down a nest of young sparrows and killing them, answered, that he had reason to do so, "Because these little birds never ceased falsely to accuse him of the murder of his father." This parricide had been till then concealed and unknown; but the revenging fury of conscience caused it to be discovered by himself, who was justly to suffer for it. That notorious sceptic and semiatheist, Hobbes, author of the "Leviathan," had been the means of poisoning many young gentlemen and others with his wicked principles, as the Earl of Rochester confessed, with extreme compunction, on his deathbed. It was remarked, by those who narrowly observed his conduct, that "though in a humour of bravado he would speak strange and unbecoming things of God, yet in his study, in the dark, and in his retired thoughts, he trembled before him." He could not endure to be left alone in an empty house. He could not, even in his old age, bear any discourse of death, and seemed to cast off all thoughts of it. He could not bear to sleep in the dark; and if his candle happened to go out in the night, he would awake in terror and amazement; a plain indication, that he was unable to bear the dismal

---

[1] Stow's Annals, p. 460.

reflections of his dark and desolate mind, and knew not how to extinguish, or how to bear the light of "the candle of the Lord" within him. He is said to have left the world with great reluctance, under terrible apprehensions of a dark and unknown futurity.

> "Conscience, the torturer of the soul, unseen,
> Does fiercely brandish a sharp scourge within.
> Severe decrees may keep our tongues in awe,
> But to our thoughts what edict can give law?
> Even you yourself to your own breast shall tell
> Your crimes, and your own Conscience be your Hell.

Many similar examples of the power of conscience in awakening terrible apprehensions of futurity, could be brought forward from the records of history both ancient and modern; and there can be no question, that, at the present moment, there are thousands of gay spirits immersed in fashionable dissipation, and professing to disregard the realities of a future world, who, if they would lay open their inmost thoughts, would confess, that the secret dread of a future retribution is a spectre which frequently haunts them while running the rounds of forbidden pleasure, and embitters their most exquisite enjoyments.

Now, how are we to account for such terrors of conscience, and awful forebodings of futurity, if there be no existence beyond the grave, especially when we consider that many of those who have been thus tormented have occupied stations of rank and power, which raised them above the fear of punishment from man? If they got their schemes accomplished, their passions gratified, and their persons and possessions secured from temporal danger, why did they feel compunction or alarm in the prospect of futurity; for every mental disquietude of this description implies a dread of something future? They had no great reason to be afraid even of the Almighty himself, if his vengeance do not extend beyond the present world. They beheld the physical and moral world moving onward according to certain fixed and immutable laws. They beheld no miracles of vengeance, no Almighty arm visibly hurling the thunderbolts of heaven against the workers of iniquity. They saw that one event happened to all, to the righteous as well as to the wicked, and that death was an evil to which they behoved sooner or later to submit. They encountered hostile armies with fortitude, and beheld all the dread apparatus of war without dismay. Yet, in their secret retirements, in their fortified retreats, where no eye but the eye of God was upon them, and when no hostile incursion was apprehended, they trembled at a shadow, and felt a thousand disquietudes from the reproaches of an inward monitor which they could not escape. These things appear altogether inexplicable if there be no retribution beyond the grave.

We are, therefore, irresistibly led to the conclusion that the voice of conscience, in such cases, is the voice of God declaring his abhorrence of wicked deeds, and the punishment which they deserve, and that his providence presides over the actions of moral agents, and gives intimations of the future destiny of those haughty spirits who obstinately persist in their trespasses. And, consequently, as the peace and serenity of virtuous minds are preludes of nobler enjoyments in a future life, so those terrors which now assail the wicked may be considered as the beginnings of that misery and anguish which will be consummated in the world to come, in the case of those who add final impenitence to all their other crimes.

SECTION VIII.

ON THE DISORDERED STATE OF THE MORAL WORLD, WHEN CONTRASTED WITH THE REGULAR AND SYSTEMATICAL ORDER OF THE MATERIAL.

The disordered state of the moral world, contrasted with the regular and systematical order of the material, affords a strong presumption of another state, in which the moral evils which now exist will be corrected.

When we take a general survey of the great fabric of the universe, or contemplate more minutely any of its subordinate arrangements, the marks of beauty, order, and harmony, are strikingly apparent. Every thing appears in its proper place, moving onward in majestic order, and accomplishing the end for which it was intended. In the planetary system, the law of gravitation is found to operate exactly in proportion to the square of the distance, and the squares of the periodic times of the planets' revolutions round the sun are exactly proportionate to the cubes of their distances. Every body in this system finishes its respective revolution in exactly the same period of time, so as not to deviate a single minute in the course of a century. The annual revolution of the planet Jupiter was ascertained two centuries ago, to be accomplished in 4330 days, 14 hours, 27 minutes, and 11 seconds, and his rotation round his axis in 9 hours, 56 minutes, and these revolutions are still found to be performed in exactly the same times. The earth performs its diurnal revolution, from one century to another, bringing about the alternate succession of day and night, in exactly the same period of 23 hours, 56 minutes, and 4 seconds. Throughout the whole of this system, there is none of the bodies of which it is composed that stops in its motion, or deviates from the path prescribed. No one interrupts another in its course, or interferes to prevent the beneficial influences of attractive power, or of light and heat. Were it otherwise, were the earth to stop in its diurnal revolution, and delay to usher in the dawn in its appointed time, or were the planets to dash one against another, and run lawlessly through the sky, the system of Nature would run into confusion, its inhabitants would be thrown into a state of anarchy, and deprived of all their enjoyments. But, in consequence of the order which now prevails, the whole presents to the eye of intelligence an admirable display of beauty and harmony, and of infinite wisdom and design.

In like manner, if we attend to the arrangements of our sublunary system, to the revolutions of the seasons, the course of the tides, the motions of the rivers, the process of evaporation, the periodical changes of the winds, and the physical economy of the animal and vegetable tribes, the same systematic order and harmony may be perceived. In the construction and movements of the human frame, there is a striking display of systematic order and beauty. Hundreds of muscles of different forms, hundreds of bones variously articulated, thousands of lacteal and lymphatic vessels, and thousands of veins and arteries, all act in unison every moment, in order to produce life and enjoyment. Every organ of sense is admirably fitted to receive impressions from its corresponding objects. The eye is adapted to receive the impression of light, and light is adapted to the peculiar construction of the eye; the ear is adapted to sound, and the constitution of the air and its various undulations are fitted to make an impression on the tympanum of the ear. Even in the construction of the meanest insect, we perceive a series of adaptations, and a system of organization, no less regular and admirable than those of man; and as much care appears to be bestowed in bending a claw, articulating a joint, or clasping the filaments of a feather, to answer its intended purpose, as if it were the only object on which the Creator was employed. And it is worthy of remark, that our views of the harmony and order of the material world become more admirable and *satisfactory*, in proportion as our knowledge of its arrangements is enlarged and extended. Whether we explore, with the telescope, the bodies which are dispersed through the boundless regions of space, or pry, by the help of the microscope, into the minutest parts of nature, we perceive traces of order, and of exquisite mechanism and design, which excite admiration and wonder in every contemplative mind. Before the invention of the microscope, we might naturally have concluded, that all beyond the limits of natural vision was a scene of confusion, a chaotic mass of atoms without life, form, or order; but we now clearly perceive, that every thing is regular and systematic, that even the dust on a butterfly's wing, every distinct particle of which is invisible to the naked eye, consists of regular organized feathers; that in the eye of a small insect, ten thousand nicely polished globules are beautifully arranged on a transparent net-work, within the compass of one-twentieth of an inch; and that myriads of living beings exist, invisible to the unassisted sight, with bodies as curiously organized, and as nicely adapted to their situations, as the bodies of men and of the larger animals. So that the whole frame of the material world presents a scene of infinite wisdom and intelligence, and a display of systematic order, beauty, and proportion. Every thing bears the marks of *benevolent* design, and is calculated to produce happiness in sentient beings.

On the other hand, when we take a survey of the moral world in all the periods of its history, we perceive throughout almost every part of its extent an inextricable maze, and a scene of clashing and of confusion, which are directly opposed to the harmony and order which pervade the material system. When we take a retrospective view of the moral state of mankind, during the ages that are past, what do we behold but a revolting scene of perfidy, avarice, injustice, and revenge; of wars, rapine, devastation, and bloodshed; nation rising against nation, one empire dashing against another, tyrants exercising the most horrid cruelties, Superstition and Idolatry immolating millions of victims, and a set of desperate villains, termed *heroes*, prowling over the world, turning fruitful fields into a wilderness, burning towns and villages, plundering palaces and temples, drenching the earth with human gore, and erecting thrones on the ruins of nations? *Here* we behold an *Alexander*, with his numerous armies, driving the ploughshare of destruction through surrounding nations, levelling cities with the dust, and massacring their inoffensive inhabitants in order to gratify a mad ambition, and to be eulogised as a hero; *there* we behold a *Xerxes*, fired with pride and with the lust of dominion, leading forward an army of three millions of infatuated wretches to be slaughtered by the victorious and indignant Greeks. *Here* we behold an *Alaric*, with his barbarous hordes, ravaging the southern countries of Europe, overturning the most spendid monuments of art, pillaging the metropolis of the Roman empire, and deluging its streets and houses with the blood of the slain; *there* we behold a *Tamerlane* overrunning Persia, India, and other regions of Asia, carrying slaughter and devastation in his train, and displaying his sportive cruelty by pounding three or four thousand people at a time in large mortars, and building their bodies with bricks and mortar into a wall. On the one hand, we behold six millions of *Crusaders* marching in wild confusion through the eastern parts of Europe, devouring every thing before them like an army of locusts, breathing destruction to Jews and Infidels, and massacring the inhabitants of Western Asia with infernal fury.

On the other hand, we behold the immense forces of *Jenghiz Kan* ravaging the kingdoms of Eastern Asia to an extent of fifteen millions[1] of square miles, beheading 100,000 prisoners at once, convulsing the world with terror, and utterly exterminating from the earth fourteen millions of human beings. At one period, we behold the ambition and jealousy of *Marius* and *Sylla* embroiling the Romans in all the horrors of a civil war, deluging the city of Rome for five days with the blood of her citizens, transfixing the heads of her senators with poles, and dragging their bodies to the Forum to be devoured by dogs. At another, we behold a *Nero* trampling on the laws of nature and society, plunging into the most abominable debaucheries, practising cruelties which fill the mind with horror, murdering his wife Octavia and his mother Agrippina, insulting Heaven and mankind by offering up thanksgivings to the gods on the perpetration of these crimes, and setting fire to Rome, that he might amuse himself with the universal terror and despair which that calamity inspired. At one epoch we behold the Goths and Vandals rushing like an overflowing torrent, from east to west, and from north to south, sweeping before them every vestige of civilization and art, butchering all within their reach, without distinction of age or sex, and marking their path with rapine, desolation, and carnage. At another we behold the emissaries of the Romish See slaughtering, without distinction or mercy, the mild and pious Albigenses, and transforming their peaceful abodes into a scene of universal consternation and horror; while the Inquisition is torturing thousands of devoted victims, men of piety and virtue, and committing their bodies to the flames.

At one period of the world,[2] almost the whole earth appeared to be little less than one great field of battle, in which the human race seemed to be threatened with utter extermination. The Vandals, Huns, Sarmatians, Alans, and Suevi, were ravaging Gaul, Spain, Germany, and other parts of the Roman empire, the Goths were plundering Rome, and laying waste the

---

[1] "The conquests of Jenghiz Kan," says Millot, "were supposed to extend to above eighteen hundred leagues from east to west, and a thousand from south to north."—Modern History, Vol. I.

[2] About the fifth, sixth, and seventh centuries of the Christian era.

cities of Italy; the Saxons and Angles were overrunning Britain and overturning the government of the Romans. The armies of Justinian and of the Huns and Vandals were desolating Africa, and butchering mankind by millions. The whole forces of Scythia were rushing with irresistible impulse on the Roman empire, desolating the countries, and almost exterminating the inhabitants wherever they came. The Persian armies were pillaging Hierapolis, Aleppo, and the surrounding cities, and reducing them to ashes, and were laying waste all Asia, from the Tigris to the Bosphorus. The Arabians under Mahomet and his successors were extending their conquests over Syria, Palestine, Persia, and India, on the east; and over Egypt, Barbary, Spain, and the islands of the Mediterranean, on the west; cutting in pieces with their swords all the enemies of Islamism. In *Europe*, every kingdom was shattered to its centre; in the Mahommedan empire in *Asia*, the Caliphs, Sultans, and Emirs, were waging continual wars; new sovereignties were daily rising and daily destroyed; and *Africa* was rapidly depopulating, and verging towards desolation and barbarism.

Amidst this universal clashing of nations, when the whole earth became one theatre of bloody revolutions, scenes of horror were displayed, over which historians wished to draw a vail, lest they should transmit an example of inhumanity to succeeding ages: the most fertile and populous provinces were converted into deserts, overspread with the scattered ruins of villages and cities; every thing was wasted and destroyed with hostile cruelty; famine raged to such a degree that the living were constrained to feed upon the dead bodies of their fellow-citizens; prisoners were tortured with the most exquisite cruelty, and the more illustrious they were, the more barbarously they were insulted; cities were left without a living inhabitant; public buildings which resisted the violence of the flames were levelled with the ground; every art and science was abandoned; the Roman empire was shattered to its centre, and its power annihilated; avarice, perfidy, hatred, treachery, and malevolence, reigned triumphant; and virtue, benevolence, and every moral principle, were trampled under foot.

Such scenes of carnage and desolation have been displayed to a certain extent, and almost without intermission, during the whole period of this world's history. For the page of the historian, whether ancient or modern, presents to our view little more than revolting details of ambitious conquerors carrying ruin and devastation in their train, of proud despots trampling on the rights of mankind, of cities turned into ruinous heaps, of countries desolated, of massacres perpetrated with infernal cruelty, of nations dashing one against another, of empires wasted and destroyed, of political and religious dissensions, and of the general progress of injustice, immorality, and crime. Compared with the details on these subjects, all the other facts which have occurred in the history of mankind are considered by the historian as *mere interludes* in the great drama of the world, and almost unworthy of being recorded.

Were we to take a survey of the moral world as it now stands, a similar prospect, on the whole, would be presented to our view. Though the shades of depravity with which it is overspread are not so thick and dark, nor its commotions so numerous and violent, as in ancient times, yet the aspect of every nation under heaven presents to our view, features which are directly opposite to every thing we should expect to contemplate in a world of systematic order, harmony, and love. If we cast our eyes towards *Asia*, we shall find the greater part of five hundred millions of human beings involved in political commotions, immersed in vice, ignorance, and idolatry, and groaning under the lash of tyrannical despots. In Persia, the cruelty and tyranny of its rulers have transformed many of its most fertile provinces into scenes of desolation. In Turkey, the avarice and fiend-like cruelty of the Grand Seignior and his Bashaws have drenched the shores of Greece with the blood of thousands, turned Palestine into a wilderness, and rendered Syria, Armenia, and Kurdistan, scenes of injustice and rapine. In China and Japan a spirit of pride and jealousy prevents the harmonious intercourse of other branches of the human family, and infuses a cold-blooded selfishness into the breasts of their inhabitants, and a contempt of surrounding nations. Throughout Tartary, Arabia, and Siberia, numerous hostile tribes are incessantly prowling among deserts and forests in quest of plunder, so that travellers are in continual danger of being either robbed or murdered, or dragged into captivity. If we turn our eyes upon *Africa*, we behold human nature sunk into a state of the deepest degradation: the States of Barbary in incessant hostile commotions, and plundering neighbouring nations both by sea and land; the petty tyrants of Dahomy, Benin, Ashantee, Congou, and Angola, waging incessant wars with neighbouring tribes, massacring their prisoners in cold blood, and decorating their palaces with their skulls; while other degraded hordes, in conjunction with civilized nations, are carrying on a traffic in man stealing and slavery, which has stained the human character with crimes at which humanity shudders. If we turn our eyes towards *America*, we shall find that war and hostile incursions are the principal employments of the native tribes, and that the malignity of infernal demons is displayed in the tortures they inflict upon the prisoners taken in battle, while anarchy, intolerance, and political commotions still agitate a great proportion of its more civilized inhabitants. If we take a survey of the Eastern Archipelago, and of the islands which are scattered over the Pacific ocean, we shall behold immense groups of human beings, instead of living in harmony and affection, displaying the most ferocious dispositions towards each other, hurling stones, spears, and darts on every stranger who attempts to land upon their coasts; offering up human sacrifices to their infernal deities, and feasting with delight on the flesh and the blood of their enemies.

If we direct our attention towards *Europe*, the most tranquil and civilized portion of the globe, even *here* we shall behold numerous symptoms of political anarchy and moral disorder. During the last fifty years, almost every nation in this quarter of the world has been convulsed to its centre, and become the scene of hostile commotions, of revolutions, and of garments rolled in blood. We have beheld France thrown from a state of aristocratical tyranny and priestly domination, into a state of popular anarchy and confusion; her ancient institutions razed to the ground, her princes and nobles banished from her territories, and her most celebrated philosophers, in company with the vilest miscreants, perishing under the stroke of the guillotine. We have beheld a *Buonaparte* riding in triumph through the nations over heaps of slain, scattering " fire-brands, arrows, and death," and producing universal commotion wherever he appeared; overturning governments, "changing times," undermining the thrones of emperors, and setting up kings at his pleasure. We have beheld his successors again attempting to entwine the chains of tyranny around the necks of their subjects, and to hurl back the moral world into the darkness which overspread the nations during the reign of Papal superstition. We have beheld Poland torn in pieces by the insatiable fangs of Russia, Austria, and Prussia; her fields drenched with blood, her patriots slaughtered, and her name blotted out from the list of nations. We have beheld Moscow enveloped in flames; its houses, churches, and palaces tumbled into ruins, the blackened carcases of its inhabitants blended with the fragments, and the road to Smolensko covered with the shattered remains of carriages, muskets, breastplates, helmets, and garments, strewed in every direction, and thousands of the dying and the dead heaped one upon another, in horrible confusion, and swimming in blood. We have beheld the demon of war raging at Borodino, Austerlitz, the Tyrol, Wilna, Smolensko, Trafalgar, Camperdown, Eglau, Jena, La Vendee, Cadiz, Warsaw, Friedland, Talavera, Sebastian, Lutzen, Leipsic, and Waterloo—demolishing cities, desolating provinces, and blending the carcases of horses and cattle with the mangled remains of millions of human beings. We have beheld Spain and Portugal thrown into anarchy and commotion, and become the scenes of bloody revolutions; Turkey waging war with religion and liberty; Greece overrun with bloodthirsty Mahometans, and her shores and islands the theatre of the most sanguinary contests.

And what do we *just now* behold when we cast our eyes on surrounding nations? Russia pushing forward her numerous armies into the confines of Persia, for the purpose of depredation and slaughter; the Grand Seignior ruling his subjects with a rod of iron, and decorating the gates of his palace with hundreds of the heads and ears of his enemies,[1] while his janisaries are

* In a communication from Odessa, dated August 8, 1824, it was stated that the five hundred heads and twelve hundred ears of the Greeks, sent by the Captain Pacha to Constantinople, after the taking of Ipsara, were exposed on the gate of the seraglio, on the 20th July, with the fol-

fomenting incessant insurrections; the Greeks engaged in a contest for liberty, surrounded with blood-thirsty antagonists, and slaughtered without mercy; Portugal the scene of intestine broils and revolutions; Spain under the control of a silly priest-ridden tyrant, to gratify whose lust of absolute power, thousands of human beings have been sacrificed, and hundreds of eminent patriots exiled from their native land; the Inquisition torturing its unhappy victims; the Romish church thundering its anathemas against all who are opposed to its interests; the various sectaries of Protestants engaged in mutual recriminations and contentions; and the princes and sovereigns on the Continent all combined to oppose the progress of liberty, and to prevent the improvement of the human mind.

If we come nearer home, and take a view of the every-day scenes which meet our eye, what do we behold? A mixed scene of bustling and confusion, in which vice and malevolence are most conspicuous, and most frequently triumphant. When we contemplate the present aspect of society, and consider the prominent dispositions and principles which actuate the majority of mankind; the boundless avaricious desires which prevail, and the base and deceitful means by which they are frequently gratified; the unnatural contentions which arise between husbands and wives, fathers and children, brothers and sisters; the jealousies which subsist between those of the same profession or employment; the bitterness and malice with which law-suits are commenced and prosecuted; the malevolence and cabaling which attend electioneering contests; the brawlings, fightings, and altercations which so frequently occur in our streets, ale-houses, and taverns; and the thefts, robberies, and murders, which are daily committed: when we contemplate the haughtiness and oppression of the great and powerful, and the insubordination of the lower ranks of society; when we see widows and orphans suffering injustice; the virtuous persecuted and oppressed; meritorious characters pining in poverty and indigence; fools, profligates, and tyrants, riot-

---

lowing inscription: "God has blessed the arms of the Mussulmans, and the detestable rebels of Ipsara are extirpated from the face of the world," etc. It was added, "*All* friendly powers have congratulated the Sublime Porte on this victory."

ing in wealth and abundance; generous actions unrewarded, crimes unpunished; and the vilest of men raised to stations of dignity and honour: we cannot but admit that the moral world presents a scene of discord and disorder, which mar both the sensitive and intellectual enjoyments of mankind.

Such, then, are the moral aspects of our world, and the disorders which have prevailed during every period of its history. They evidently present a striking contrast to the beauty and harmony which pervade the general constitution of the material system; to the majestic movements of the planetary orbs, the regular succession of day and night, and the vicissitudes of the seasons; the changes of the moon; the ebbing and flowing of the sea; the admirable functions of the human system; and the harmonious adaptations of light and heat, air and water, and the various objects in the mineral and vegetable kingdoms, to the wants and the comfort of animated beings. And can we for a moment suppose, that this scene of moral disorder and anarchy was the ultimate end for which the material system was created? Can we suppose that the earth is every moment impelled in its annual and diurnal course by the hand of Omnipotence, that it presents new beauties every opening spring, brings forth the treasures of autumn, and displays so many sublime and variegated landscapes; that the sun diffuses his light over all its regions, that the moon cheers the shades of night, and the stars adorn the canopy of the sky, from one generation to another, merely that a set of robbers and desperadoes, and the murderers of nations, might prowl over the world for the purpose of depredation and slaughter, that tyrants might gratify their mad ambition, that vice might triumph, that virtue might be disgraced, that the laws of moral order might be trampled under foot, and that the successive generations of mankind might mingle in this bustling and discordant scene for a few years, and then sink for ever into the shades of annihilation? Yet such a conclusion we are obliged to admit, if there is no future state, in which the present disorders of the moral world will be corrected, and the plan of the Divine government more fully developed. And if this conclusion be admitted, how shall we be able to perceive or to vindicate the *wisdom* of the Creator in his moral administration? We account it folly in a human being when he constructs a machine, either for no purpose at all, or for no *good* purpose, or for the promotion of mischief. And how can we avoid ascribing the same imperfection to the Deity, if the present state of the moral world be the ultimate end of all his physical arrangements? But his wisdom is most strikingly displayed in the adaptations and arrangements which relate to the material system; and a Being possessed of boundless intelligence must necessarily be supposed to act *in consistency* with himself. He cannot display wisdom in the material system, and folly in those arrangements which pertain to the world of mind. To suppose the contrary, would be to divest him of his moral attributes, and even to call in question his very existence.

We are therefore necessarily led to conclude, that the present state of the moral world is only a small part of the great plan of God's moral government; the commencement of a series of dispensations to be completed in a future scene of existence, in which his *wisdom*, as well as all his other attributes, will be fully displayed before the eyes of his intelligent offspring. If this conclusion be admitted, it is easy to conceive how the moral disorders which now exist may be rectified in a future world, and the intelligent universe restored to harmony and happiness, and how those moral dispensations which now appear dark and mysterious, will appear illustrative of Divine Wisdom and Intelligence, when contemplated as parts of one grand system, which is to run parallel in duration with eternity itself. But, if this be rejected, the moral world presents to our view an inextricable maze, a chaos, a scene of interminable confusion, and no prospect appears of its being ever restored to harmony and order. The conduct of the Deity appears shrouded in impenetrable darkness; and there is no resisting of the conclusion, that imperfection and folly are the characteristics of the Almighty: a conclusion from which the mind shrinks back with horror, and which can never be admitted by any rational being who recognises a Supreme Intelligence presiding over the affairs of the universe.

SECTION IX.

ON THE UNEQUAL DISTRIBUTION OF REWARDS AND PUNISHMENTS IN THE PRESENT STATE.

The unequal distribution of rewards and punishments in the present state, viewed in connection with the justice and other attributes of the Deity, forms another powerful argument in support of the doctrine of a future state.

It is admitted, to a certain extent, that "virtue is its own reward, and vice its own punishment." The natural tendency of virtue, or an obedience to the laws of God, is to produce happiness; and were it universally practised, it would produce the greatest degree of happiness of which human nature in the present state is susceptible. In like manner, the natural tendency of vice is to produce misery; and were its prevalence universal and uncontrolled, the world would be transformed into a society of demons, and every species of happiness banished from the abodes of men. By connecting happiness with the observance of his laws, and misery with the violation of them, the Governor of the world, in the *general course* of his providence, gives a display of the rectitude of his character, and the impartiality of his allotments towards the subjects of his government.

But, although these positions hold true in the general course of human affairs, there are innumerable cases in which the justice of God, and the impartiality of his procedure, would be liable to be impeached, if this world were the only scene of rewards and punishments. We behold a poor starving wretch, whom hunger has impelled to break open a house in order to satisfy his craving appetite, or to relieve the wants of a helpless family, dragged with ignominy to the scaffold, to suffer death for his offence. We behold, at the same time, the very tyrant by whose order the sentence was executed, who has plundered provinces, and murdered millions of human beings, who has wounded the peace of a thousand families, and produced universal consternation and despair wherever he appeared, regaling himself in the midst of his favourites in perfect security from human punishment. Instead of being loaded with fetters and dragged to a dungeon, to await in hopeless agony the punishment of his crimes, he dwells amidst all the luxuries and splendours of a palace; his favour is courted by surrounding attendants; his praises are chanted by orators and poets; the story of his exploits is engraved in brass and marble; and historians stand ready to transmit his fame to future generations. How does the equity of the Divine government appear, in such cases, in permitting an undue punishment to be inflicted on the least offender, and in loading the greatest miscreant with unmerited enjoyments?

Again, in almost every period of the world, we behold men of piety and virtue who have suffered the most unjust and cruel treatment from the hands of haughty tyrants and bloodthirsty persecutors. It would require volumes to describe the instruments of cruelty which have been invented by these fiend-like monsters, and the excruciating torments which have been endured by the victims of their tyranny, while justice seemed to slumber, and the perpetrators were permitted to exult in their crimes. The Waldenses, who lived retired from the rest of the world, among the bleak recesses of the Alps, were a people distinguished for piety, industry, and the practice of every moral virtue. Their incessant labour subdued the barren soil, and prepared it both for grain and pasture. In the course of two hundred and fifty years they increased to the number of eighteen thousand, occupying thirty villages, besides hamlets, the workmanship of their own hands. Regular priests they had none, nor any disputes about religion; neither had they occasion for courts of justice; for brotherly love did not suffer them to go to law. They worshipped God according to the dictates of their conscience and the rules of his word, practised the precepts of his law, and enjoyed the sweets of mutual affection and love. Yet this peaceable and interesting people became the victims of the most cruel and bloody persecution. In the year 1540, the parliament of Provençe condemned nineteen of them to be burned for heresy, their trees to be rooted up, and their houses to be razed to the ground. Afterwards a violent persecution commenced against the whole of this interesting people, and an army of banditti was sent to carry the hellish purpose into effect. The soldiers began with massacring the old men, women and children, all having fled who were able to fly; and then proceeded to burn their houses, barns, corn, and whatever else appertained to them. In the town of Cabriere sixty men and thirty women, who had surrendered upon promise of life, were butchered each of them without mercy. Some women, who had taken refuge in a church, were dragged out and burned alive. Twenty-two villages were reduced to ashes; and that populous and flourishing district was again turned into a cheerless desert. Yet, after all these atrocities had been committed, the proud pampered priests, at whose instigation this persecution was commenced, were permitted to live in splendour, to exult over the victims of their cruelty, to revel in palaces, and to indulge in the most shameful debaucheries. If the present be the only state of punishments and rewards, how shall we vindicate the rectitude of the Almighty in such dispensations?

In the reign of Louis XIV, and by the orders of that despot, the Protestants of France were treated with the most wanton and diabolical cruelty. Their houses were rifled, their wives and daughters ravished before their eyes, and their bodies forced to endure all the torments that ingenious malice could contrive. His dragoons, who were employed in this infamous expedition, pulled them by the hair of their heads, plucked the nails off their fingers and toes, pricked their naked bodies with pins, smoked them in their chimneys with wisps of wet straw, threw them into fires, and held them till they were almost burnt, slung them into wells of water, dipped them into ponds, took hold of them with red-hot pincers, cut and slashed them with knives, and beat and tormented them to death in a most unmerciful and cruel manner. Some were hanged on the gallows, and others were broken upon wheels, and their mangled bodies were either left unburied, or cast into lakes and dunghills, with every mark of indignation and contempt. Mareschal Montrevel acted a conspicuous part in these barbarous executions. He burned five hundred men, women and children, who were assembled together in a mill to pray and sing psalms; he cut the throats of four hundred of the new converts at Montpelier, and drowned their wives and children in the river, near Aignes

Moters. Yet the haughty tyrant by whose orders these barbarous deeds were committed, along with his mareschals and grandees, who **assisted** in the execution, instead **of** suffering the visitations **of** retributive justice, continued for thirty **years** after this **period, to** riot in all **the** splendours of absolute **royal**ty, entering **into** solemn treaties, and breaking them when he pleased, **and** arrogating to himself divine honours; and his historians, instead of branding his memory **with** infamy, have **procured for** him the appellation of *Louis the Great.*

A thousand examples of this description might be collected from the records even **of modern** history, **were** it necessary for the illustration of this topic. The horrible cruelties which were committed on the Protestant inhabitants in the Netherlands by the agents of Charles V **and** Philip II of Spain, where **more** than a hundred thousand persons of respectable character were butchered without mercy by the Dukes of Alva and Parma, for their **adherence to the** religion of the Reformers; the dreadful **massacres** which took place on St. Bartholomew's day, in Paris **and** throughout **every province of France;** the persecutions of **the** Protestants in England, during the reign of Queen Mary, when the fires of Smithfield were kindled to consume the bodies **of the** most pious and venerable men; the Irish massacre in the reign of Charles I, when more than 40,000 inoffensive individuals were slaughtered without distinction of age, sex, or condition, and with every **circumstance of** ferocious **cruelty;** the persecutions endured by the Scottish Presbyterians, when they were driven from their dwellings, **and** hunted like wild **beasts by the** blood-thirsty Claverhouse and his savage dragoons; **the many** thousands of worthy men who have fallen **victims to** the **flames, and** the cruel tortures inflicted **by** the Inquisitors of Spain, while their haughty persecutors were permitted **to riot on the** spoils of nations; the fiend-like cruelties of the Mogul emperors in their bloody wars; **the** devastations and atrocities committed by the Persian despots; the massacre **of** the Gardiotes by Ali Pacha, and of the inhabitants of Scio by the ferocious Turks: are only a few instances out of many thousands, which the annals of **history** record of human beings suffering the most unjust and cruel treatment, while their tyrannical persecutors were permitted to prosecute their diabolical career without suffering the punishment due to their crimes. When the mind takes a deliberate review of all the revolting details connected with such facts, it is naturally led to exclaim, "Wherefore do the wicked live, become old, yea, are mighty in power? Is there no reward for the righteous? is there no punishment for the workers of iniquity? is there no God that judgeth in the earth? And, indeed, were there no retributions beyond the limits of the present life, we should be necessarily obliged to admit one or other of the following conclusions: either that no Moral Governor of the world exists, or that justice and judgment are not the foundation of his throne.

When we take a survey of the moral world around us, as it exists in the present day, the same conclusion forces itself upon the mind. When we behold, on the one hand, the virtuous and upright votary of religion struggling with poverty and misery, treated with scorn and contempt, persecuted on account of his integrity and piety, despoiled of his earthly enjoyments, or condemned to an ignominious death; and on the other, the profligate and oppressor, the insolent despiser of God and religion, passing his days in affluence and luxurious ease prosecuting with impunity his unhallowed courses, and robbing the widow and the fatherless of their dearest comforts: when we behold hypocrisy successful in all its schemes, and honesty and rectitude overlooked and neglected; the destroyers of our species loaded with wealth and honours, while the benefactors of mankind are pining in obscurity and indigence; knaves and fools exalted to posts of dignity and honour, and men of uprightness and intelligence treated with scorn, and doomed to an inglorious obscurity; criminals of the deepest dye escaping with impunity, and generous actions meeting with a base reward: when we see young men of virtue and intelligence cut off in early life, when they were just beginning to bless mankind with their philanthropic labours, and tyrants and oppressors continuing the pests of society, and prolonging their lives to old age in the midst of their folly and wickedness; human beings torn from their friends and their native home, consigned to perpetual slavery, and reduced below the level of the beasts, while their oppressors set at defiance the laws of God and man, revel in luxurious abundance, and prosper in their crimes;

when we behold one nation and tribe irradiated with intellectual light, another immersed in thick darkness; one enjoying the blessings of civilization and liberty, another groaning under the lash of despotism, and doomed to slavery and bondage: when we contemplate such facts throughout every department of the moral world, can we suppose, for a moment, that the Divine administration is bounded by the visible scene of things, that the real characters of men shall never be brought to light, that vice is to remain in eternal concealment and impunity, and that the noblest virtues are never to receive their just "recompence of reward?" To admit such conclusions would be in effect to deny the wisdom, goodness, and rectitude of the Ruler of the world, or to suppose, that his all-wise and benevolent designs may be defeated by the folly and wickedness of human beings. But such conclusions are so palpably and extravagantly absurd, that the only other alternative, the reality of a future state of existence, may be pronounced to have the force of a *moral demonstration*. So that, had we no other argument to produce in support of the doctrine of a future state of retribution, this alone would be sufficient to carry conviction to every mind that recognises the existence of a Supreme Intelligence, and entertains just views of the attributes which must necessarily be displayed in his moral administration.

When this conclusion is once admitted, it removes the perplexities, and solves all the difficulties, which naturally arise in the mind, when it contemplates the present disordered state of the moral world, and the apparently capricious manner in which punishments and rewards are dispensed. Realizing this important truth, we need not be surprised at the unequal distribution of the Divine favours among the various nations and tribes of mankind; since they are all placed on the first stage of their existence, and eternity is rich in resources, to compensate for all the defects and inequalities of fortune which now exist. We need not be overwhelmed with anguish when we behold the pious and philanthropic youth cut down at the commencement of his virtuous career, since those buds of virtue which began to unfold themselves with so much beauty in the present life, will be fully expanded and bring forth nobler fruits of righteousness in that life which will never end. We need not wonder when we behold tyrants and profligates triumphing, and the excellent ones of the earth trampled under foot, since the future world will present a scene of equitable administration, in which the sorrows of the upright will be turned into joy, the triumphs of the wicked into confusion and shame, and every one rewarded according to his works. We need not harass our minds with perplexing doubts respecting the wisdom and equity of the dispensations of Providence; since the moral government of God extends beyond the limits of this world, and all its dark and intricate mazes will be fully unravelled in the light of eternity.

> ———— " *The great eternal scheme*
> Involving all, and in *a perfect whole*
> Uniting, as the prospect wider spreads,
> To Reason's eye will then clear up apace.
> ———— Then shall we see the cause
> Why unassuming Worth in secret lived,
> And died neglected; why the good man's share
> In life was gall and bitterness of soul;
> Why the lone widow and her orphans pined
> In starving solitude, while Luxury,
> In palaces, lay straining her low thought,
> To form unreal wants; why heaven-born Truth
> And Moderation fair, wore the red marks
> Of Superstition's scourge; why licensed Pain,
> That cruel spoiler, that embosom'd foe,
> Embitter'd all our bliss.—Ye good distrest!
> Ye noble Few! who here unbending stand
> Beneath life's pressure, bear yet up a while,
> And what your bounded view, which only saw
> A little part, deemed evil, is no more:
> The storms of Wintry time will quickly pass,
> And one unbounded Spring encircle all."
>
> THOMSON.

Thus it appears, that, although God, in the general course of his providence, has connected happiness with the observance of his laws, and misery with the violation of them, in order to display the rectitude of his nature, and his hatred of moral evil: yet he has, at the same time, in numerous instances, permitted vice to triumph, and virtue to be persecuted and oppressed, to convince us that his government of human beings is not bounded by the limits of time, but extends into the eternal world, where the system of his moral administration will be completed, his wisdom and rectitude justified, and the mysterious ways of his providence completely unravelled.

This argument might have been further illustrated from a consideration of those moral perceptions implanted in the human constitution, and which may be considered as having the force of moral laws proceeding from the Governor of the universe. The difference between right and wrong, virtue and vice, is founded upon the nature of things, and is perceptible by every intelligent agent whose moral feelings are not altogether blunted by vicious indulgences. Were a man to affirm that there is no difference between justice and injustice, love and hatred, truth and falsehood: that it is equally the same whether we be faithful to a friend or betray him to his enemies, whether servants act with fidelity to their masters or rob them of their property, whether rulers oppress their subjects or promote their interests, and whether parents nourish their children with tenderness, or smother them in their cradles: he would at once be denounced as a fool and a madman, and hooted from society. The difference between such actions is eternal and unchangeable; and every moral agent is endued with a faculty which enables him to perceive it. We can choose to perform the one class of actions and to refrain from the other; we can comply with the voice of conscience which deters us from the one, and excites us to the other, or we can resist its dictates, and we can judge whether our actions deserve reward or punishment. Now, if God has endued us with such moral perceptions and capacities, is it reasonable to suppose, that it is equally indifferent to him whether we obey or disobey the laws he has prescribed? Can we ever suppose, that He who governs the universe is an unconcerned spectator of the good or evil actions that happen throughout his dominions? or that he has left man to act, with impunity, according to his inclinations, whether they be right or wrong? If such suppositions cannot be admitted, it follows that man is accountable for his actions, and that it must be an essential part of the Divine government to bring every action into judgment, and to punish or reward his creatures according to their works. And if it appear, in point of fact, that such retributions are not fully awarded in the present state, nor a visible distinction made between the righteous and the violators of his law, we must necessarily admit the conclusion, that the full and equitable distribution of punishments and rewards is reserved to a future world, when a visible and everlasting distinction will be made, and the whole intelligent creation clearly discern between him that served God and him that served him not.

SECTION X.

ON THE ABSURDITY OF SUPPOSING THAT THE THINKING PRINCIPLE IN MAN WILL EVER BE ANNIHILATED.

It is highly unreasonable, if not absurd, to suppose that the thinking principle in man will ever be annihilated.

In so far as our knowledge of the universe extends, there does not appear a single instance of annihilation throughout the material system. There is no reason to believe, that, throughout all the worlds which are dispersed through the immensity of space, a single atom has ever yet been or ever will be annihilated. From a variety of observations, it appears highly probable, that the work of creation is still going forward in the distant regions of the universe, and that the Creator is replenishing the voids of space with new worlds and new orders of intelligent beings; and it is reasonable to believe, from the incessant agency of Divine Omnipotence, that new systems will be continually emerging into existence while eternal ages are rolling on. But no instance has yet occurred of any system or portion of matter, either in heaven or earth, having been reduced to annihilation. *Changes* are indeed incessantly taking place, in countless variety, throughout every department of nature. The spots of the Sun, the belts of Jupiter, the surface of the Moon, the rings of Saturn, and several portions of the starry heavens, are frequently changing or varying their aspects. On the earth, mountains are crumbling down, the caverns of the ocean are filling up, islands are emerging from the bottom of the sea, and again sinking into the abyss; the ocean is frequently shifting its boundaries, and trees, plants, and waving grain, now adorn many tracts which were once overwhelmed with the foaming billows. Earthquakes have produced frequent devastations, volcanoes have overwhelmed fruitful fields with torrents of burning lava, and even the solid strata within the bowels of the earth have been bent and disrupted by the operation of some tremendous power. The invisible atmosphere is likewise the scene of perpetual changes and revolutions, by the mixture and decomposition of gases, the respiration of animals, the process of evaporation, the action of winds, and the agencies of light, heat, and the electric and magnetic fluids. The vegetable kingdom is either progressively advancing to maturity or falling into decay. Between the plants and the seeds of vegetables there is not the most distant similarity. A small seed, only one-tenth of an inch in diameter, after rotting for a while in the earth, shoots forth a stem ten thousand times greater in size than the germ from which it sprung, the branches of which afford an ample shelter for the fowls of heaven. The tribes of animated nature are likewise in a state of progressive change, either from infancy to maturity and old age, or from one state of existence to another. The caterpillar is first an egg, next a crawling worm, then a nymph or chrysalis, and afterwards a butterfly adorned with the most gaudy colours. The May-bug beetle burrows in the earth, where it drops its egg, from which its young creeps out in the shape of a maggot, which casts its skin every year, and, in the fourth year, it bursts from the earth, unfolds its wings, and sails in rapture "through the soft air." The animal and vegetable tribes are blended, by a variety of wonderful and incessant changes. Animal productions afford food and nourishment to the vegetable tribes, and the various parts of animals are compounded of matter derived from the vegetable kingdom. The wool of the sheep, the horns of the cow, the teeth of the lion, the feathers of the peacock, and the skin of the deer; nay, even our hands and feet, our eyes and ears, with which we handle and walk, see and hear, and the crimson fluid that circulates in our veins; are derived from plants and herbs which once grew in the fields; which demonstrates the literal truth of the ancient saying, "All flesh is grass."

Still, however, amidst these various and unceasing changes and transformations, no example of annihilation has yet occurred to the eye of the most penetrating observer. When a piece of coal undergoes the process of combustion, its previous *form* disappears, and its component parts are dissolved, but the elementary particles of which it was composed still remain in existence. Part of it is changed into caloric, part into gas, and part into tar, smoke, and ashes, which are soon formed into other combinations. When vegetables die, or are decomposed by heat or cold, they are resolved into their primitive elements, caloric, light, hydrogen, oxygen, and carbon; which immediately enter into new combinations, and assist in carrying forward the designs of Providence in other departments of nature. But such incessant changes, so far from militating against the idea of the future existence of man, are, in reality, presumptive proofs of his immortal destination. For, if amidst the perpetual transformations, changes, and revolutions, that are going forward throughout universal nature in all its departments, no particle of matter is ever lost, or reduced to nothing, it is in the highest degree improbable, that the thinking principle in man will be destroyed, by the change which takes place at the moment of his dissolution. That change, however great and interesting to the individual, may be not more wonderful, nor more mysterious, than the changes which take place in the different states of existence to which a caterpillar is destined. This animal, as already stated, is first an *egg*, and how different does its form appear when it comes forth a crawling worm? After living sometime in the caterpillar state, it begins to languish, and apparently dies; it is encased in a tomb, and appears devoid of life and enjoyment. After a certain period it acquires new life and vigour, bursts its confinement, appears in a more glorious form, mounts upwards on expanded wings, and traverses the regions of the air. And is it not reasonable, from analogy, to believe, that man, in his present state, is only the *rudiments* of what he shall be hereafter in a more expansive sphere of existence? and that, when the body is dissolved in death, the soul takes its ethereal flight into a celestial region, puts on immortality, and becomes "all eye, all ear, all ethereal and divine feeling?"

Since, then, it appears that annihilation forms no part of the plan of the Creator in the material world, is it reasonable to suppose, that a system of annihilation is in incessant operation in the world of mind? that God is every day creating thousands of minds, endued with the most capacious powers, and, at the same time, reducing to eternal destruction thousands of those which he had formerly created? Shall the material universe exist amidst all its variety of changes, and shall that noble creature, *for whose sake the universe was created*, be cut off for ever in the infancy of its being, and doomed to eternal forgetfulness? Is it consistent with the common dictates of reason to admit, that *matter* shall have a longer duration than *mind*, which gives motion and beauty to every material scene? Shall the noble structures of St. Paul and St. Peter survive the ravages of time, and display their beautiful proportions to successive generations, while Wren and Angelo, the architects that planned them, are reduced to the condition of the clods of the valley? Shall the "Novum Organum" of BACON, and the "Optics" and "Principia" of NEWTON, descend to future ages, to unfold their sublime conceptions, while the illustrious minds who gave birth to these productions are enveloped in the darkness of eternal night? There appears a palpable absurdity and inconsistency in admitting such conclusions. We might almost as soon believe that the universe would continue in its present harmony and order, were its Creator ceasing to exist. "Suppose that the Deity, through all the lapse of past ages, has supported the universe by such miracles of power and wisdom as have already been displayed, merely that he might please himself with letting it fall to pieces, and enjoy the spectacle of the fabric lying in ruins:" would such a design be worthy of Infinite Wisdom, or conformable to the ideas we ought to entertain of a Being eternal and immutable in his nature, and possessed of boundless perfection? But suppose, further, that he were to *annihilate* that *rational nature* for whose sake he created the universe, while the material fabric was still permitted to remain in existence, would it not appear still more incompatible with the attributes of a Being of unbounded goodness and intelligence? To blot out from existence the rational part of his creation, and to cherish desolation and a heap of rubbish, is such an act of inconsistency, that the mind shrinks back with horror at the thought of attributing it to the All-Wise and Benevolent Creator.

We are, therefore, necessarily led to the following conclusion: "That, when the human body is dissolved, the immaterial principle, by which it was animated, continues to think and act, either in a state of separation from all body, or in some material vehicle to which it is intimately united, and which goes off with it at death; or else, that it is preserved by the Father of spirits, for the purpose of animating a body in some future state." The soul contains no principle of dissolution within itself, since it is an immaterial uncompounded substance; and, therefore, although the material creation were to be dissolved and to fall into ruins, its energies might still remain unimpaired, and its faculties

> ———— "Flourish in immortal youth,
> Unhurt amidst the war of elements,
> The wreck of matter, and the crash of worlds!"

And the Creator is under no necessity to annihilate the soul for want of power to support its faculties, for want of objects on which to exercise them, or for want of space to contain the innumerable intelligencies that are incessantly emerging into existence; for the range of immensity is the theatre of his Omnipotence, and that powerful Energy which has already brought millions of systems into existence, can as easily replenish the universe with ten thousand millions more. If room were wanted for new creations, ten thousand additional worlds could be comprised within the limits of the solar system, while a void space of more than a hundred and eighty thousand miles would still intervene between the orbits of the respective globes; and the immeasurable spaces which intervene between our planetary system and the nearest stars would afford an ample range for the revolutions of millions of worlds. And, therefore, although every soul, on quitting its mortal frame, were clothed with a new material vehicle, there is ample scope in the spaces of the universe, and in the omnipotent energies of the Creator, for the full exercise of all its powers, and for every enjoyment requisite to its happiness. So that, in every point of view in which we can contemplate the soul of man and the perfections of its Creator, it appears not only improbable, but even absurd in the highest degree, to suppose that the spark of intelligence in man will **ever** be extinguished.

SECTION XI.

ON THE GLOOMY CONSIDERATIONS AND ABSURD CONSEQUENCES INVOLVED IN THE DENIAL OF A FUTURE STATE.

The denial of the doctrine of a future state involves in it an immense variety of gloomy considerations and absurd consequences.

If the doctrine of a future existence be set aside, man appears an enigma, a rude abortion, and a monster in nature; his structure is inexplicable, and the end for which he was created an unfathomable mystery; the moral world is a scene of confusion, the ways of providence a dark impenetrable maze; the universe a vast, mysterious, and inexplicable system, and the Deity a Being whose perfections and purposes can never be traced nor unfolded.

Let us suppose, for a few moments, that there is no state of existence beyond the grave, and consequently, that the supposed discoveries of Revelation are a mere delusion; and consider some of the gloomy prospects and absurd consequences to which such a supposition necessarily leads. I shall suppose myself standing in an attitude of serious contemplation, and of anxious inquiry respecting the various scenes and objects which surround me, and the events that pass under my review:

I first of all look into myself, and inquire, whence I came? whither I am going? who produced me? of what my body is composed? what is the nature of my senses? of the thinking principle I feel within me? and for what purpose was I ushered into being? I perceive in my body a wonderful mechanism which I cannot comprehend: I find by experience that my will exercises a sovereign power over my muscular system, so that my hands, feet, arms, and limbs are disposed to obey every impulse, and, at the signal of a wish, to transport my body from one place to another. I find my thinking principle intimately connected with my corporeal frame, and both acting reciprocally on each other; but I cannot fathom the manner in which these operations are effected. I feel ardent desires after enjoyments in which I never shall participate, and capacities for knowledge and improvement which I never can attain. I feel restless and uneasy, even amidst the beauties of nature and the pleasures of the senses. I ask whence proceeds the want I feel amidst all my enjoyments? Wherefore can I never cease from wishing for something in addition to what I now possess? Whence arises the disgust that so quickly succeeds every sensitive enjoyment, and the want I feel even in the midst of abundance? I ask why I was called into existence at this point of duration, rather than at any other period of that incomprehensible eternity which is past, or of that which is yet to come? why, amidst the vast spaces with which I am encompassed, and the innumerable globes which surround me, I was chained down to this obscure corner of creation, from which I feel unable to transport myself? why I was ushered into life in Britain, and not in Papau or New Zealand? and why I was formed to walk erect and not prone, as the inferior animals? To all such inquiries I can find no satisfactory answers; the whole train of circumstances connected with my existence appears involved in impenetrable darkness and mystery. Of one thing only I am fully assured, that my body shall, ere long, be dissolved and mingled with the dust, and my intellectual faculties, desires, and capacities for knowledge, be for ever annihilated in the tomb. I shall then be reduced to nothing, and be as though I never had been, while myriads of beings, like myself shall start into existence, and perish in like manner, in perpetual succession, throughout an eternity to come.

I look backward through ages past; I behold every thing wrapped in obscurity, and perceive no traces of a beginning to the vast system around me: I stretch forward towards futurity, and perceive no prospect of an end: all things appear to continue as they were from generation to generation, invariably subjected to the same movements, revolutions, and changes, without any distinct marks which indicate either a beginning or an end. I look around on the scene of terrestrial nature; I perceive many beauties in the verdant landscape, and many objects the mechanism of which is extremely delicate and admirable: I inhale the balmy zephyrs, am charmed with the music of the groves, the splendour of the sun, and the variegated colouring spread over the face of creation. But I behold other scenes, which inspire melancholy and terror; the tempest, the hurricane, and the tornado; the sirocco, the samiel, and other poisonous winds of the desert; the appalling thunder-cloud, the forked lightnings, the earthquake shaking kingdoms, and the volcano pouring fiery streams around its base, which desolate villages and cities in their course. I behold in one place a confused assemblage of the ruins of nature in the form of snow-capped mountains, precipices. chasms, and caverns; in another, extensive marshes and immense deserts of barren sand; and, in another, a large proportion of the globe a scene of sterile desolation, and bound in the fetters of eternal ice. I know not what opinion to form of a world where so many beauties are blended with so much deformity, and so many pleasures mingled with so many sorrows and scenes of terror, or what ideas to entertain of Him who formed it. But I need give myself no trouble in inquiring into such subjects; for my time on earth is short and uncertain, and when I sink into the arms of death, I shall have no more connection with the universe.

I take a retrospective view of the moral world in past ages, in so far as authentic history serves as a guide, and perceive little else but anarchy, desolation, and carnage; the strong oppressing the weak, the powerful and wealthy trampling under foot the poor and indigent; plunderers, robbers, and murderers, ravaging kingdoms, and drenching the earth with human gore. I behold the virtuous and innocent persecuted, robbed, and massacred, while bloody tyrants and oppressors roll in their splendid chariots, and revel amidst the luxuries of a palace. In such scenes I perceive nothing like regularity or order, nor any traces of justice or equity in the several allotments of mankind; for since their whole existence terminates in the grave, the virtuous sufferer can never be rewarded, nor the unrighteous despot suffer the punishment due to his crimes. The great mass of human beings appear to be the sport of circumstances, the victims of oppression, and the dupes of knavery and ambition, and the moral world at large an assemblage of discordant elements tossed about like dust before the whirlwind. I hear virtue applauded, and vice denounced as odious and hateful. But what is virtue? A shadow, a phantom, an empty name! Why should I follow after virtue if she interrupts my pleasures, and why should I forsake vice if she points out the path to present enjoyment? It is my wisdom to enjoy life during the short period it continues; and if riches be conducive to my enjoyment of happiness, why should I fear to procure them either by deceit, perjury, or rapine? If sensual indulgence contribute to my pleasure, why should I refrain from drunkenness and debauchery, or any other action that suits my convenience or gratifies my passions, since present enjoyments are all I can calculate upon, and no retributions await me beyond the grave.

I feel myself subjected to a variety of sufferings, disappointments, and sorrows; to poverty and reproach, loss of friends, corporeal pains and mental anguish. I am frequently tortured by the recollection of the past, the feelings of the present, and the dread of approaching sufferings. But I see no object to be attained, no end to be accomplished, by my subjection to such afflictions: I suffer merely for the purpose of feeling pain, wasting my body and hastening its dissolution; I am sick only to languish under the burden of a feeble emaciated frame, perplexed and downcast only to sink into deeper perplexities and sorrows; oppressed with cares and difficulties only to enter on a new scene of danger and suffering. No drop of comfort mingles itself with the bitter cup of sorrow; no affliction is sweetened and alleviated by the prospect of a better world; for the gloomy mansions of the grave bound my views and terminate all my hopes and fears. How, then, can I be easy under my sufferings? how can I be cordially resigned to the destiny which appointed them? or how can I trace the benevolence of a superior Being in permitting me thus to be pained and tormented for no end? I will endeavour to bear them with resolute desperation, merely because I am borne down by necessity to pain and affliction, and cannot possibly avoid them.

I lift my eyes to the regions above, and contemplate the splendours of the starry frame. What an immensity of suns, and systems, and worlds, burst upon my view, when I apply the telescope to the spaces of the firmament! How incalculable their number! how immeasurable their distance! how immense their magnitude! how glorious their splendour! how sublime their movements! When I attempt to grasp this stupendous scene, my imagination is bewildered, and my faculties overpowered with wonder and amazement. I gaze, I ponder; I feel a longing desire to know something further respecting the nature and destination of these distant orbs; but my vision is bounded to a general glimpse, my powers are limited, and when I would fly away to those distant regions, I feel myself chained down, by an overpowering force, to the diminutive ball on which I dwell. Wherefore, then, were the heavens so beautifully adorned, and so much magnificence displayed in their structure, and why were they ever presented to my view, since I am never to become further acquainted with the scenes they unfold? Perhaps this is the last glance I shall take of the mighty concave, before my eyes have closed in endless night. "Wherefore was light given to him that is in misery; to a man whose way is hid, and whom God hath hedged in?" Had I been enclosed in a gloomy dungeon, my situation had been tolerable; but here I stand as in a splendid palace, without comfort and without hope, expecting death every moment to terminate my prospects; and when it arrives, the glories of the heavens to me will be annihilated for ever.

I behold science enlarging its boundaries, and the arts advancing towards perfection; I see numerous institutions organizing, and hear lectures on philosophy delivered for the improvement of mankind, and I am invited to take a part in those arrangements which are calculated to produce a general diffusion of knowledge among all ranks. But of what use is knowledge to beings who are soon to lose all consciousness of existence! It requires many weary steps and sleepless nights to climb the steep ascent of science; and when we have arrived at the highest point which mortals have ever reached, we descry still loftier regions which we never can approach; our footing fails, and down we sink into irretrievable ruin. If our progress in science here were introductory to a future scene of knowledge and enjoyment, it would be worthy of being prosecuted by every rational intelligence; but to beings who are uncertain whether they shall exist in the universe for another day, it is not only superfluous, but unfriendly to their present enjoyments. For, the less knowledge they acquire of the beauties and sublimities of nature, and the more brutish, ignorant, and sottish they become, the less will they feel at the moment when they are about to be launched into non-existence. Let the mass of mankind, then, indulge themselves in whatever frivolous amusements they may choose; do not interrupt their sensual pleasures, by vainly attempting to engage them in intellectual pursuits; let them eat and drink, and revel and debauch, for to-morrow they die. All that is requisite is, to entwine the chains of despotism around their necks, to prevent them from aspiring after the enjoyments of their superiors.

In short, I endeavour to form some conceptions of the attributes of that Great Unknown Cause which produced all things around me. But, my thoughts become bewildered amidst a maze of unaccountable operations, of apparent contradictions and inconsistencies. I evidently perceive that the Creator of the universe is possessed of boundless *power*, but I see no good reason to conclude that he exercises unerring wisdom, unbounded goodness, and impartial justice. I perceive, indeed, some traces of wisdom in the construction of my body and its several organs of sensation; and of goodness in the smiling day, the flowery landscape, and the fertile plains; but I know not how to reconcile these with other parts of his operations. How can I attribute the perfection of wisdom to One who has implanted in my constitution desires which will never be gratified, and furnished me with moral and intellectual faculties which will never be fully exercised, and who has permitted the moral world in every age to exhibit a scene of disorder? I perceive no evidences of his benevolence in subjecting me to a variety of sorrows and sufferings which accomplish no end but the production of pain; in tantalizing me with hopes, and alarming me with fears of futurity which are never to be realized, and in throwing a vail of mystery over all his purposes and operations. Nor can I trace any thing like impartial justice in the bestowment of his favours, for disappointments and sorrows are equally the lot of the righteous and the wicked, and frequently it happens that the innocent are punished and disgraced, while villains and debauchees are permitted to glory in their crimes. All that I can plainly perceive, is, the operation of Uncontrollable Power, directed by no principle but caprice, and accomplishing nothing that can inspire ardent affection, or secure the permanent happiness of rational beings.

Such are some of the gloomy reflections of a hopeless mortal whose prospect is bounded by the grave; and such are some of the horrible consequences which the denial of a future state necessarily involves. It throws a vail of darkness over the scenes of creation, and wraps in impenetrable mystery the purposes for which man was created; it exhibits the moral world as a chaotic mass of discordant elements, accomplishing no end, and controlled by no intelligent agency; it represents mankind, as connected with each other merely by time and place, as formed merely for sensual enjoyment, and destined to perish with the brutes; it subverts the foundations of moral action, removes the strongest motives to the practice of virtue, and opens the floodgates of every vice; it removes the anchor of hope from the anxious mind, and destroys every principle that has a tendency to support us in the midst of sufferings; it throws a damp on every effort to raise mankind to the dignity of their moral and intellectual natures, and is calculated to obstruct the progress of useful science; it prevents the mind from investigating and admiring the beauties of creation, and involves in a deeper gloom the ruins of nature which are scattered over the globe; it terminates every prospect of becoming more fully acquainted with the glories of the firmament, and every hope of beholding the plans of Providence completely unfolded; it involves the character of the Deity in awful obscurity, it deprives Him of the attributes of infinite wisdom, benevolence, and rectitude, and leaves him little more than boundless Omnipotence, acting at random, and controlled by no beneficent agency. In short, it obliterates every motive to the performance of noble and generous actions, damps the finest feelings and affections of humanity, leads to universal scepticism, cuts off the prospect of every thing which tends to cheer the traveller in his pilgrimage through life, and presents to his view nothing but an immense blank, overspread with the blackness of darkness for ever.

Such being the blasphemous and absurd consequences which flow from the denial of the doctrine of a future state of retribution, the man who obstinately maintains such a position, must be considered as unworthy not only of the name of a philosopher, but of that of a rational being, and as one who would believe against demonstration, and swallow any absurdity, however extravagant, which quadrates with his grovelling appetites and passions. Mathematicians frequently demonstrate a truth by showing that its contrary is impossible, or involves an absurdity. Thus *Euclid* demonstrates the truth of the fourth proposition of the first book of his Elements, by showing that its contrary implies this obvious absurdity: "that two straight lines may inclose a space." This mode of proving the truth of a proposition is considered by every geometrician, as equally conclusive and satisfactory as the *direct* method of demonstration; because the contrary of every falsehood must be truth, and the contrary of every truth, falsehood. And if this mode of demonstration is conclusive in mathematics, it ought to be considered as equally conclusive in moral and theological reasoning. If, for example, the denial of a future existence involves in it the idea that God is not a Being possessed of impartial justice, and of perfect wisdom and goodness, notwithstanding the striking displays of the two last mentioned attributes in the system of nature, we must, I presume, either admit the doctrine of the immortality of man, or deny that a Supreme Intelligence presides over the affairs of the universe. For, a Being divested of these attributes is not entitled to the name of Deity, nor calculated to inspire intelligent minds with adoration and love; but is reduced to something like *uncontrollable fact* or mere physical force, impelling the movements of universal nature without a plan, without discrimination, and without intelligence. On the same principle (the *reductio ad absurdum*) we demonstrate the earth's annual revolution round the sun. The motions of the planets, as **viewed** from the earth, present an inexplicable maze, contrary **to** every thing we should expect in a well arranged and orderly system. These bodies appear sometimes to move backwards, sometimes forwards, sometimes to remain stationary, and to describe **looped** curves, so anomalous or confused, that we cannot suppose **an** Infinite Intelligence the contriver of a system of such **inextricable** confusion. Hence the astronomer concludes, on **good** grounds, *that the earth is a moving body;* and no one thoroughly acquainted with the subject ever calls it in question: for when our globe is considered as revolving round the centre of the system in concert with the other planetary orbs, all the apparent irregularities in their motions are completely accounted for, and the whole system appears reduced to a beautiful and harmonious order, in accordance with every idea we ought to form of the wisdom and intelligence of its Author.

In the same way, the admission of the doctrine of a future state accounts for the apparent irregularities of the moral world, **and** affords **a key for** the solution **of** all the difficulties that may arise **in the mind** respecting the equity of the Divine administration in the present state. In opposition to the desponding reflections and gloomy views of the sceptic, it inspires the virtuous mind with a lively hope, and throws a glorious radiance over the scenes of creation, and over every part of the government of the Almighty. It exhibits the Self-existent and Eternal Mind as an object **of** ineffable sublimity, **grandeur,** and loveliness, invested with unerring wisdom, impartial justice, and boundless benevolence, presiding over an endless train of intelligent minds formed after his image, go**verning** them with just and equitable laws, controlling all things by **an** almighty and unerring hand, and rendering all his dispensations ultimately conducive to **the** happiness of the moral universe. It presents before us an unbounded scene, in which we **may** hope to contemplate the scheme of Providence in all its objects and bearings, where **the** glories of the divine perfections will be illustriously displayed, where the powers of the human mind will be perpetually expanding, and new objects **of** sublimity and beauty incessantly rising to the view, in boundless perspective, world without end. It dispels the clouds that hang over the present and future destiny of man, and fully accounts for those longing looks into futurity which accompany us at every turn, and those capacious powers of intellect, which cannot be fully exerted in the present life. It presents the most powerful motives to a life of virtue, to the performance of beneficent and heroic actions, to the prosecution of substantial science, and to the diffusion of useful knowledge among all the ranks of mankind. It affords the strongest consolation and support amidst the trials of life, and explains the reasons of those sufferings to which we are here exposed, as being incentives to the exercise of virtue, and as "working out for us a far more exceeding and eternal weight of glory." It affords us ground to hope that the vail which now intercepts our view of the distant regions of creation will be withdrawn, and that the amazing structure of the universe, in all its sublime proportions and beautiful arrangements, will be more clearly unfolded to our view. It dispels the terrors which naturally surround the messenger of death, and throws a radiance over the mansions of the tomb. It cheers the gloomy vale of death, and transforms it into a passage which leads to a world of perfection and happiness, where moral evil shall be for ever abolished, where intellectual light shall beam with effulgence on the enraptured spirit, and where celestial virtue, now so frequently persecuted and contemned, shall be enthroned in undisturbed and eternal empire.

Since, then, it appears, that the denial of a future state involves in it so many difficulties, absurd consequences, and blasphemous assumptions, and the admission of this doctrine throws a light over the darkness that broods over the moral world, presents a clue to unravel the mazes of the divine dispensations, and solves every difficulty in relation to the present condition of the human race: the pretended philosopher who rejects this important truth must be considered as acting in direct opposition to those principles of reasoning which he uniformly admits in his physical and mathematical investigations, and as determined to resist the force of every evidence which can be adduced in proof of his immortal destination.

Thus I have endeavoured, in the preceding pages, to prove and illustrate the immortality of man, from a consideration of the universal belief which this doctrine has obtained among all nations; the **desire** of immortality implanted in the human breast; the **strong** desire *of knowledge,* and the *capacious intellectual powers* with which man is furnished; the capacity **of making** *perpetual progress* towards intellectual and moral perfection; *the unlimited range of view* which is opened to the human mind throughout the *immensity of space* and *duration;* the *moral powers* of action with which man is endued; the *forebodings* and apprehensions **of the** mind when under the influence of remorse; the disordered state **of** the *moral* world when contrasted with the systematical order **of the** material; **the** *unequal distribution of rewards and punishments,* viewed in connection with the justice of God; the *absurdity* of **admitting** that *the thinking principle in man will be annihilated;* and the *blasphemous and absurd consequences* which would follow if the idea of a future state of retribution were rejected.

Perhaps there are some of these arguments, *taken singly,* that would be insufficient fully to establish the truth of man's eternal destiny; but when taken in combination with each other, they carry irresistible evidence to the mind of every unbiassed inquirer. They all reflect **a mutual** lustre on each other; they hang together in perfect **harmony;** they are fully consistent with the most amiable and sublime conceptions we **can** form **of** the Deity; they **are congenial** to the sentiments entertained by the wisest and **best of** men in every age; they **are** connected with all the improvements and discoveries in the moral **and** physical worlds; and, like the radii of a circle, **they** all converge to the same point, and lead directly to the **same** conclusion. It appears next to impossible, that such a **mutual** harmony, consistency, and dependence, could exist among a **series** of propositions that had no foundation in truth; and, therefore, they ought to be considered, when taken conjunctly, as having all the force **of a** *moral demonstration.* They rest on the same principles and process of reasoning from which we deduce the being **of** a God; and I see no way of eluding their force, but by erasing from the mind every idea of **a** Supreme Intelligence. Hence, it has generally, I might **say** uniformly, been found, that all nations that have acknowledged the existence of a Divine Being, have likewise recognised the idea of a future state of retribution. These two fundamental propositions are so intimately connected, and the latter is so essentially dependent on the former, that they must stand or fall together. And consequently, we find, that the man who obstinately rejects the doctrine of a future state, either avows himself a downright atheist, or acts precisely in the same way as a person would do, who believes that a supreme Moral Governor has no existence.

But even the principles of atheism itself, though frequently embraced by vicious characters to allay their fears, are not sufficient to remove all apprehensions in regard to a future existence. For, if the universe be the production merely of an eternal succession of causes and effects, produced by blind necessity impelling the atoms of matter through the voids of immensity, what should hinder that, amidst the infinite combinations arising from perpetual motion, men should be created, destroyed, and again ushered into existence, with the same faculties, reminiscences, perceptions, and relations as in their former state of existence? And, although thousands or millions of years should intervene between such tranformations, yet such periods might appear as short and imperceptible as the duration which passes while our faculties are absorbed in a sound repose. The idea of infinity, immensity, and an endless succession of changes, renders such a supposition not altogether impossible. But what a dreadful futurity might not the mind be left to picture to itself in such a case! If the movements of the universe were the production of chance, directed by no intelligent agency, we should incessantly be haunted with the most dreadful anticipations. We should see the images of death, annihilation, and reproduction advancing before us in the most terrific forms, and should find it impossible to determine on what foundation the hopes and the destiny of intelligences reposed. We should be uncertain whether mankind were doomed to perish irrecoverably, or, by the operation of some unknown cause or accident, to be reproduced, at some future period in duration, and devoted to endless torments. The comparative order and tranquillity which now subsists, or have subsisted for ages past, could afford us no ground of hope that such consequences would not take place; for all the revolutions of time to which we can look back, are but as a moment in the midst of infinite duration, and the whole earth but a point in the immensity of space. So that, during the lapse of infinite ages, changes, revolutions, and transformations might be effected, which might overwhelm all **the** intelligent beings that ever existed, in eternal misery. **Hence** it appears, that **even** atheism itself, with all its mass of contradictions and absurdities, cannot entirely shelter its **abettors** from the terrors of an unknown futurity.

I shall only remark further, on this part of my subject: that, although the arguments now adduced in support of **the** immortality of man were less powerful than they really **are**, they ought to make a deep impression on the mind of every reflecting person, and determine the line of conduct which he ought to pursue. If they were only probable; if they possessed no greater degree of weight than simply to overbalance the opposite arguments; still it would be every man's interest to act on the supposition, that a future world has a real existence. For in the ordinary affairs of human life, and even in the sciences, our opinions and conduct are generally determined by a series of probabilities, and in a concurrence of reasons, which supply the want of more conclusive evidence on subjects which are not susceptible of strict demonstration. A merchant, when he purchases a certain commodity, has no demonstrative evidence that the sale of it shall ultimately turn to his advantage; but, from a consideration of its price and quality, of the circumstances of trade, and of his immediate prospects, he determines on the purchase; and, by acting on the ground of similar probabilities, he conducts his affairs, so as to issue in his prosperity and success. A philosopher has no *demonstrative* arguments to support the one half of the opinions he has formed, in relation to the phenomena of human society, and of the material world. His deductions respecting the causes of the winds, of thunder and lightning, of volcanic eruptions, of the nature of light, sound, electricity, galvanism, and other operations in the system of nature, are grounded on that species of reasoning which is termed *analogical*, and which, at best, amounts to nothing more than a high degree of probability. Notwithstanding, he feels no hesitation in prosecuting his experiments and researches, under the guidance of such reasoning, confident that it will ultimately lead him to the innermost recesses of the temple of truth; for we know, that the most splendid discoveries of modern times have originated from inquiries and observations, conducted on the ground of analogical reasoning. In like manner, in the important subject under consideration, we ought to be determined in our views and conduct, even by *probabilities*, although the arguments adduced should leave the question at issue in some measure undetermined. For, if an eternal world has a real existence, we only embrace an error in rejecting this idea, but, by acting in conformity with our erroneous conceptions, run the risk of exposing ourselves to the most dreadful and appalling consequences. Whereas, if there be no future state, the belief of it, accompanied with a corresponding conduct, can produce no bad effect either upon our own minds or those of others. On the contrary, it would prove a pleasing illusion during our passage through a world of physical and moral evil, and would revive the downcast spirit, when overwhelmed with the disappointments and sorrows which are unavoidable in our present condition. So that, even in this case, we might adopt the sentiment of an ancient philosoper,[1] and say, "If I am wrong in believing that the souls of men are immortal, I please myself in my mistake; nor while I live will I ever yield, that this opinion, with which I am so much delighted, should be wrested from me. But if, at death, I am to be annihilated, as some minute philosophers suppose, I am not afraid lest those wise men, when extinct too, should laugh at my error."

But, if the arguments we have brought forward, amount, not only to bare probability, but to *moral certainty*, or, at least, to something nearly approximating to moral demonstration; if the opposite opinion involves a train of absurdities, if it throws a dismal gloom over the destiny of man, and over the scenes of the universe, and if it robs the Almighty of the most glorious and distinguishing attributes of his nature; no words are sufficient to express the folly and inconsistency of the

[1] Cicero.

man, by whatever title he may be distinguished, who is determined to resist conviction, and who resolutely acts, as if the idea of a future world were a mere chimera. To pass through life with indifference and unconcern, to overlook the solemn scenes of the invisible world, and to brave the terrors of the Almighty, which may be displayed in that state, in the face of such powerful arguments as even reason can produce, is not only contrary to every prudential principle of conduct, but the height of infatuation and madness. Such persons must be left to be aroused to consideration, by the awful conviction which will flash upon their minds, when they are transported to that eternal state which they now disregard, and find themselves placed at the bar of an Almighty and impartial Judge.

Among the considerations which have been adduced to prove the immortality of man, I have taken no notice of an argument, which is almost exclusively dwelt upon by some writers; namely, that which is founded on the *immateriality* of the human soul. I have declined entering upon any illustrations of this topic, 1. Because the proof of the soul's immateriality involves a variety of abstract metaphysical discussions, and requires replies to various objections which have been raised against it, which would tend only to perplex readers endowed with plain common sense. 2. Because the doctrine of the immateriality of the thinking principle, however clearly it may be proved, can add nothing to the weight of the considerations already brought forward; nor, when considered by itself, can it afford any conclusive argument in favour of the soul's immortality. It simply leads to this conclusion, that, since the soul is an uncompounded substance, it cannot perish by a decomposition of its parts; **and** consequently *may* exist, in a **separate** state, in the full exercise of its **powers**, after its corporeal tenement is dissolved. But its immortality cannot necessarily be inferred from its natural capacity of existing in a state of separation from the body; for that Being who created it may, if he pleases, reduce it to annihilation, since all the works of God, whether material or immaterial depend wholly on that power by which they were originally brought into existence. Its immortality depends **solely on the** will **of** its Creator, without whose sustaining energy the whole creation would sink into its original nothing. If it could be proved, that God will employ his power to annihilate the soul, in vain should we attempt to demonstrate that it is naturally immortal. But whether God *wills* that the soul should be destroyed at death, is a very different question from that which relates to its nature as an immaterial substance. The whole train of argument illustrated in the preceding pages, affords, I presume, satisfactory evidence, that the Creator will never annihilate the human soul, but has destined it to remain in the vigorous exercise of its noble faculties to all eternity.

Hence it follows, that it is a matter of trivial importance, when considering the arguments which prove our immortal destiny, whether we view the soul as a *material*, or as an *immaterial* substance. Suppose I were to yield to the sceptic, for a moment, the position, " that the soul is a material substance, and cannot exist but in connection with a material frame," what would he gain by the concession? It would not substract a single atom from the weight of evidence which has already been brought forward to prove the immortality of man. For, if we can prove that God has willed the immortality of the soul, and consequently, has determined to interpose his almighty power, in order to support its faculties throughout an eternal existence, in vain shall he have proved that it is not immortal *in its nature.* He who created the human soul, and endued it with so many noble faculties, can continue its existence, through an unlimited extent of duration, in a thousand modes incomprehensible to us. If a material system of organical powers be necessary for the exercise of its energies, he can either clothe it with a fine ethereal vehicle, at the moment its present tenement is dissolved, or connect it, in another region of the universe, with a corporeal frame of more exquisite workmanship, analagous to that which it now animates. For any thing we know to the contrary, there may be some fine material system, with which it is essentially connected, and which goes off with it at death, and serves as a medium through which it may hold a direct communication with the visible universe. Even although its consciousness of existence were to be suspended for thousands of years, its Creator can afterwards invest it with a new organical frame, suited to the expansive sphere of action to which it is destined; and the intervening period of its repose may be made to appear no longer than the lapse of a few moments. In short, if God has sustained the material universe hitherto, and will in all probability, continue it for ever in existence, so that not a single atom now existing shall at any future period be annihilated; the same Power and Intelligence can, with equal ease, support the thinking principle in man, whatever may be its nature or substance, and however varied the transformations through which it may pass. If the Creator is both able and willing to perpetuate the existence of the rational spirit through an endless duration, and if his wisdom, benevolence, and rectitude, require that this object should be accomplished, all difficulties arising from its nature or the mode of its subsistence, must at once evanish. The preceding arguments in support of a future state, are, therefore, equally conclusive, whether we consider the soul as a pure immaterial substance, or as only a peculiar modification of matter; so that the sceptic who adopts the absurd idea of the materiality of mind, cannot even on this ground invalidate the truth of man's eternal destination.

CHAPTER II.

PROOFS OF A FUTURE STATE FROM DIVINE REVELATION.

The evidences of a future state, which we have endeavoured, in the preceding pages, to investigate on the principles of human reason, are amply confirmed and illustrated in the Revelation contained in the Sacred Scriptures. It is one of the distinguishing characteristics of that revelation, that, in every important point, it harmonises with the deductions of sound reason, and the principles of common sense. This was naturally to be presumed; since God is the author both of the reasoning faculty, and of the declarations contained in the volume of inspiration; and this consideration forms a strong presumptive argument in support of the Divine authority of the Scriptures, and should excite us to receive, with cordial veneration and esteem, a revelation which confirms the law of nature, and is congenial to the sentiments of the wisest and the best of mankind in all ages. If any serious inquirer, who had entertained doubts on this subject, has been led to a conviction of the reality of his immortal destiny, by such arguments as the preceding, he will naturally resort to the Sacred Records for more full information on this important point; and I should have no fear of any one remaining long an enemy of Revelation, when once a powerful conviction of a future state has been deeply impressed on his mind. If a man is fully convinced that he is standing every moment on the verge of an eternal state, he cannot but feel anxious to acquire the most correct information that can be obtained respecting that world which is to constitute his everlasting abode; and if he is altogether careless and insensible in this respect, it is quite clear, that he has no thorough conviction of the realities of a life to come.

The Christian Revelation has "brought life and immortality to light," not so much on account of the express assurance it gives of the reality of a future world, but chiefly, as it clearly exhibits the nature and the employments of that state, its endless duration, the ground on which we can expect happiness in it, and the dispositions and virtues which qualify us for relishing its exercises and enjoying its felicities; and particularly, as it opens to our view the glorious scene of a "*resurrection from the dead*," and the reunion of soul and body in the mansions of bliss.

In illustrating this topic, it would be quite unnecessary to enter into any lengthened details. When the Divine authority of the Scriptures is recognised, a single proposition or assertion, when it is clear and express, is sufficient to determine the reality of any fact, or the truth of any doctrine; and, therefore, I shall do little more than bring forward a few passages bearing on the point under consideration, and intersperse some occasional remarks. As some have called in question the position, "that the doctrine of a future state was known to the Jews," I shall, in the first place, bring forward a few passages and considerations to show that the doctrine of immortality was recognised under the Jewish as well as under the Christian dispensation.

As the belief of a future state lies at the very foundation of religion, it is impossible to suppose, that a people whom the Almighty had chosen to be his worshippers, and the depositaries of his revealed will, should have remained ignorant of this interesting and fundamental truth, and have had their views confined solely to the fleeting scenes of the present world. "Faith," says Paul, in his Epistle to the Hebrews, "is the confident expectation of things hoped for, and the conviction of things not seen."[1] It includes a belief in the existence of God, and of the rewards of a life to come; for, says the same apostle, "He that cometh to God must believe that he is, and that he is the rewarder of them that diligently seek him."

[1] Doddrige's translation of Heb. xi. 1.

Having stated these principles, he proceeds to show, that the ancient patriarchs were animated in all their services by their conviction of the realities of a future and **invisible** world. With respect to Abraham, he informs us, **that** "he expected a city which had foundations, whose builder and maker is God." He obtained **no such** city in the earthly Canaan; and therefore we **must** necessarily suppose, that his views were directed to mansions **of** perpetuity beyond the confines of the present world. With respect to Moses, he says, that under all his persecutions **and** afflictions, "**he** endured as seeing Him who **is** inviable; for he had respect to the recompence of reward." That *reward* did not consist in temporal grandeur, otherwise he might have enjoyed it in much more splendour and security in Egypt, as the son of Pharaoh's daughter; nor did it consist in the possession of Canaan, for he was not permitted to enter into that goodly land. It must, therefore, have been the celestial inheritance to which the eye of his faith looked forward, as the object of his joyful anticipation. With regard to **all the** other patriarchs whose names stand high on the records **of the** Old Testament Church, he declares, that "they confessed that they were strangers and pilgrims on earth," that "they declared plainly that they sought a *better country,* that is, an heavenly;" and that those who "were tortured" to induce **them** to renounce their religion, endured their sufferings with invincible fortitude, "not accepting deliverance" when it **was** offered them, "*that they might obtain a better resurrection.*"

In accordance with these declarations, the prophets, in many parts of their writings, speak **decisively of** their expectations of a future life, and of the **consolation** the prospect of it afforded them under **their sufferings.** "As for me," says the Psalmist, "I shall **behold thy face** in righteousness; I shall be satisfied when I **awake** with thy likeness." "My flesh shall **rest** in hope; for thou wilt not leave my **soul** in the grave. **Thou wilt** show me the path of life: in thy **presence is** fulness of joy; **at thy** right hand are pleasures for evermore." "Yea, though I **walk** through the valley **of the** shadow of death, I will fear no evil: for thou art with **me.** Surely goodness and mercy will follow me all the days of my life, *and I shall dwell* in *the house of the Lord for ever.*" " God will redeem my soul from the grave; for he will receive me." " Whom have I in heaven but thee? and there is none upon earth that I desire besides thee. Thou wilt guide me with thy counsel, and afterwards receive me to glory. My flesh and my heart shall fail; but God is the strength of my heart and *my portion for ever.*" Nothing can be more clear and express than such declarations. If the Psalmist had no belief in a future state, and no hopes of enjoying its felicities, after the termination of his earthly pilgrimage, his language is absolutely without meaning. What rational interpretation can be given to the expressions of " dwelling in the house of God for ever," after his days on earth are numbered; of " Jehovah being his everlasting portion," after his heart had ceased to beat; and of his being " redeemed from the grave," and put in possession of "fulness of joy" and "everlasting pleasures," if his views were confined to the narrow limits of time, and the boundaries of the earthly Canaan! Such expressions would be a species of bombast and hyperbole, altogether inconsistent with the dignity and veracity of an inspired writer.

Job, that illustrious example of patience under affliction, consoled his spirit in the midst of adversity by the hopes he entertained of a blessed immortality. "I know," says he, " that my Redeemer liveth, and that he shall stand at the latter day upon the earth: and, after I shall awake, though this body shall be destroyed, yet out of my flesh shall I see God." In various other passages of the prophets, not only a future state, but a resurrection from the grave and the solemnities of a day of judgment, are plainly intimated. " Thy dead men shall live, together with my dead body shall they arise. Awake and sing, ye that dwell in dust; for thy dew is as the dew of herbs, and the earth shall cast out the dead." " Rejoice, O young man in thy youth, and walk in the ways of thy heart, and in the sight of thine eyes: but know thou, that for all these things God will bring thee into judgment." " For God shall bring every work into judgment, with every secret thing, whether it be good, or whether it be evil." " Many of them that sleep in the dust of the earth shall awake, some to everlasting life, and some to shame and everlasting contempt. And they that be wise shall shine as the brightness of the firmament; and they that turn many to righteousness, as the stars for ever and ever."

One reason, among others, why the doctrine of a future state is not frequently adverted to, and treated in detail, in the writings of the Old Testament, undoubtedly is, that it was a truth so well understood, so generally recognised, and so essential to the very idea of religion, that it would have been superfluous to have dwelt upon it in detail, or to have brought it forward as a new discovery. This doctrine is implied in the phraseology of the Old Testament, in many cases where there is no direct reference to a future world, as in such passages as the following: "I am the God of thy father, the God of Abraham, the God of Isaac, and the God of Jacob:" Exod. iii, 6. Our Saviour has taught us to consider this and similar passages as embodying the doctrine of a future life. "For God is not the God of the dead, but of the living." If the holy patriarchs whose names are here commemorated with so much honour, were reduced to the condition of the clods of the valley, and if their intellectual part were not in existence, Jehovah would never own the high relation of a God to those whom he has finally abandoned, and suffered to sink into non-existence. Consequently, Abraham, Isaac, and Jacob were living and intelligent beings, in another state, when this declaration was made to Moses at the burning bush. The phrase, "He was gathered to his people," implies a similar sentiment. In Gen. xxv, it is said, "Abraham gave up the ghost, and was *gathered to his people*." This expression is not to be viewed as importing that he was buried with his fathers; for the fathers of Abraham were buried several hundreds of miles from the cave of Machpelah, in which Abraham's mortal remains were deposited, some of them in the land of Chaldea, and some of them in the country of Mesopotamia, which lay at a considerable distance from the land of Canaan. The true meaning must therefore be, that he was "gathered" to the assembly of the righteous, to the blessed society of those congenial spirits, eminent for their piety, who had passed before him into the invisible world. Hence, says the Psalmist, "*Gather* not my soul with sinners." Hence, says Job, when describing the miseries of the wicked,

"The rich man shall lie down" in the grave, "but *he shall not be gathered;*" and the prophet, when personating the Messiah, declares, "Though Israel be not *gathered*, yet **shall** I be glorious in the eyes of Jehovah."

These remarks may suffice to show, that the doctrine of a future state was known, and generally recognised, by the venerable patriarchs, and other illustrious characters that flourished under **the** Jewish dispensation.

That this doctrine is exhibited in the clearest light in the *Christian* Revelation, has never been disputed by any class of religionists, nor even by infidels themselves. In this revelation, however, the doctrine of immortality is **not** attempted to be proved by any laboured arguments, or supernatural evidences, nor is it brought forward as a new discovery. It is evidently taken for granted, and incidently interwoven through all the discourses of our Saviour and his apostles, as a truth which lies at the foundation of religion, and which never ought for a moment to be called in question. In elucidating this topic, it will be quite sufficient simply to quote a few passages from the New Testament writers.

Paul, when looking forward to the dissolution of his mortal frame, declares, in his own name, and in the name of all Christians: "Our light affliction, which is but for a moment, worketh out for us a far more exceeding and eternal weight of glory; while we aim not at the things which are visible, but at those which are invisible: for the things which are visible are temporary, but those which are invisible are eternal. For we know, that, **if** this earthly house of our tabernacle were dissolved, we **have** a building of God, an house not made with hands, eternal in **the** heavens." When the time of his departure from the body was at hand, he declared, "I have fought the good fight, I have finished my course, I have kept the faith: henceforth there is laid up for **me a** crown of righteousness, which the righteous Judge shall give me at that day; and not to me only, but to all them that love his appearing." The apostle Peter declares, that believers " are regenerated to the lively hope of an inheritance incorruptible, undefiled, and that fadeth not away, reserved in heaven for them." When the chief Shepherd shall appear, "we shall receive a crown of **glory**, which fadeth not away." Our Saviour declares, in reference to his servants, "I give unto them *eternal life,* and they shall never perish." "In my Father's house are many mansions: if it were not so, I would have told you. I go to prepare a place for you. And I will come again and receive you to myself, that where I am there you may be also." And again, "Many shall come from the east and from the west, and shall sit down with Abraham, and Isaac, and Jacob, in the kingdom of heaven." "Then shall the righteous shine forth as the sun in the kingdom of their Father."

While these and similar passages clearly demonstrate the certainty of an eternal world, and the future happiness of the righteous, the apostles and evangelists are equally explicit in asserting the future misery of the wicked. "The unrighteous shall not inherit the kingdom of God," but "shall go away into everlasting punishment." "The Lord Jesus shall be revealed from heaven, with his mighty angels, in flaming fire, taking vengeance on them that know not God, and who obey not the Gospel: who shall be punished with everlasting destruction from the presence of the Lord, and from the glory of his power." "At the end of the world, the angels shall come forth and sever the wicked from among the just, and shall cast them into a furnace of fire, where shall be weeping and gnashing of teeth." "The fearful, and unbelieving, and murderers, and whoremongers, and sorcerers, and idolaters, and all liars, shall have their part in the lake which burneth with fire and brimstone. There shall in no wise enter into the heavenly Jerusalem any thing that defileth, neither whatsoever worketh abomination, or maketh a lie."

The way by which happiness in the future world may be obtained, is also clearly exhibited. "Eternal life is the gift of God, through Jesus Christ our Lord." "For God so loved the world, that he gave his only begotten Son, that whosoever believeth in him should not perish, but have everlasting life." "This is the record, that God hath given to us eternal life, and this life is in his Son." "The God of all grace hath called us unto his eternal glory, by Christ Jesus." The dispositions of those on whom this happiness will be conferred, and the train of action which prepares us for the enjoyment of eternal bliss, are likewise distinctly described. "Whatsoever a man soweth, that shall he also reap. He that soweth to the flesh, shall of the flesh reap corruption: but he that soweth to the Spirit, shall of the Spirit **reap** life everlasting." "To them who by patient continuance in well-doing, seek for glory, honour, and immortality, God will recompense eternal life." "The **pure in heart** shall see God." "He that *doeth the will of God abideth for ever.*" "*Him that overcometh* will I make **a** pillar in the temple of my God, **and** he shall go no more out." "Blessed are they that **do** his commandments, **that** they might have a right to the tree of **life**, and may enter through the gates into the city."

The nature of the heavenly felicity, and the employments of the future world, are likewise incidentally stated and illustrated. The foundation of happiness in that state is declared to consist in perfect freedom from moral impurity, and in the attainment of moral perfection. "No one who worketh abomination can enter the gates of the new Jerusalem." "Christ Jesus gave himself for the Church, that he might sanctify and cleanse it, and that he might present it to himself a glorious Church, holy, and without blemish." The honour which awaits the faithful, in the heavenly world, is designated "a crown of *righteousness.*" The inheritance to which they are destined is declared to be "undefiled" with moral pollution; and it is "an inheritance *among them that are sanctified.*" "When Christ, who is our life, shall appear," says the apostle John, "*we shall be like him,*" adorned with all the beauties of holiness which he displayed on earth as our pattern **and** exemplar. The *employments* of that world are represented as consisting in adoration of the Creator of the universe, **in** the celebration of his praises, in the contemplation of his works, **and in** those active services, flowing from the purest love, which have a tendency to promote the harmony and felicity of the intelligent creation. "I beheld," said John, when a vision of the future world was presented to his view, " and, lo, a great multitude, which no man could number, of all nations, and kindreds, and people, and tongues, stood before the throne, clothed in white robes, crying with a **loud voice**, Salvation to our God that sitteth upon the throne, and unto the Lamb. Blessing, and glory, and wisdom, and thanksgiving, and honour, and power, be ascribed to our God for ever and ever," That the contemplation of the works of God is one leading part of the exercises of the heavenly inhabitants, appears, from the scene presented to the same apostle, in another vision, where the celestial choir are represented as falling down before Him that sat on the throne, and saying, "Thou art worthy, O Lord, to receive glory, and honour, and power; for thou hast created all things, and for thy pleasure they are, and were created." Such sublime adorations and ascriptions of praise, are the natural results of their profound investigations of the wonderful works of God. In accordance with the exercises of these holy intelligences, another chorus of the celestial inhabitants is exhibited as singing the song of Moses the servant of God, and the song of the Lamb, saying, "Great and marvellous are thy works, Lord God Almighty, just and true are thy ways, thou King of saints."

The resurrection of the body to an immortal life, is also declared in the plainest and most decisive language. This is one of the peculiar discoveries of Revelation; for, although the ancient sages of the Heathen world generally admitted the immortality of the soul, they seem never to have formed the most distant conception, that the bodies of men, after putrifying in the grave, would ever be reanimated; and hence, when Paul declared this doctrine to the Athenian Philosophers, he was pronounced to be a babbler. This sublime and consoling truth, however, is put beyond all doubt by our Saviour and his apostles: "The hour is coming," says Jesus, "when all that are in the graves shall hear the voice of the Son of God, and shall come forth: they that have done good to the resurrection of life; and they that have done evil, to the resurrection of condemnation." "I am the Resurrection and the Life; he that believeth in me, though he were dead, yet shall he live." "Why should it be thought a thing incredible that God should raise the dead?" "We look for the Saviour, who shall change our vile body, that it may be fashioned like unto his glorious body, according to the energy by which he is able even to subdue all things to himself." "We shall all be changed, in a moment, in the twinkling of an eye, at the last trump; for the trumpet shall sound, and the dead shall be raised incorruptible, and we shall be changed:" the nature of this change, and the *qualities* of the resurrection-body, are likewise particularly described by Paul in the fifteenth chapter of the First Epistle to the Corinthians. "It is sown," or committed to the grave, "in corruption; it is raised in *incorruption*," liable no more to decay, disease, and death, but immortal as its Creator. "It is raised in *power*," endued with strength and vigour incapable of being weakened or exhausted, and fitted to accompany the mind in its most vigorous activities. "It is raised in glory," destined to flourish in immortal youth and beauty, and arrayed in a splendour similar to that which appeared on the body of Christ when "his face did shine as the sun, and his raiment became white and glistering." "It is raised a *spiritual* body," refined to the highest pitch of which matter is susceptible, capable of the most vigorous exertions and of the swiftest movements, endued with organs of perception of a more exquisite and sublime nature than those with which it is now furnished, and fitted to act as a suitable vehicle for the soul in all its celestial services and sublime investigations.

Such is a brief summary of the disclosures which the Christian Revelation has made respecting the eternal destiny of mankind: a subject of infinite importance to every rational being; a subject of ineffable sublimity and grandeur, which throws into the shade the most important transactions, and the most splendid pageantry, of this sublunary scene; a subject which should be interwoven with all our plans, pursuits, and social intercourses, and which ought never for a moment to be banished from our thoughts.

I shall, therefore, conclude this department of my subject with a remark or two

ON THE PRACTICAL INFLUENCE WHICH THE DOCTRINE OF A FUTURE STATE OUGHT TO HAVE UPON OUR AFFECTIONS AND CONDUCT.

When we look around us on the busy scene of human life, and especially when we contemplate the bustle and pageantry which appear in a populous city, we can scarcely help concluding, that the great majority of human beings that pass in review before us, are acting as if the present world were their everlasting abode, and as if they had no relation to an invisible state of existence. To indulge in sensual gratifications, to acquire power, wealth, and fame, to gratify vanity, ambition, and pride, to amuse themselves with pictures of fancy, with fantastic exhibitions, theatrical scenes and vain shows, and to endeavour to banish every thought of death and eternity from the mind, appear to be in their view the great and ultimate ends of existence. This is the case, not merely of those who openly avow themselves "men of the world," and call in question the reality of a future existence; but also of thousands who regularly frequent our worshipping assemblies, and profess their belief in the realities of an eternal state. They listen to the doctrines of eternal life and of future punishment, without attempting to question either their reality or their importance, but as soon as they retire from " the place of the holy," and mingle in the social circle, and the bustle of business, every impression of invisible realities evanishes from their minds, as if it had been merely a dream or a vision of the night. To cultivate the intellectual faculties, to aspire after moral excellence, to devote the active powers to the glory of the Creator, and the benefit of mankind; to live as strangers and pilgrims upon earth, to consider the glories of this world as a transient scene that will soon pass away, and to keep the eye constantly fixed on the realities of an immortal life: are characteristics of only a comparatively small number of individuals scattered amidst the swarming population around us, who are frequently regarded by their fellows as a mean-spirited and ignoble race of beings. Though death is making daily havoc around them, though their friends and relatives are, year after year, dropping into the grave, though poets and orators, princes and philosophers, statesmen and stage-players, are continually disappearing from the living world; though sickness and disease are raging around, and laying their victims of every age prostrate in the dust, and though they frequently walk over the solemn recesses of the burying ground, and tread upon the ashes of " the mighty man, and the man of war, the judge and the ancient, the cunning artificer, and the eloquent orator:"

yet they prosecute the path of dissipation and vanity with as much keenness and resolution, as if every thing around them were unchangeable, and as if their present enjoyments were to last for ever.

If this representation be founded on fact, we may assuredly conclude, that the great bulk of mankind have no fixed belief of the reality of a future world, and that more than the one half of those who profess an attachment to religion, are as little influenced in their general conduct by this solemn consideration, as if it were a matter of mere fancy or of "doubtful disputation." It is somewhat strange, and even paradoxical, that, amidst the never-ceasing changes which are taking place among the living beings around us, men should so seldom look beyond the grave to which they are all advancing, and so seldom make inquiries into the certainty and the nature of that state into which the tide of time has carried all the former generations of mankind. If a young man were made fully assured that, at the end of two years, he should obtain the sovereignty of a fertile island in the Indian ocean, where he should enjoy every earthly pleasure his heart could desire, his soul would naturally bound at the prospect; he would search his maps to ascertain the precise position of his future residence, he would make inquiries respecting it at those travellers who had either visited the spot or passed near its confines, he would peruse with avidity the descriptions which geographers have given of its natural scenery, its soil and climate, its productions and inhabitants; and, before his departure, he would be careful to provide every thing that might be requisite for his future enjoyment. If a person, when setting out on a journey which he was obliged to undertake, were informed that his road lay through a dangerous territory, where he should be exposed, on the one hand, to the risk of falling headlong into unfathomable gulphs, and, on the other, to the attacks of merciless savages, he would walk with caution, he would look around him at every step, and he would welcome with gratitude any friendly guide that would direct his steps to the place of his destination. But, in relation to a future and invisible world, there exist, in the minds of the bulk of mankind, a most unaccountable apathy and indifference; and not only an indifference, but, in many instances, a determined resolution not to listen to any thing that may be said respecting it. To broach the subject of immortality, in certain convivial circles, would be considered as approaching to an insult; and the person who had the hardihood to do so, would be regarded as a rude sanctimonious intruder. How unaccountably foolish and preposterous is such a conduct! especially when we consider, that those very persons who seem to be entirely regardless whether they shall sink into the gulph of annihilation, or into the regions of endless perdition, will pass whole days and nights in chagrin and despair for the loss of some employment, for a slight affront, or for some imaginary reflection on their reputation and honour.

Were it necessary to bring forward additional proofs that the greater part of mankind have no belief in a future state; or, which amounts nearly to the same thing, that it has no influence whatever on the general tenor of their thoughts and actions, the prominent features of their conduct afford abundant evidence of this melancholy truth. Would a man, who firmly believes that he is destined to an everlasting state, pass fifty or sixty years of his life without spending one serious thought about that unknown futurity into which he is soon to enter, or making the least inquiry respecting its nature and employments? Would he toil from morning to night, with incessant care, to lay up a few fleeting treasures, and never spend a single hour in considering what preparations are requisite for an endless existence? Would he spurn at that book which has unvailed the glories and the terrors of eternity, and "brought life and immortality to light?" Would he sneer at the person who is inquiring the way to a blessed immortality, and count him as an enemy when he wished to direct his attention to the concerns of an unseen world? Can that man be supposed to believe that a crown of glory awaits him in the heavens, whose whole soul is absorbed in the pursuits of ambition, and who tramples on every principle of truth and justice, in order to gain possession of a post of opulence and honour? Can those parents believe that in heaven there is "a treasure which fadeth not,' while they teach their children to conclude, that the acquisition of a *fortune*, and the favour of the great, are the grand objects to which they should aspire? Can that old hoary-headed votary of pleasure consider himself as standing on the verge of an eternal world, who still indulges himself in all the fashionable follies and frivolities of the age, and never casts an eye beyond the precincts of the grave? Can that hard-hearted worldling, who shuts his ears at the cry of the poor **and needy, and** who grasps his treasures with eagerness even amidst the agonies of dissolution, believe that "a recompence of reward" awaits the benevolent "at the the resurrection of **the** just?" Can that man be impressed with the solemnities of the eternal world, who, the moment after he has committed the remains of a relative to the grave, violates **every** humane **and** friendly feeling; and, **for the** sake of **a few** paltry pounds or shillings, deprives the widow and the orphan of every earthly enjoyment? Can that courtly sycophant, who is continually hunting after places and pensions, fawning upon his superiors, and whose whole life is a continued course of treachery, adulation, and falsehood, believe that "all liars shall have their portion in the lake that burneth with fire and brimstone?" Can that thoughtless debauchee believe that future punishment awaits the workers of iniquity, who runs from one scene of dissipation to another, who wastes his time in folly and extravagance, and whose life is but one continued crime? Or can we even suppose that that clergyman, who is unremittingly aspiring after preferment, who is mercilessly fleecing his flock, yet neglecting their instruction, and engaged in incessant litigations about some paltry tithes, seriously believes, that the treasures of this world are unworthy to be compared with that "exceeding great and eternal weight of glory which is about to be revealed" in the life to come? Such conduct plainly indicates, whatever professions certain descriptions of these characters may make, that the solemn realities of the eternal world have no more practical influence on their minds than if they regarded them as unsubstantial phantoms or as idle dreams.

The doctrine of a future state is not a mere speculative proposition, to serve **as a** subject of metaphysical investigation, or to be admitted merely to complete a system of philosophical or theological belief. It is a truth of the highest *practical* *importance,* which ought to be interwoven with the whole train of our thoughts and actions. Yet how many are there, even of those who bear the Christian name, who are incessantly engaged in boisterous disputes respecting the nature of *faith,* who have never felt the influence of that faith which is "the confident expectation of things hoped for, and the conviction of things which are not seen," and which realizes to the mind, as if actually present, the glories of the invisible world! If we really believe the doctrine of immortality, it will manifest itself in our thoughts, affections, and pursuits. *It will lead us to form a just estimate of the value of all earthly enjoyments.* For, in the light of eternity, all the secular pursuits in which men now engage, appear but as vanity, and all the dazzling objects which fascinate their eyes, as fleeting shadows. A realizing view of an eternal state dissipates the illusion which the eye of sense throws over the pageantry and the splendours of this world, and teaches us that all is transitory and fading, and that our most exquisite earthly enjoyments will ere long be snatched from our embrace. For, not a single mark of our sublunary honours, not a single farthing of our boasted treasures, not a single trace of our splendid possessions, nor a single line of the beauty of our persons, can be carried along with us to the regions beyond the grave. *It will stimulate us to set our affections on things above, and to indulge in heavenly contemplations.* "Where our treasure is, there will our hearts be also." Rising superior to the delights of sense, and to the narrow boundaries of time, we will expatiate at large in those boundless regions which eye hath not seen, and contemplate, in the light of reason and of revelation, those scenes of felicity and grandeur, which will burst upon the disembodied spirit when it has dropped its earthly tabernacle in the dust. Like Seneca, when he contemplated, in imagination, the magnitude and beauty of the orbs of heaven, we will look down, with a noble indifference, on the earth as a scarcely distinguishable atom, and say, "Is it to this little spot that the great designs and vast desires of men are confined? Is it for this there is such disturbance of nations; so much carnage, and so many ruinous wars. O folly of deceived men; to imagine great kingdoms in the compass of an atom, to raise armies to divide a *point* of earth with their swords! It is just as if the *ants* should divide their molehills into provinces, and conceive a field to be several kingdoms, and fiercely contend to enlarge their borders, and celebrate a triumph in gaining a foot of earth, as a new province to their empire." In the light of heaven all sublunary glories fade away, and the mind is refined and ennobled, when, with the eye of faith, it penetrates within the vail, and descries the splendours of the heaven of heavens.

Again, if we believe the doctrine of immortality, we will be careful to avoid those sins which would expose us to misery in the future world, and to cultivate those dispositions and virtues which will prepare us for the enjoyment of eternal felicity. Between virtue and vice, sin and holiness, there is an essential and eternal distinction; and this distinction will be fully and visibly displayed in the eternal world. He whose life is a continued scene of vicious indulgence, and who has **devoted** himself to " work all manner of uncleanness with greediness," becomes, by such habits, " a vessel of wrath *fitted for destruction;*" and, from the very constitution of things, there is no possibility of escaping misery in the future state, if his existence be prolonged. Whereas, he who is devoted to the practice of holiness, who loves his Creator with supreme affection, and his neighbour as himself, who adds to his faith " virtue, knowledge, temperance, patience, brotherly-kindness, and charity," is, by such graces, rendered fit for everlasting communion with the Father of spirits, and for delightful association with all the holy intelligences that people his immense empire. Again, the belief of a future world should excite us to the exercise of *contentment,* and *reconcile our minds to whatever privations or afflictions Providence may allot* to us in the present world. " For the sufferings of the present time are not worthy to be compared with the glory which is to be revealed." If we believe that the whole train of circumstances connected with our present lot is arranged by Infinite Wisdom and Benevolence, everything that befals us here must have a certain bearing on the future world, and have a tendency to prepare us for engaging in its exercises and for relishing its enjoyments. In short, if we recognise the idea of an immortal life, we will endeavour to acquire clear and comprehensive views of its nature, its pleasures, and its employments. We will not rest satisfied with vague and confused conceptions of celestial bliss; but will endeavour to form as precise and definite ideas on this subject as the circumstances of our sublunary station will permit. We will search the Oracles of Divine Revelation, and the discoveries of science, and endeavour to deduce from both the sublimest conceptions we can form of the glories of that "inheritance which is incorruptible, undefiled, and that fadeth not away, which is reserved in heaven for the faithful."

In a word, if our minds are as deeply impressed with this subject as its importance demands, we shall experience feelings similar to those which affected the mind of Hieronymus when he contemplated the dissolution of the world, and the solemnities of the last judgment. "Whether I eat or drink, or in whatever other action or employment I am engaged, that solemn voice always seems to sound in my ears, 'Arise, ye dead, and come to judgment!' As often as I think of the day of judgment, my heart quakes, and my whole frame trembles. If I am to indulge in any of the pleasures of the present life, I am resolved to do it in such a way, that the solemn realities of a future judgment may never be banished from my recollection."

PART II.

ON THE CONNECTION OF SCIENCE WITH A FUTURE STATE.

A GREAT outcry has frequently been made, by many of those who wish to be considered as pious persons, about *the vanity of human science*. Certain divines in their writings, and various descriptions of preachers, in their pulpit declamations, not unfrequently attempt to embellish their discourses, and to magnify the truths of Scripture, by contrasting them with what they are pleased to call " the perishing treasures of scientific knowledge." " The knowledge we derive from the Scriptures," say they, " is able to make us wise unto salvation; all other knowledge is but comparative folly. The knowledge of Christ and him crucified will endure for ever; but all human knowledge is transitory, *and will perish for ever when this world comes to an end.* Men weary themselves with diving into human science, while all that results to them is vanity and vexation of spirit. Men may become the greatest philosophers, and have their understandings replenished with every kind of human knowledge, and yet perish for ever. What have we to do with the planets and the stars, and whether they be be peopled with inhabitants? Our business is to attend to the salvation of our souls."

Now, although some of the above, and similar assertions, when properly modified and explained, may be admitted as true, the greater part of them, along with hundreds of similar expressions, are either ambiguous or false. But, although they were all admitted as strictly true, what effect can the frequent reiteration of such comparisons and contrasts have on the mass of the people to whom they are addressed, who are already too much disinclined to the pursuit of general knowledge, but to make them imagine, that it is useless, and in some cases dangerous, to prosecute any other kind of knowledge than what is derived *directly* from the Scriptures? And what is the knowledge which the great majority of those who attend the public services of religion have acquired of the contents of the sacred Oracles? It is too often, I fear, exceedingly vague, confused, and superficial; owing, in a great measure, to the want of those habits of mental exertion, which a moderate prosecution of useful science would have induced.

Such declamations as those to which I have now adverted, obviously proceed from a very limited sphere of information, and a contracted range of thought. It is rather a melancholy reflection, that any persons, particularly preachers of the Gospel, should endeavour to apologize for their own ignorance, by endeavouring to undervalue what they acknowledge they have never acquired, and, therefore, cannot be supposed to understand and appreciate. For, although several well informed and judicious ministers of religion have been led, from the influence of custom, and from copying the expressions of others, to use a phraseology which has a tendency to detract from the utility of scientific knowledge, yet it is generally the most ignorant, those whose reading and observation have been confined within the narrowest range, who are most forward in their bold and vague declamations on this topic. We never find, in any part of the Sacred Records, such comparisons and contrasts as those to which I allude. The inspired writers never attempt to set the *word* of God in opposition to his *works*, nor attempt to deter men from the study of the wonders of his creation, on the ground that it is of less importance than the study of his word. On the contrary, they take every proper opportunity of directing the attention to the mechanism and order, the magnificence and grandeur, of the visible world; and their devotional feelings are kindled into rapture by such contemplations. When the Psalmist had finished his survey of the different departments of nature, as described in the 104th Psalm, he broke out into the following devotional strains: " How manifold are thy works, O Lord! in wisdom hast thou made them all: the earth is full of thy riches, so is the great and wide sea. The glory[1] of the Lord shall endure for ever, the Lord shall rejoice in all his works. I will sing unto the Lord as long as I live; I will sing praises to my God while I have my being." For the visible works of God display the same essential attributes of Deity, and of his superintending providence, as the revelations of his word; and it is one great design of that word to direct men to a rational and devout contemplation of these works, in which his glory is so magnificently displayed. And, therefore, to attempt to magnify the word of God by degrading his works, or to set the one in opposition to the other, is to attempt to set the Deity in opposition to himself, and to prevent mankind from offering a certain portion of that tribute of adoration and thanksgiving which is due to his name.

It is true, indeed, that the mere philosopher has frequently been disposed to contemplate the universe as if it were a self-acting and independent machine. He has sometimes walked through the magnificent scenes of creation, and investigated the laws which govern the motions of the celestial orbs, and the agencies which produce the various phenomena of our sublunary system, without offering up that tribute of thanksgiving and praise which is due to the great First Cause, or feeling those emotions of adoration and reverence which such studies have a tendency to inspire. But it is no less true, that the mere theologian has, likewise, not unfrequently walked through the field of revelation, studied its doctrines, and facts, and moral requisitions, written volumes in support of its heavenly origin, and defended its truths against the cavils of adversaries, without feeling that supreme love to God and affection towards his neighbour which is the great object of the Scriptures to produce, and displaying a disposition and conduct directly repugnant to its holy precepts. An argument founded on the impiety of certain pretended philosophers, to dissuade us from the study of the material world, would, therefore, be equally powerful to deter us from the study of divine revelation, when we consider that many who profess to receive it doctrines, live in open defiance of its most sacred requisitions. In both cases,

---

[1] That is, the display of the divine perfections in the material world, as the connection of the passage plainly intimates.

such examples merely show that man is a frail inconsistent being, and too frequently disposed to overlook his Creator, and to wander from the source of happiness.

In the Work, entitled *The Christian Philosopher*, I have endeavoured to illustrate this subject at considerable length, and to show that the investigation of the works of creation, under the guidance of true science, has a tendency to expand our conceptions of the power, wisdom, benevolence, and superintending providence of God; and that the various sciences and the inventions of art may be rendered subservient in promoting the objects of true religion, and diffusing its influence among the nations. At present, I shall confine my views, in the few following remarks, to the illustration of the following position: "That science has a relation to a future state."

It is a very vague, and in many points of view, a *false* assertion, which has so frequently been reiterated: that, what is generally termed human knowledge, or the sciences, have no connection with an immortal existence, and that they will be of no utility whatever when this world comes to an end. Truth of every description is, from its very nature, eternal and unchangeable; and, consequently, it cannot be supposed a preposterous opinion, that the established principles of several of our sciences will be the basis of reasoning and of action in a future state as well as in the present. That a whole is greater than any of its parts; that the three angles of a triangle are equal to two right angles; that the sides of a plain triangle are to one another, as the sides of the angles opposite to them: these and many similar propositions are equally true in heaven as in earth, and may probably be as useful truths there as in our present abode.

OBJECT OF SCIENTIFIC INVESTIGATION.

In order to avoid misconception, and a confusion of thought on this subject, it may not be improper in the first place, to define and illustrate what is meant by the term *Science*.

Science, in its most general acceptation, denotes *knowledge* of every description; in a more restricted sense, it denotes that species **of** knowledge which is acquired chiefly by the exercise of the human faculties; and in a still more restricted sense, it denotes that systematic species of knowledge which consists of rule and order: such as geometry, arithmetic, algebra, natural philosophy, geography, astronomy, chemistry, mineralogy, and botany. In the observations which follow, the **term may** be taken in any one of these senses; but particularly in the last, which is its most common and appropriate meaning.

By means of scientific investigation, the **powers of** the human mind have been wonderfully strengthened and expanded, and our knowledge of the operations of the Creator extensively enlarged. Science has enabled us to transport ourselves from one continent to another, to steer our course through the pathless ocean, and to survey all the variety of scenery which the terraqueous globe displays; it has taught us to mount upwards to the region of the clouds, and to penetrate into the bowels of the earth, to explore the changes which the earth has undergone since the period of its creation. It has laid open to our view the nature and constitution of the atmosphere, the principles of which it is composed, and its agency in supporting fire and flame, and vegetable and animal life. On the principles which science has established, we have been enabled to ascertain the distances of many of the heavenly bodies, to compute their magnitudes, and to determine the periods of their revolutions; and by means of the instruments it has invented, we have been enabled to take a nearer survey of distant worlds, to contemplate new wonders of creating power in regions of the **sky** which lie far beyond the utmost stretch **of the** unassisted eye, and **to explore those** invisible regions **where** myriads of living beings are concentrated within the compass **of a** visible point. In consequence of such discoveries, **we** have been enabled to acquire **more clear** and ample conceptions of the amazing energies of Omnipotence, of the inscrutable depths of infinite wisdom, of the overruling providence of the Almighty, of the benevolent care he exercises over all his creatures, and of the unlimited extent of those dominions over which he eternally **presides.**

The *faculties* by which man has been enabled to make the discoveries to which I have alluded, were implanted in his constitution by the hand of his Creator; and the *objects* on which these faculties are exercised, are the works of the Creator, which, the more minutely they are investigated, the more strikingly do they display the glory of his character and perfections. Consequently, it must have been the intention of the Creator that man should employ the powers he has given him in scientific researches; otherwise, he would neither have endowed him with such noble faculties, nor have opened to his view so large a portion of his empire. Scientific investigations, therefore, are to be considered as nothing less than inquiries into the plans and operations of the Eternal, in order to unfold the attributes of his nature, his providential procedure in the government of his creatures, and the laws by which he directs the movements of universal nature. It is true, indeed, that every one who calls himself a philosopher may not keep this end in view in the prosecution of scientific acquirements. He may perhaps be actuated merely by a principle of curiosity, by a love of worldly gain, or by a desire to acquire reputation among the learned by the discoveries he may bring to light, just in the same way as some theologians are actuated in prosecuting the study of the Christian system. But the discoveries which have been made by such persons, are, notwithstanding, real developments of the plans of the Deity, and open to a devout mind a more expansive view of the power, wisdom, and benevolence of Him who is " wonderful in counsel and excellent in working." It is our own fault if we do not derive useful instruction from the investigations and discoveries of philosophy; it is owing to our want of intelligence to discriminate between the experiments of men, and the operations of God, and to the want of that reverence, humility and devotion, which ought to accompany us in all our studies and contemplations of nature. Science, therefore, from whatever motives it may be prosecuted, is in effect and in reality, *an inquiry after God.* It is the study of angels and other superior intelligences; and we cannot suppose there is a holy being throughout the universe, that is not employed in one mode or another, in scientific research and investigation; unless we can suppose that there are moral intelligences who are insensible to the displays of the Divine glory, and altogether indifferent, whether or not they make progress in the knowledge of their Creator.

OBJECTS ON WHICH THE FACULTIES OF CELESTIAL INTELLIGENCES WILL BE EMPLOYED.

Let us now consider the objects on which the faculties of celestial intelligences will be employed in the way of scientific investigation.

The grand scene of universal nature, that august theatre on which the Almighty displays to countless myriads his glorious perfections, will remain substantially the same as it is at present, after all the changes in reference to our globe shall have taken place; and the clear and expansive view of its economy, its movements, and its peculiar glories, which will then be laid open to their inspection, will exercise the faculties, and form a considerable portion of the felicity of renovated moral agents.

That the general system of nature will remain materially the same, when the present fabric of our globe is dissolved, may be argued, 1. From the *immense number and magnitude of the bodies of* which it is composed. In every direction to which we can turn our eyes, the universe appears to be replenished with countless orbs of light, diffusing their splendours from regions immeasurably distant. Nearly one hundred millions of these globes are visible through telescopes of the greatest magnifying power; and it is more than probable, that beyond the reach of the finest glasses that art has ever constructed, thousands of millions exist in the unexplored regions of immensity, which the eye of man, while he remains in this lower world, will never be able to descry. All these luminous globes, too, are bodies of immense magnitude; compared with any one of which, the whole earth dwindles into an inconsiderable ball. It is probable that the smallest of them is at least one hundred thousand times larger than the globe on which we live. 2. All these bodies are *immensely distant from the earth*. Although we could wing our course with a swiftness equal to ten thousand miles a-day, it would require more than five millions of years before we could reach the nearest star; and the more distant of these orbs are placed in regions so immensely distant, that the imagination is bewildered and overpowered when it attempts to grasp the immeasurable extent which intervenes between us and them. This circumstance proves, that these bodies are of an immense size and splendour, since they are visible at such distances; and consequently demonstrates, that each of them is destined, in its respective sphere, to accomplish some noble purpose, worthy of the plans of a Being of infinite wisdom and goodness. 3. The whole of this vast assemblage of suns and worlds *has no immediate connection* with the present constitution and arrangement of our globe. There are no celestial bodies that have any immediate connection with the earth, or direct influence upon it, except the sun, the moon, and several of the planets; and therefore, those more distant orbs, to which I allude, cannot be supposed to be involved in the physical evils which the fall of man has introduced into our world; or to have the least connection with any future change or catastrophe that may befall the terraqueous globe. Though this globe, and "all that it inherits," were dissolved; yea, although the sun himself and his surrounding planets were set in a blaze, and blotted for ever out of creation; the innumerable and vast bodies which replenish the distant regions of the universe, would still exist, and continue to illuminate the voids of creation with undiminished splendour.

EXTENT OF THE GENERAL CONFLAGRATION.

From the considerations now stated, it is evident, that the changes which are predicted to take place at the general conflagration, will not extend beyond the environs of our globe, or, at farthest, beyond the limits of the solar system. There is, indeed, no reason to conclude, that they will extend beyond the terraqueous globe itself, and its surrounding atmosphere; for since all the revelations of Scripture have a peculiar reference to the inhabitants of this globe, the predicted changes which are to take place in its physical constitution, at the close of the present economy of Providence, must be considered as limited to the same sphere. As the world was formerly destroyed by a deluge of waters, in consequence of the depravity of man, so its destruction by fire will take place, for the same reason, in order that it may be purified from all the effects of the *curse* **which** was originally pronounced upon **the** ground for man's sake, and restored to its former order **and beauty.** But there is not the smallest reason to conclude, either from Scripture or the general constitution of the universe, that this **destruction** will extend beyond that part of the frame of nature which was subjected to the curse, and is physically connected with the sin of man; and, consequently, will be entirely confined to certain changes which will be effected throughout the continents, islands, and oceans, and in the higher and lower regions of the atmosphere.

This appears to be the sense in which the most judicious expositors of Scripture interpret those passages which have a particular reference to this event. Dr. Guyse, in his "Paraphrase on the New Testament," interprets 2 Peter iii, 7, 12, precisely in this sense: "When that final decisive day of the Lord Jesus shall come, the *aerial heavens*, being all in a flame, shall be destroyed, and the constituent principles of the atmosphere, together with the earth and all things in it, shall be melted down by an intense dissolving heat, into a confused chaos, like that out of which they were originally formed." And **in** a note on this paraphrase he remarks, " By **the** *heavens* is meant **here** the *aerial heavens.* For the **heavens and** the earth are **here** spoken of in opposition to those of the old world, which could mean nothing more than the earth and its former atmosphere, the state of which underwent a great alteration **by** the flood." " By the *heavens and the earth*, in such passages as these," says the learned Dr. Mede, " is to be understood, that part of nature which was subjected to the curse, or that is inhabited by Christ's enemies, and includes in it the earth, water, and air, but not the heavenly bodies, which are not only at a vast distance from it, but it is little more than a point, if compared to them for magnitude." Dr. Dwight, when adverting to this subject, expresses the same sentiment: "The phrase *heavens and earth* (says he) in Jewish phraseology denoted the universe. In the present case, however, (2 Peter iii, 10, 12, 13,) the words appear to be used with a meaning less extended, where it is declared, that that which is intended by both terms, shall be consumed, dissolved, and pass away. This astonishing event, we are taught, shall take place at the final judgment; *and we have no hint in the Scriptures, that the judgment will involve any other beings besides angels and men.*"

From the preceding considerations, it is obvious, that when the inspired writers use such expressions as these: "The stars shall fall from heaven," "the powers of heaven shall be shaken," and, "the heaven departed as a scroll," they are to be understood not in a *literal*, but in a *figurative* sense, as denoting changes, convulsions, and revolutions in the moral world. And when, in reference to the dissolution of our globe and its appendages, it is said, that "the heavens shall pass away with a mighty noise," the aerial heaven, or the surrounding atmosphere, is to be understood. How this appendage to our world may be dissolved, or pass away *with a mighty noise*, it is not difficult to conceive, now that we have become acquainted with the nature and energies of its constituent parts. One essential part of the atmosphere contains the principle of flame; and if this principle were not counteracted by its connection with another ingredient, or were it let loose to exert its energies without control, instantly one immense flame would envelope the terraqueous globe, which would set on fire the foundation of the mountains, wrap the ocean in a blaze, and dissolve, not only coals, wood, and other combustibles, but the hardest substances in nature. It is more than probable, that when the last catastrophe of our globe arrives, the oxygen and nitrogen, or the two constituent principles of the atmosphere, will be separated by the interposition of almighty power. And the moment this separation takes place, it is easy to conceive, that a tremendous concussion will ensue, and the most dreadful explosions will resound throughout the whole of the expanse which surrounds the globe, which will stun the assembled world, and shake the earth to its foundations. For if, in chemical experiments conducted on a small scale, the separation of two gases, or their coming in contact with the principle of flame, is frequently accompanied with a loud and destructive explosion; it is impossible to form an adequate idea of the loud and tremendous explosions which would ensue *were the whole atmosphere at once dissolved*, and its elementary principles separated from each other and left to exert their native energies. A sound as if creation had burst asunder, and accompanied the next moment with a universal blaze, extending over sea and land, would present a scene of sublimity and terror, which would more than realize all the striking descriptions given in Scripture of this solemn scene.

Again, when in reference to this tremendous event, it is said, that "the earth and the heaven fled away," (Rev. xx, 11,) we are not to imagine, that the distant bodies of the universe shall be either annihilated, or removed from the spaces they formerly occupied; but that all sublunary nature shall be thrown into confusion and disorder, and that the celestial orbs, during this universal uproar of the elements, will be eclipsed from the view, and appear as if they had fled away. The appearance of the heavens whirling with a confused and rapid motion, at this period, would be produced, were the Almighty (as will probably be the case) suddenly to put a stop to the diurnal rotation of the earth, or to increase the rate of its motion; in which case, the celestial luminaries would appear either to stop in their courses, or to be thrown into rapid and irregular agitations. And the appearance of the heavens in reality receding from the view, would be produced, were the earth to leave its present station among the planets, and to be impelled with a rapid motion towards the distant parts of the solar system, or beyond its boundaries; in which case, the sun would appear to fly off with a rapid motion to a distant part of space, till he had diminished to the size of a twinkling star, and the moon and the nearest planets would, in a short time, entirely disappear. Whether these suppositions exactly correspond with the arrangements which Divine Wisdom has made in reference to the general conflagration, I do not take upon me positively to determine. But I have stated them in order to show, that all the descriptions contained in Scripture of the dissolution of our globe, and of the circumstances connected with it, can be easily accounted for, and may be fully realized, without supposing any change to take place in the universe beyond the limits of the earth and its atmosphere.

To suppose, as some have done, that the whole fabric of creation will be shattered to pieces, that the stars will literally fall from their orbs, and the material universe be blotted out of existence, is a sentiment so absurd and extravagant, and so contrary to the general tenor of Scripture, and the character of God, that it is astonishing it should ever have been entertained by any man, calling himself a divine or a Christian preacher.[1] I have already had occasion to remark, that there is no example of annihilation, or an entire destruction of material substances, to be found in the universe, and that it is to the last degree improbable, that any one particle of matter which now exists will ever be completely destroyed, however numerous the changes that may take place in the universe.[2] We have no reason to believe, that even those changes to which our world is destined, at the general conflagration, will issue in its entire destruction. The materials of which the earth and its atmosphere are composed will still continue to exist, after its present structure is deranged, and will, in all probability,

---

[1] As a specimen of the vague and absurd declamations on this subject, which have been published both from the pulpit and the press, the following extract from a modern and elegantly printed volume of sermons may suffice: "The blast of the seventh trumpet, thundering with terrific clangour through the sky, and echoing from world to world, shall fill the universe, and time shall be no more! The six trumpets have already sounded: when the seventh shall blow, a total ruin shall take place throughout the creation; the vast globe which we now inhabit shall dissolve, and mingle with yon beauteous azure firmament, with sun and moon, and all the immense luminaries flaming there, *in one undistinguished ruin;* all shall vanish away like a fleeting vapour, a visionary phantom of the night, and *not a single trace of them be found!* Even the last enemy, Death, shall be destroyed, and time itself shall be no more!" etc. When such bombastic rant is thundered in the ears of Christian people, it is no wonder that their ideas on this subject become extremely incorrect and even extravagantly absurd.

[2] See Sect. X, page 95.

be employed in the arrangement of a new system, purified from the physical evils which now exist, and which may continue to flourish as a monument of Divine power and wisdom, throughout an indefinite lapse of ages.

In accordance with these sentiments, we find the inspired writers asserting the stability and perpetuity of the material universe. In a passage formerly alluded to, the Psalmist after having contemplated the scenes of the material creation declares, in reference to these visible manifestations of the divine perfections: "The glory of the Lord *shall endure for ever*, the Lord shall rejoice in all his works." And the apostle Peter, when describing the dissolution of the elementary parts of our globe, intimates, at the same time, the continued existence of the visible fabric of nature. "We look," says he, "for new heavens and a new earth, wherein dwelleth righteousness." The same truth is incidentally declared in many other portions of Scripture. In the prophecies respecting the Messiah and the duration of his kingdom, it is declared, that "His name shall endure for ever, his name shall be continued *as long as the sun:*" "His seed shall endure for ever, and his throne *as the sun before me:*" which expressions evidently imply that the sun will not be blotted out of creation, but continue to hold a station in the universe as long as the Redeemer and his subjects exist. It is also stated, in reference to the same illustrious personage, "His seed will I make to endure for ever, and his throne *as the days of heaven;*" which intimates, that the heavens will endure as long as the government of Immanuel. In reference to the stability and perpetuity of the celestial luminaries, it is declared, that "Jehovah hath *prepared his* THRONE *in the heavens.*" And when the Psalmist calls upon all the beings in the universe to celebrate the praises of the Creator, he says in reference to the orbs of heaven, "Praise ye him, sun and moon, praise him, all ye stars of light: Let them praise the name of the Lord; for he commanded, and they were created. *He hath also established them for ever and ever; he hath made a decree which shall not pass;*"[1] which expressions evidently imply, that, whatever changes may hap-

---

[1] See Psalms lxxii, 17; lxxxix, 36, etc.; ciii, 19; cxlviii, 3–7.

pen in particular systems, the great body of the celestial orbs, which constitute some of the grandest scenes of the universe, will remain stable and permanent as the throne of the Eternal. But, not to multiply quotations, the following declaration of Jehovah by the prophet Jeremiah is quite decisive on this point: "Thus saith the Lord, who giveth the sun for a light by day, and the ordinances of the moon and of the stars for a light by night; the Lord of Hosts is his name: *if those ordinances depart from before me, saith the Lord,* then the seed of Israel also shall cease from being a nation before me for ever:"[2] which words plainly imply, that if these luminaries continue in existence, the accomplishment of the divine promise is secured to all the spiritual seed of Israel; but should they be blotted out of creation, or depart from before Jehovah, the happiness of the "ransomed of the Lord," and their relation to him as the source of their felicity, would be terminated for ever. And have not these luminaries continued in their stations, since this prediction was announced, during a period of more than two thousand years? And do they not still shine with undiminished lustre? Yes, and they will still continue to display the glory of their Creator, while countless ages are rolling on. Hence it is declared, with respect to "the saints of the Most High," "They that be teachers of wisdom shall shine as the brightness of the firmament, and they that turn many to righteousness, *as the stars for ever and ever.*"

In short, when we consider the boundless extent of the starry firmament, the scenes of grandeur it displays, the new luminaries, which, in the course of ages, appear to be gradually augmenting its splendour, and the countless myriads of exalted intelligences which doubtless people its expansive regions; when we consider that it constitutes the principal portion of the empire of the Eternal, the most astonishing scene of his operations, and the most striking display of his omnipotence and wisdom; it would be one of the most extravagant notions that can possibly be entertained, and inconsistent with every rational and Scriptural idea we can form of the goodness and intelligence of the Deity, to suppose that these vast dominions of his, in which

---

[2] Jeremiah, xxxi, 35, 36.

his perfections shine with a splendour so ineffable, will ever be suffered to fall to pieces, or to sink into non-existence. With almost equal reason might we suppose, that the Creator himself would cease to exist, and infinite space be left as a boundless blank without matter and intelligence.

If the considerations now adduced be admitted to have any force, and if the position I have endeavoured to establish, cannot be overthrown, either on Scriptural or rational grounds, many of our sermons and *poems* which profess to give a description of the scenes of the "*Last day*," must be considered as containing a species of bombast which has a tendency to bewilder the mind, and to produce distorted views of the perfections of the Creator, and of the wise arrangements he has established in the system of the universe. A celebrated Poet, when expatiating on this subject, in order to give effect to his descriptions, breaks out in the following extravagant exclamations, when alluding to the starry firmament:

> "How far from east to west! The lab'ring eye
> Can scarce the distant azure bounds descry;
> So vast, this world's a grain; yet myriads grace
> With golden pomp the throng'd ethereal space.
> How great, how firm, how sacred all appears!
> How worthy an immortal round of years!
> Yet all must drop, as autumn's sickliest grain.
> And earth and firmament be sought in vain!
> Time shall be slain, all nature be destroy'd,
> Nor leave an atom in the mighty void;
> One universal ruin spreads abroad,
> Nothing is safe beneath the throne of God!"

Again,

> "The flakes aspire, and make the heavens their prey,
> The sun, the moon, the stars, all melt away;
> All, all is lost, no monument, no sign,
> Where once so proudly blazed the gay machine," etc.

If such descriptions were to be literally realized, *a resurrection from the dead would be an absolute impossibility;* the universe would be reduced to an immense blank; and the visible glories of the Creator, by which alone his perfections are recognised by infinite intelligences, would be eclipsed in the darkness of eternal night. Poetical scraps of this description are, however, frequently reiterated by flaming orators, in order to give effect to their turgid declamations, while they have no other tendency than to lead their hearers into a maze of error and extravagancy, to prevent them from thinking soberly and rationally on the scenes predicted in Scripture, and to excite the sneer of philosophical infidels.

The only passage of Scripture which, at first view, seems to militate against the position I have endeavoured to establish, is that contained in Psalm cii, 25, 26. "Of old hast thou laid the foundation of the earth; and the heavens are the work of thy hands: they shall perish, but thou shalt endure; yea, all of them shall wax old like a garment; as a vesture shalt thou change them, and they shall be changed; but thou art the same," etc. Some commentators, as Mr. Pierce and others, suppose, that by "the earth and heavens," in this passage, are to be understood, *governments*, or *civil and ecclesiastical states*, as these words, in their figurative sense, sometimes denote. But this does not appear to be the sense in which they are here used. Taken in their literal sense, they may refer to the same objects and events alluded to by the apostle Peter, in his Second Epistle, chap. iii, 7, 10, formerly explained; namely, to the dissolution of the earth and the *aerial* heavens, at the close of time. But supposing that the words were taken in their most extensive sense, as denoting *the whole fabric of the material universe*, it would not in the least invalidate the proposition I am now supporting. The main design of the passage is to assert the eternal immutability of God, in opposition to the mutable nature of created beings. All material things are liable to change; but *change* does not imply *destruction* or *annihilation*. When it is said, "the righteous *perish*, and no man layeth it to heart;" and "they that are far from God shall *perish*," it is not to be understood, that either the one or the other shall be blotted out of existence. So, when it is said that the heavens and the earth *shall perish*, a change or revolution is implied, but not an entire destruction. It is further said, "As a vesture they shall be folded up," etc. This appears to be spoken in allusion to the custom which obtains in the Eastern nations, among the grandees, of frequently changing their garments as a mark of respect; and seems to import, the *ease* and *celerity* with which the Divine Being can accomplish important changes in the universe. He can accomplish the revolutions of worlds and of systems, with an ease similar to that of a **prince** changing his apparel, or laying aside his vestments. But his changing any particular system from its original **state,** implies **only** his opening a new scene, and **varying the course** of his dispensations in relation to a certain order **of his** creatures. Nor does the passage under consideration **lead us** to conclude, that **the** changes alluded to shall all take place throughout the whole universe *at the same period;* but they may be considered as happening **at** different periods throughout the lapse of infinite duration, according to the designs which his wisdom has determined to accomplish.

That all material objects are subject to decomposition and changes, we have abundance of evidence in every department of nature. With respect to the earth on which we tread, we perceive the soil in the higher grounds gradually washed down **by the action of winds** and rains, and carried by the rivers to the bed **of the ocean.** Banks are accumulating at the mouths **of** rivers, and reefs in the midst of the seas, which are the terror of mariners, and **obstructions** to navigation. In every pit and quarry, and on the face of every crag and broken precipice, we perceive the marks of disorder, and the effects of former changes and convulsions **of nature;** while around the bases of volcanic mountains, we **behold** cities buried under a **mass** of solid lava, orchards and vineyards laid waste, and fertile fields transformed into **a** scene of barrenness and desolation. Observation likewise demonstrates, that even the luminaries of heaven are not exempted from revolutions and changes. The **law** of gravitation, which extends its influence through all the celestial orbs, has a tendency, in the course of ages, to draw together all the spacious globes in the universe, and to condense them into one solid mass; and were it not for the counteracting and sustaining hand of God, this effect, at some distant period in duration, **would** inevitably take place, and creation be reduced to one vast and frightful ruin. Many **of the** stars are ascertained to be subjected to periodical changes, varying their lustre, and appearing and disappearing at certain intervals; while others, which formerly shone with superior brilliancy, have gradually disappeared, and their place in the heavens is no longer to be found. Other stars, unknown to the ancients and to preceding observers, have made their appearance in modern times; and various nebulous spots, in the distant regions of space, appear to be increasing both in lustre and extent. These, and many other similar facts, indicate changes and revolutions as great, and even much greater than those which are predicted to befall the earth when its atmosphere shall be dissolved, its "elements melt with fervent heat," and a new world arise out of its ruins. It is probable, that, in the lapse of infinite duration, all the systems which now exist, some at one period and some at another, will undergo changes and transformations which will astonish the intelligent creation, and open new and sublimer scenes of Divine operation to an admiring universe. But such changes will be altogether different from annihilation or utter destruction; altogether different from the ideas embodied in the language of poets, when they tell us that "not one atom shall be left in the mighty void," and that "earth and firmament will be sought in vain." Those stars which appeared, the one in 1572, and the other in 1604, which shone with a brightness superior to Venus, and afterwards disappeared, we have no reason to believe are blotted out of creation. They may either have been changed, from flaming suns to opake globes, like the planets, and may still be existing in the same region of space; or they may have been carried forward, with a rapid motion, to a region of the universe, altogether beyond the utmost limits of our vision, or some other transformation, beyond the reach of human conception, may have been effected. For the annihilation of matter appears to form no part of the plan of the Creator's arrangements; at least, we have no proof of it, in any one instance, and the very idea of it seems to imply an inconsistency, which is repugnant to what we already know of the Divine character and operations.

Such changes, then, so far from diminishing the visible glory of the universe, will present to the view of the intelligent creation, a *greater variety of sublime scenery*, than if all things "continued as they were from the beginning of the creation," and will exhibit the attributes of the Almighty in all their varied aspects and diversified modes of operation. While they demonstrate the mutable nature of created beings, and the immutability of the Creator, they will enliven the scenes of the universe, and excite the admiration and praises of countless multitudes of enraptured intelligences.

From the considerations now stated, it will follow, that the various relations which now subsist among the great bodies which compose the universe, will not be materially altered by any changes or revolutions which may take place in our terrestrial sphere: nor will the general aspect of creation be sensibly altered by any changes that may occasionally happen among the celestial luminaries. What ever may be the nature of such changes, or however important they may be to the inhabitants of the systems in which they happen, they bear no sensible proportion to the whole fabric of the universe. Though stars have, at different periods, disappeared from the visible concave of the firmament, and have, doubtless, undergone amazing revolutions, yet the general appearance of the heavens, in all ages, has been nearly the same, and will probably continue so for an indefinite lapse of ages yet to come. Although our earth were just now transported to a point of space a hundred thousand millions of miles beyond the sphere we presently occupy, the general aspect, and the relative positions of the starry orbs, and the figures of the different constellations, would appear, on the whole, the same as they now do, when we lift our eyes to the nocturnal sky. The constellations of *Orion* and *Charles' Wain*, for example, would present the same shape, the same number of stars, and the same relation to neighbouring constellations, when viewed from a region 1,000,000,000,000,000[1] of miles distant from the earth, as they now do from the sphere in which we are placed.[2] Extension,

---

[1] That is, *a thousand billions;* a billion being equal to ten hundred thousand millions.

[2] This will appear quite evident to any one who considers the immense distance of the stars from the earth, and from one another. We know, by experience, that a change of place, equal to 190 millions of miles, or the diameter of the earth's annual orbit, produces no sensible difference in the appearance of the starry heavens; and it is certain, that if this

magnitude, relative position, attraction, gravitation, central forces, rectilineal and circular motions, and other properties and relations of matter, will still subsist in the universe, after we are transported to another state and to a different region: and, consequently, the *sciences* founded on the various combinations of these properties, and of the laws which govern them, will be cultivated by intelligent beings, and carried forward to that measure of perfection, which they cannot attain in the present state; unless we suppose, what is evidently absurd and contrary to Scripture, that our knowledge *will be more limited* in the future than in the present world.

For example, the laws which direct the motions of falling bodies, the appearances produced by bodies in the heavens moving with different degrees of velocity, the apparent motions of the sun and of the starry heavens, and the general principles of geography and astronomy, on the planet Jupiter, or any other similar globe, with the exception of a few local modifications, are materially the same as on the surface of the earth; which is evident from the consideration of his spheroidal figure, his diurnal and annual motions, and from the consideration that gravitation is regulated by the same general laws on that body, and on similar globes, as on the surface of the earth or the moon. The laws of *vision*, and the nature and properties of *light* and *colours*, are essentially the same throughout all that portion of the universe which lies within the sphere of our observation; and we have no reason to believe that the general laws of the universe will be unhinged, for the sake of man, or on account of any changes that happen in his present abode, or in reference to his future destination. For, to use the words of an eminent Scottish philosopher, " The light by which the fixed stars are seen, is the same with that by which we behold the sun and his attending planets. It moves with the same velocity, as we observe by comparing the aberrations of the

distance were multiplied by ten hundred thousand, the case would be nearly the same. The nearest star is, at least, 20 billions of miles distant, and remoter stars, several thousands of billions; and, therefore, the relative positions of bodies so widely dispersed from each other, would not be sensibly altered, by a change of place, equal in extent to a thousand billions of miles.

fixed stars with the eclipses of Jupiter's satellites. It is refracted and reflected by the same laws. It consists of the same colours. **No** opinion, therefore, can be formed of the solar light which must not also be adopted with respect to the light of the fixed stars. The medium of vision must be acted on in the same manner by both, whether we suppose it the undulations of an **ether,** or the emission of matter from the luminous body." From these facts we may conclude, that the general and fundamental principles of the science of *Optics* are recognised and acted upon in the remotest regions which the telescope has explored, and form a portion of that knowledge which is possessed by the intelligences which occupy those **distant** provinces of the Creator's empire; always, however, making **proper** allowances for those local varieties and modifications, which must produce an infinite diversity of scenery throughout the universe, although the same general laws operate throughout the whole.

What has been now stated in reference to light, gravitation, and other affections **of** matter, might be extended to various other properties, **and to** the sciences which have been founded upon them; such as, the pressure and motions of fluids, the properties of gaseous bodies, the phenomena of electricity and magnetism, and all those affinities, decompositions, and changes, which are the objects of *chemical* research. For, in a *material* fabric, in whatever portion of space it may be placed, there must, from the very nature of things, be a diversity of objects for the investigation of the naturalist, the chemist, and the **philosopher, in** which the wisdom and goodness of the Deity will always be displayed. Every system of matter, wherever existing in infinite space, has a determinate size and figure; it is composed of an infinite number of atoms, variously modified and **arranged; it** has certain diversities of surface and internal arrangement; **it is** susceptible of certain motions; it stands in certain relations to surrounding bodies, and it is destined to accomplish some wise designs corresponding to the eternal plan of the infinite Creator. There is no portion of organized matter now existing, or which may hereafter exist, but which must be considered in these and similar points of view. **Now,** the object of every rational intelligence, whether designated by the appellations of philosopher, astronomer, or chemist, when contemplating any material system, **is**, or ought to be, to trace the various properties and arrangements **which** exist in that system, in order to perceive the intelligence, wisdom, and benevolence, that appear in its construction, and thus to acquire a more correct and comprehensive view of the plans and perfections of his Creator. But such contemplations necessarily suppose, the cultivation of those sciences which will enable him to make such investigations with spirit and effect, without which he would be unable to trace either the qualities and relations of material objects, or to perceive the admirable designs of the all-wise Creator in the works which his Almighty power has produced.

SCIENCES WHICH WILL BE CULTIVATED IN A FUTURE STATE.

In order to illustrate this subject a little further, **I shall** offer a few brief remarks on some of those sciences which will be recognised and prosecuted in a future world.

ARITHMETIC.

Arithmetic, or the knowledge of numbers, and their various powers and combinations, is a science which must be understood in a greater or less degree by all intelligent beings, wherever existing, without some knowledge of which, no extensive progress could be made in the study of the works of **God,** and in forming just conceptions of the immense number and variety of beings which exist within the limits of his empire. **By** the application of the science of numbers, the bulk of the earth has been ascertained; the distances and magnitudes of many of the heavenly bodies have been computed; the proportion which one part of the universe bears to another has been determined; the inconceiveable minuteness of the particles of effluvia, of animalculæ, and of the atoms of light, has been brought within the limits of our contemplation; and we have been enabled to form some faint conceptions of the amazing velocities with which the celestial orbs are carried forward in their courses. The universe presents to our view an assemblage of objects, relations, and movements, calculated to draw forth into exercise all the knowledge of numbers we can possibly acquire. We are presented with magnitudes so stupendous, and with spaces and distances so vast, that the mind is obliged to summon up all its powers of calculation, and all its knowledge of proportions, progressions, and equations, and to add one known magnitude to another, in a long mental process, before it can approximate to any thing like a well-defined idea of such sublime and expansive objects; and, after all its mental efforts, computations, and comparisons, it is frequently under the necessity of resting satisfied with ideas which are vague, inaccurate, and obscure. With regard to the *multiplicity* and *variety* of the objects which creation contains, our present knowledge of the powers of numbers is altogether inadequate to convey to the mind anything approaching to a distinct and comprehensive conception. The *number* of systems of the heavens which lie within the range of our telescopes, is reckoned to be at least a hundred millions (100,000,000.) In the regions of infinite space, beyond the boundaries of all these, it is not improbable, that ten thousand times ten thousand millions of other systems are running their ample rounds. With each of these systems, it is probable that at least a hundred worlds are connected.[1] Every one of these worlds and systems, we have reason to believe, differs from another, in its size, splendour, and internal arrangements, in the peculiar beauties and sublimities with which it is adorned, and in the organization and capacities of the beings with which it is furnished. The immense multitude of rational beings and other existences with which creation is replenished, is an idea which completely overpowers the human faculties, and is beyond the power of our arithmetical notation to express. Even the multiplicity of objects in *one* world or system is beyond our dis-

---

[1] With the solar system to which we belong, there are connected more than a hundred globes of different sizes, if we take into account the planets both *primary* and *secondary*, and likewise the *comets*.

tinct conception. How very feeble and imperfect conceptions have we attained of the immensity of radiations of light incessantly emitted from the sun and falling upon our globe, and of the innumerable crossings and recrossings of these rays from every object around, in order to produce vision to every beholder! of the incalculable myriads of invisible animalculæ which swim in the waters and fly in the air, and pervade every department of nature! of the particles of vapour which float in the atmosphere, and of the drops of water contained in the caverns of the ocean! of the many millions of individuals belonging to every species of vegetables, of which 50,000 different species have already been discovered, and of the number of trees, shrubs, flowers, and plants of every description, which have flourished since the creation! of the countless myriads of the lower animals, and of the human species, which have been brought into existence since the commencement of time, and of those which are yet to appear in regular succession till time shall be no more! of the immense variety of movements, adjustments, and adaptations connected with the structure of an animal body, of which fourteen thousand may be reckoned as belonging to the system of bones and muscles comprised in the human frame, besides a distinct variety of as numerous adaptations in each of the 60,000 different species of animals which are already known to exist! of the countless globules contained in the eyes of the numerous tribes of beetles, flies, butterflies, and other insects, of which 27,000 have been counted in a single eye! And, if the multiplicity of objects in one world overwhelms our powers of conception and computation, how much more the number and variety of beings and operations connected with the economy of millions of worlds! No finite intelligence, without a profound knowledge of numbers in all their various combinations, can form even a rude conception of the diversified scenes of the universe; and yet, without some faint conception, at least, of such objects, the perfections of the Creator and the glories of his kingdom cannot be appreciated.

It is evident, therefore, that superior intelligences, such as angels, and redeemed men, in a future state, must have their attention directed to the science of numbers, unless we suppose, what is contrary to Scripture, that their knowledge and capacities of intellect will be more limited than ours are in the present state. They may not stand in need of the aids of any thing similar to slates, pencils, or numerical characters, to direct them in their computations, or to give permanency to the results of their arithmetical processes. The various steps of their calculations may be carried **forward** with inconceivable rapidity, **by a** mental process which **will** lead to unerring certainty; but the same general principles on which we proceed in **our** notations and calculations, must, from the nature of things, be recognised in all their numerical **processes** and sublime investigations.

The Scriptures occasionally give us some intimations of objects and scenes calculated to exercise the numerical powers of the heavenly inhabitants. When Daniel beheld the vision of the "Ancient of Days" sitting on his throne, a numerous **retinue** of glorious beings appeared in his train to augment the grandeur of the scene. "Thousand thousands ministered **unto** him, and **ten** thousand times ten thousand stood before him." We are told, in the sixty-eighth Psalm, that "the chariots of God are twenty-thousand, even many thousands of angels;" and, in the epistle to the Hebrews, we read of "an innumerable company of angels." The apostle John, when narrating his visions of the celestial world, tells us that he "beheld and heard the voice of many angels round about the throne, and the number of them was **ten** thousand times ten thousand, and thousands of thousands. And, again, "After **this I** beheld, and, lo, a great multitude, which no man could number, of all nations and kindreds, and people, and tongues; **and** all the angels stood round about the throne, and fell on their faces and worshipped God." These expressions are the strongest which the inspired writers make use of, in order to express a countless multitude of objects; and they lead us to conclude, that, in the heavenly world, vast assemblages of intelligent beings will be occasionally presented to the view; and, consequently, a countless variety of scenes, objects, and circumstances, connected with their persons, stations and employments. And, therefore, if celestial beings were not familiarized with numerical calculations and proportions, such scenes, instead of being contemplated with intelligence and rational admiration, would confound the intellect, and produce an effect, similar to that which is felt by a savage, when he beholds, for the first time, some of the splendid scenes of civilized life.

It is owing, in a great measure, to ignorance of the powers of numbers, and the mode of applying them, that we find it impossible to convey any distinct ideas of the velocities, distances, and magnitudes of the heavenly bodies to the illiterate ranks of mankind. We are told by travellers, that there are some untutored tribes, whose knowledge of numbers is so limited, that they cannot count beyond a *hundred*, and that there are others, whose notation is limited to *twenty*, or the number of fingers and toes on their hands and feet. While such ignorance of numbers exists, it is quite evident that such persons are entirely unqualified for surveying, with an eye of intelligence, the grand and *diversified* operations of the Creator, and for appreciating their number and magnificence. Even the most cultivated minds, from an imperfect knowledge of this subject, find it difficult to form distinct conceptions of the plans of the Creator, and of the various relations which subsist in the universe. After familiarizing our minds to the classification and arrangement of numbers, we can form a tolerable notion of a *thousand*, or even of a *hundred thousand;* but it is questionable, whether we have any distinct and well-defined idea of *a million*, or ten hundred thousand. And, if our conceptions of such a number be imperfect, how exceedingly vague must be our ideas of *a thousand millions*, of *billions*, *trillions*, and *quartillions*, when used to express the number or distances of the heavenly bodies? It is evident, then, that beings of a superior order, or in a higher state of existence, must have more profound and comprehensive knowledge of numbers than man: in consequence of which they are enabled to survey the universe with more intelligence, and to form more distinct and ample conceptions of the designs and operations of Infinite wisdom and omnipotence.

MATHEMATICS.

Mathematics, including geometry, trigonometry, conic sections, and other branches, is another department of science, which will be recognised by superior beings in a future state. It is the science of *Quantity*, and treats of magnitude, or local extension, as lines, surfaces, solids, etc. The demonstrated truths of this science are eternal and unchangeable, and are applicable to the circumstances of all worlds, wherever they may exist, and in every period of duration, so long as the material fabric of the universe remains. Guided by the truths which this science unfolds and demonstrates, we have been enabled to determine the figure and dimensions of the earth, to direct our course from one continent to another across the pathless deep, to ascertain the distance and magnitude of the sun and planets, and the laws which the Almighty has ordained for preserving their order, and directing them in their movements; and have been led to form more correct ideas of the immense distances, and the vast extent of the starry heavens. It was owing to his profound knowledge of the truths of this science that the illustrious Sir Isaac Newton determined the properties and the composition of light, the causes of the alternate movements of the ocean, and the mechanism of the planetary system; and expanded our views of the grandeur of the universe, and the perfections of its Almighty Contriver.

Some of the truths of this science may appear, to a superficial thinker, as extremely trivial, and almost unworthy of regard. The properties of a *triangle*, such as, "that the square of the hypotenuse of a right-angled triangle, is equal to the squares of the other two sides;" "that the three angles of a triangle are equal to two right angles;" and "that the sides of a plain triangle are to one another as the sines of the angles opposite to them;" may appear to some minds as more curious than useful, and scarcely deserving the least attention. Yet these truths, when applied to the relations of the universe, and traced to all their legitimate consequences, have led to the most important and sublime results. On the ground of such truths, we have ascertained, that the moon is 240,000 miles distant from the earth; that the sun is thirteen hundred thousand times larger than our globe; that the planet Herschel is removed to the distance of eighteen hundred millions of miles; and that the nearest star is at least two hundred thousand times farther from us than the sun. When the length of any one side of a triangle is known, however large that triangle may be, and the quantity of its angles determined, the length of the other sides can easily be found: we know the extent of the earth's diameter; we can ascertain under what angle that diameter appears at the moon, and from these *data* we can, by an easy calculation, determine the length of any of the other two sides of this triangle, which gives the distance of the moon.

We have every reason to conclude, that angels and other superior intelligences proceed on the same general principles in estimating the distances and magnitudes of the great bodies of the universe. They may not, indeed, require to resort to the same tedious calculations, nor to the same instruments and geometrical schemes which we are obliged to use. Without such aids, *they* may arrive at the proper results with unerring precision, and their computations may be performed almost in the twinkling of an eye; and, while *we* are obliged to confine our calculations to lines and triangles of only a few thousands or millions of miles in extent, *they* may be enabled to form triangles of inconceivable extent, on *base lines* of several thousands of trillions of miles in length. We are informed, in the book of Daniel, that "the angel Gabriel, being commanded to fly swiftly from the celestial regions, reached the prophet about the time of the evening sacrifice." This fact implies, not only that angelic beings are endued with powers of rapid motion, but that they are intimately acquainted with the directions, distances, and positions of the bodies which compose the material universe. This heavenly messenger, having been previously stationed far beyond the limits of our planetary system, had to shape his course in that direction, to discriminate the orbit of the earth from the orbits of the other planets, and the particular part of its orbit in which it was then moving; and, having arrived at the confines of our atmosphere, he required to discriminate the particular region in which

Daniel resided, and to direct his flight to the house in which he was offering up his devotions. Now, since angels are neither omniscient nor omnipresent, as they are limited beings, possessed of *rational* faculties, and, as it is probable, are invested with bodies, or fine material vehicles,[1] they must be guided in such excursions by their reasoning powers, and the faculty of rapid motion with which they are endued. Such excursions imply the recognition of certain mathematical principles, and I have already had occasion to notice, that these principles are applicable throughout every part of the universe, and must be recognised, more or less, by all intelligent beings.

The Creator himself has laid the foundation of the mathematical sciences. His works consist of globes and spheroids of all different dimensions, and of immense concentric rings revolving with a rapid motion. These globes are carried round different centres, some of them in circles, some in ellipses, and others in long eccentric curves. Being impelled in their courses by different degrees of velocity, their real motions cannot be traced, nor the beautiful simplicity and harmony of the different systems made apparent, without the application of mathematical investigations. To an observer untutored in this science, many of the celestial motions would appear to display inextricable confusion, and lead him to conclude, that the Framer of the universe was deficient in wisdom and intelligent design. The principles of mathematics are also exhibited in the numerous and diversified figures into which diamonds, crystals, salts, and other bodies, are formed; in the hexagonal cells of bees, wasps, and hornets, in the *polygons* and *parallel lines* which enter into the construction of a spider's web, and in many other objects in nature. Now, since God has exhibited the elements of this science before us in his works; since he has endued us with rational faculties to appreciate and apply these elements to useful investigations; and since his wisdom and intelligence, and the beauty and order of his works, cannot be fully understood without such investigations; it is evident, that he must have intended, that men should be occasionally exercised in such studies, in order to

---

[1] The Author will afterwards have an opportunity of illustrating this position, in Part III of this Work.

perceive the depths of his wisdom, and the admirable simplicity of his diversified operations. And as the applications of this science are extremely limited in the present world, its more extensive applications, like those of many other branches of knowledge, must be considered as reserved for the life to come. To suppose, therefore, that such studies will be abandoned, and such knowledge obliterated in a future state, would be to suppose, that the works of God will not be contemplated in that state, and that redeemed men in the heavenly world will lose a part of their rational faculties, and remain inferior in their acquirements to the inhabitants of the earth, even in their present imperfect and degraded condition.

ASTRONOMY.

Astronomy is another science which will occupy the attention of pure intelligences in the future world. The object of this science is, to determine the distances and magnitudes of the heavenly bodies, the form of the orbits they describe, the laws by which their motions are directed, and the nature and destination of the various luminous and opake globes of which the universe appears to be composed. It is the most noble and sublime of all the sciences, and presents to our view the most astonishing and magnificent objects; whether we consider their immense magnitude, the splendour of their appearance, the vast spaces which surround them, the magnificent apparatus with which some of them are encompassed, the rapidity of their motions, or the display they afford of the omnipotent energy and the intelligence of the Creator. In consequence of the cultivation of this science, our views of the extent of creation, and of the sublime scenery it unfolds, are expanded far beyond what former ages could have conceived. From the discoveries of astronomy it appears, that our earth is but as a point in the immensity of the universe; that there are worlds a thousand times larger, enlightened by the same sun which "rules our day;" that the sun himself is an immense luminous world, whose circumference would enclose more than twelve hundred thousand globes as large as ours; that the earth and its inhabitants are carried forward through the regions of space, at the rate of a thousand miles every minute; that motions exist in the great bodies of the universe, the force and rapidity of which astonish and overpower the imagination; and that beyond the sphere of the sun and the planets, creation is replenished with millions of luminous globes, scattered over immense regions to which the human mind can assign no boundaries.

These objects present an immense field for the contemplation of every class of moral intelligences, and a bright mirror in which they will behold the reflection of the Divine attributes. Of this vast universe, how small a portion has yet been unvailed to our view! With respect to the bodies which compose our planetary system, we know only a few general facts and relations. In regard to the fixed stars, we have acquired little more than a few rude conceptions of their immense distance and magnitudes. In relation to the *comets*, we only know that they move in long eccentric orbits, that they are impelled in their courses with immense velocity, and appear and disappear in uncertain periods of time. Of the numerous systems into which the stars are arranged, of the motions peculiar to each system, of the relations which these motions have to the whole universe as one vast machine, of the nature and arrangement of the numerous nebulæ which are scattered throughout the distant regions of space; of the worlds which are connected with the starry orbs; of the various orders of beings which people them; of the changes and revolutions which are taking place in different parts of the universe, of the new creations which are starting into existence, of the number of *opake* globes which may exist in every region of space, of the distance to which the material world extends, and of the various dispensations of the Almighty towards the diversified orders of intelligences which people his vast empire; we remain in almost profound ignorance, and must continue in this ignorance, so long as we are chained down to this obscure corner of creation. There will, therefore, be *ample scope* in the future world for further researches into this subject, and for enlarging our knowledge of those glorious scenes which are at present so far removed beyond the limits of natural vision, and the sphere of human investigation.

The heavens constitute the principal part of the *divine empire*, compared with which our earth is but as an atom, and " all nations are as nothing, and are accounted to Jehovah as less than nothing and vanity." Vast as this world may appear to the frail beings that inhabit it, it probably ranks among the smallest globes in the universe; but, although it were twenty thousand times more spacious than it is, it would be only as a grain of sand when compared with the immensity of creation, and all the events that have passed over its inhabitants as only a few of those *ephemeral* transactions which crowd the annals of eternity. It is throughout the boundless regions of the firmament that God is chiefly seen, and his glory contemplated by unnumbered intelligences. It is there that the moral grandeur of his dispensations, and the magnificence of his works, are displayed in all their variety and lustre to countless orders of his rational offspring, over which he will continue eternally to preside. Hence the numerous allusions to " the heavens," by the inspired writers, when the majesty of God and the glory of his dominions are intended to be illustrated. " All the gods of the nations are idols; but Jehovah *made the heavens*." " The Lord hath *prepared his throne in the heavens*, and his kingdom ruleth over all." " By his Spirit he hath garnished the heavens." " The heavens declare the glory of Jehovah." " When I consider thy heavens, the work of thy fingers, the moon and the stars, which thou hast ordained; what is man, that thou art mindful of him, or the son of man, that thou visitest him!" " The heavens, even the heaven of heavens cannot contain thee." " By the word of Jehovah were the heavens made, and *all the host of them* by the spirit of his mouth." " The heavens shall declare his righteousness." " Our God is in the heavens, he hath done whatsoever he hath pleased." " *The heavens shall declare thy wonders, O Lord!*" " I lift up mine eyes to thee, O thou that *dwellest in the heavens.*" " Thus saith God the Lord, *he that created the heavens* and stretched them out." " The heavens for height are unsearchable." " As the heaven is high above the earth, so great is his mercy toward them that fear him." He is " *the God of heaven;* he rideth on the *heaven of heavens*, which he founded of old; heaven is his *throne*, and the earth his footstool." When the **folly** of idolaters is exposed, when the coming of Messiah is announced, and when motives are presented to invigorate the faith and hope of the saints, Jehovah is represented as that omnipotent Being who "meteth out the heavens with a span, who spreadeth them out as a curtain, and bringeth forth their hosts by the greatness of his might." "Thus saith God the Lord, he that created the heavens and stretched them out, I will give thee for a covenant of the people, for a light of the Gentiles."[1] "Thus saith the Lord that created the heavens, I said not to the seed of Jacob, seek ye me in vain," etc.[2] These, and hundreds of similar passages, evidently imply, that we ought to contemplate the attributes of God chiefly in relation to the display which is given of them in the firmament of his power; that the heavens are by far the most extensive portion of his dominions; and that the power and intelligence displayed in the formation and arrangement of the host of heaven, lay a sure foundation for the hope and joy, and the future prospects of the people of God.

In order to form just conceptions of the beauty and grandeur of the heavens, and of the intelligence of Him who arranged their numerous hosts, some of the fundamental facts and principles of astronomy require to be understood and recognised. The order of the bodies which compose the solar system, or other systems which exist in the universe; the form of their orbits, their proportional distances and periods of revolution; their magnitudes, rotations, velocities, and the various phenomena which are observed on their surfaces; the arrangement and positions of the different clusters of stars; of the stellar and planetary *nebulæ*, of double, triple, and variable stars, and many other general facts: require to be known before the mind can receive further information respecting the structure of the universe. It may be also necessary, even in a higher state of existence, to be acquainted with those contrivances or artificial helps by which very distant objects may be brought near to view. We know, by experience, in our present state, that, by means of telescopes, millions of stars, which the unas-

---

[1] **Isa. xliv,** 5, 6.   [2] Isa. xlv, 18, 19.

sisted eye cannot discern, are brought within the sphere of our observation, and numerous other splendid objects, which, without the aid of these instruments, would have been altogether concealed from our view. The organs of vision, indeed, of the redeemed inhabitants of our globe, after the resurrection, there is every reason to believe, will be capable of taking in a much more extensive range of view than at present. They may be endowed with qualities which will enable them to penetrate into the depths of space far beyond the reach of our most powerful telescopes, and to perceive with distinctness, objects at a distance of many billions of miles. Still, however, they may require artificial aids to their natural organs, in order to enable them to contemplate objects at still greater distances. And although such helps to natural vision, analogous to our telescopes, may be conceived as incomparably superior to ours, yet the same general principles must be recognised in their construction. For, as has been already noticed, the light which emanates from the most distant stars, consists of the same colours, and is refracted and reflected by the same laws, as the light which is emitted from the sun, and which illuminates our terrestrial abode; and, consequently, must operate on the organs of sentient beings, in those remote regions, in a manner similar to its effects on the eyes of men.

It is highly probable, that, in the future world, a considerable portion of our knowledge respecting the distant provinces of the Divine empire, will be communicated by superior beings who have visited the different systems dispersed through the universe, and have acquired information respecting their history and their physical and moral scenery. We learn from Scripture, that there are intelligences who can wing their way, in a short period of time, from one world to another. Such beings, in the course of a thousand centuries, must have made many extensive tours through the regions of creation, and acquired a comprehensive knowledge of the most striking scenes which the universe displays. And, since they have occasionally mingled in the society of men, and communicated intelligence from heaven to earth, it is reasonable to believe, that they will have more frequent intercourse with redeemed men in a future state, and communicate the discoveries they have made respecting the economy and grandeur of God's universal empire. But, at the same time, it ought carefully to be observed, that such communications would neither be fully understood nor appreciated, unless the mind had a previous acquaintance with the leading facts, and the grand outlines of astronomical science. To enter into the spirit of those sublime details which angels or archangels might communicate respecting other systems and worlds, the mind *must be prepared* by a knowledge of those principles which have already been ascertained, and of those discoveries which have already been made in relation to the system of the universe. Suppose a group of the native tribes of New Holland, or Van Dieman's Land, were assembled for the purpose of listening to a detail of the principal discoveries which modern astronomers have made in the heavens; it would be impossible to convey to their minds a clear conception even of the prominent and leading facts of this science, from the want of those general ideas which are previously necessary in order to the right understanding of such communications. Such would be the case of men in a future state, in regard to the communications of angelic messengers from distant worlds, were their minds not imbued with a certain portion of astronomical knowledge. They might stare, and wonder at some of the facts detailed; but their ideas would be vague and confused, and they would be unable to form clear and comprehensive conceptions of the various circumstances connected with the scenes described, in all their bearings, aspects, and relations, and of the indications they afford of exquisite skill and intelligent design.

As the objects which astronomy explores are unlimited in their range, they will afford an *inexhaustible* subject of study and contemplation to superior beings, and to mankind when placed in a higher sphere of existence. Astronomical science, as having for its object to investigate and explore the facts and relations peculiar to all the great bodies in the universe, can never be exhausted; unless we suppose that finite minds will be able, at some future period in duration, to survey and to comprehend all the plans and operations of the Infinite Creator. But this is evidently impossible: for, "Who can by searching find out God? Who can find out the Almighty unto per fection?" After millions of centuries have run their rounds, new scenes of grandeur will be still bursting on the astonished mind, new regions of creation, and new displays of divine power and wisdom will still remain to be explored; and, consequently, the science of astronomy will never arrive at absolute perfection, but will be in a progressive course of improvement through all the revolutions of eternity. In the prosecution of such investigations, and in the contemplation of such objects as this science presents, the grand aim of celestial intelligences will be, to increase in the knowledge and the love of God; and in proportion as their views of the glories of his empire are enlarged, in a similar proportion will their conceptions of his boundless attributes be expanded, and their praises and adorations ascend in sublimer strains to Him who sits upon the throne of the universe, who alone is "worthy to receive glory, honour, and power," from every order of his creatures.

Since, then, it appears, that astronomy is conversant about objects the most wonderful and sublime; since these objects tend to amplify our conceptions of the Divine attributes; since a clear and distinct knowledge of these objects cannot be attained without the acquisition of a certain portion of astronomical science; since the heavens constitute the principal part of God's universal empire; since our present views of the magnificence of this empire are so obscured and circumscribed; since even the information that may be communicated on this subject, by other intelligences, could not be fully understood without some acquaintance with the principles of this science; and since the boundless scenes it unfolds present an inexhaustible subject of contemplation, and afford motives to stimulate all holy beings to incessant adoration: it would be absurd to suppose that renovated men, in a superior state of existence, will remain in ignorance of this subject, or that the study of it will ever be discontinued while eternity endures.

NATURAL PHILOSOPHY.

Natural Philosophy is another subject which will doubtless engage the attention of regenerated men in a future state.

The object of this science is to describe **the** phenomena of the material world, to explain their causes, to investigate the laws by which the Almighty directs the operations of nature, and to trace the exquisite skill and benevolent design which are displayed **in the** economy of the universe. It embraces investigations into the several powers and properties, qualities and attributes, motions and appearances, causes and effects, **of all the** bodies with which we are surrounded, and which are obvious to our senses: such as light, **heat,** colours, air, water, **sounds,** echoes; the electrical and magnetical fluids; hail, rain, **snow,** dew, thunder, lightnings, the rainbow, parhelia, winds, luminous and fiery meteors, the Aurora **Borealis, and** similar objects in the system of nature.

From the discoveries of experimental philosophers, **we** have been made acquainted with a variety of striking facts and agencies in the system of the universe, which display the amazing energies of the Creator, and which tend to excite our admiration of the depths of his wisdom and intelligence. We learn that the *light* emitted from the sun and other luminous bodies moves with a velocity equal to 200,000 miles in a *second* of time; that every **ray of** white light is composed of all the colours in nature, blended in certain proportions; that the immense variety of shades of colours which adorns the different landscapes **of** the earth, is not in the objects themselves, but in the light that falls upon them; and that thousands of millions of rays are incessantly **flying off** from all visible objects, crossing and recrossing each other in an infinity of directions, and yet conveying to every eye that is open to **receive** them, a distinct picture of the objects whence they proceed. We learn that the atmosphere which surrounds us presses our bodies with **a** weight equal **to** thirty thousand pounds, **that it contains** the principles of fire and flame; that, in one **combination, it** would raise our animal spirits to the highest pitch **of ecstacy, and** in another, cause our immediate destruction; **that it is capable** of being compressed into 40,000 times less space **than it** naturally occupies; and that the production of sound, the **lives of** animals, and the growth of vegetables, depend upon its various **and** unceasing agencies. We **learn** that a certain fluid pervades all nature, which is capable of giving a *shock* to the animal frame, which shock may be communicated in an instant to a thousand individuals; that this fluid moves with inconceivable rapidity; that it can be drawn from the clouds in the form of a stream of fire; that it melts iron wire, increases the evaporation of fluids, destroys the polarity of the magnetic needle, and occasionally displays its energies among the clouds in the form of fire-balls, lambent flames, and forked lightnings. We learn that the bodies of birds, fishes, quadrupeds, and insects, in relation to their eyes, feet, wings, fins, and other members, are formed with admirable skill, so as to be exactly adapted to their various necessities and modes of existence, and that they consist of an infinite number of contrivances and adaptations in order to accomplish the purpose intended; and that the beaver, the bee, the ant, and other insects, construct their habitations, and perform their operations, with all the skill and precision of the nicest mathematical science. The bee, in particular, works as if it knew the highest branches of mathematics, which required the genius of Newton to discover. In short, the whole of nature presents a scene of wonders, which, when seriously contemplated, is calculated to expand the intellectual powers, to refine the affections, and to excite admiration of the attributes of God, and the plan of his providence.

Natural Philosophy may, therefore, be considered as a branch both of the religion of nature, and of the religion of revelation. It removes in part the vail which is spread over the mysterious operations of nature, and discloses to our view the wonders which lie concealed from the sottish multitude, "who regard not the works of the Lord, nor consider the operations of his hands." It enables us to perceive the footsteps of the Almighty, both in his majestic movements and in his most minute designs; for there is not a step we can take in the temple of nature, under the guidance of an enlightened philosophy, in which we do not behold traces of inscrutable wisdom and design, and of a benevolence which extends its kind regards to every rank of sensitive and intelligent existence. It shows us the beauty and goodness of the Divine administration; and demonstrates, that the communication of happiness is the final cause of all the admirable arrangements which pervade the material system. It teaches us, that the several operations of nature are carried on by means uncontrollable by human power, and far transcending finite skill to plan or to execute. It discovers those laws by which the Sovereign of the universe governs his vast dominions, and maintains them in undecaying beauty and splendour throughout all ages. It thus **enables** us to consecrate the universe into one grand **temple,** and, from the contemplation of every object it presents, to elevate our minds, and to raise our voices in grateful **praises** to Him, " who created all things, and for whose pleasure they are and were created."

In the future world, there will be *abundant scope* for the prosecution of this subject to an indefinite extent. With respect to the state of separate spirits, after their departure from this world, the employments in which they engage, **and the** connection in which they stand to the material system, we can form no distinct conception, **and must** remain in ignorance, till the period arrive when we shall be actually ushered into that mysterious scene of existence. But, **we are** assured, that, after the resurrection, a *material* world will be prepared for the habitation of the just, in which their connection with the visible universe will, doubtless, **be far more** extensive than it is at present; and where ever a material system exists, it affords scope for physical investigations, and for the application of the principles of Natural Philosophy. This new world will be prepared and arranged by Divine wisdom; and, consequently, will exhibit scenes of beauty and grandeur, of exquisite contrivance **and** benevolent design. For, if **the** world we now inhabit, amidst all the deformities and physical derangements which sin **has** introduced, displays so many beautiful arrangements and marks of intelligence and skill, much more may we conclude, that **the world in** which " righteousness shall dwell," will abound **in every** thing that can charm the eye, the ear, or the imagination, **and** illustrate **the** manifold wisdom of God; and, of course, will **present a** boundless field for the most sublime investigations of science. This world, in many of its arrangements, will doubtless present a variety of objects and scenes altogether different from those we now behold, even although the same physical laws, which govern our terrestrial system, should still continue in operation. The inflection, refraction, and reflection of light will be directed by the same general laws, and will produce effects analogous to those we now perceive in the scene around us; but the mediums through which it passes, and the various objects by which it is refracted and reflected, and many other modifications to which it may be subjected, may produce a variety of astonishing effects, surpassing every thing we now behold, and exhibit scenes of beauty and magnificence, of which we can, at present, form no distinct conception. The science of optics, in unfolding to us the nature of light, and the various properties of prisms, mirrors, and lenses, has enabled us to exhibit a variety of beautiful and surprising effects, and to perceive traces of infinite intelligence in relation to this element, beyond what former ages could have believed. And, therefore, we have reason to conclude, that, in the hand of Omnipotence, when arranging other worlds, the element of light is capable of being modified in a thousand forms, of which we are now ignorant, so as to produce the most glorious and transporting effects. There will probably be no such phenomena as thunder, lightning, and fiery meteors in the world to which I allude, but the electrical fluid, which is the principal agent in producing these appearances, and which pervades every part of nature, may operate in that world in a different manner, and, instead of producing effects that are terrific and appalling, may be an agent for creating scenes which will inspire the soul with admiration and delight. Some of the mechanical, pneumatical, and hydrostatical principles which enter into the construction of mills, wheel-carriages, forcing-pumps, and steam-engines, may not be applied to the same purposes in the future world; but they may be applicable to a variety of other unknown purposes, corresponding to the nature of the world, and the character and employments of its inhabitants.

In such cases as those now alluded to, and in thousands of others, there will be ample scope for the application of all the principles of natural science; and thousands of facts and principles, to us unknown, will doubtless be brought to light by the superior sagacity of the heavenly inhabitants. To maintain the contrary, would be, in effect, to suppose, that the inhabitants of heaven are endowed with powers of intellect *inferior* to those of the inhabitants of the earth; that their knowledge is less extensive than ours, or that they make no progress in moral and intellectual attainments; and that they have no desire to explore "the works of the Lord, and to consider the operations of his hands."

What has been now stated in relation to Natural Philosophy, will equally apply to the science of *Chemistry*. This science has for its object to ascertain the first principles of all bodies, their various properties and combinations, their mode of operation, and the effects they produce in the economy of nature. Its discoveries have not only unfolded many of the admirable processes which are going forward in the animal, vegetable, and mineral kingdoms, but have opened to our view many striking displays of the wisdom and goodness of God, in producing, by the most simple means, the most astonishing and benevolent effects. The principles of this science must therefore be applicable *where ever matter exists*, under whatever shape or modification it may present itself: and as all the worlds throughout the universe are composed of *matter*, compounded into various forms, they must afford an ample range for the investigations and researches of chemical science.

ANATOMY AND PHYSIOLOGY.

Anatomy and Physiology are subjects which, we may reasonably conclude, will occasionally occupy the attention of the inhabitants of heaven. The object of these sciences is, to investigate the general structure and economy of the animal frame, and especially the parts and functions of the human body. The system of organization connected with the human frame is the most admirable piece of mechanism which the mind can contemplate; whether we consider the immense number and variety of its parts, the numerous functions they perform, the rapid movements which are incessantly going forward throughout every part of this system, the amazing force exerted by the heart and muscles, the processes of digestion and respiration, the system of veins and arteries, the articulation of the bones, the structure and course of the lymphatics, the ramifications of the nerves, the circulation of the blood, the wonderful changes, dissolutions, and combinations, continually going on; the chemical apparatus adapted for effecting these purposes; the organs of sense, by which an intercourse is maintained with the external world; or, the harmonious correspondence of all its parts and functions with the agencies of the surrounding elements. From the researches of physiologists we learn, that there are in the human body two hundred and forty-five bones, variously articulated, each of them having above forty distinct scopes or intentions; and four hundred and forty-six muscles of various figures and magnitudes, connected with the bones, for producing the numerous movements of the animal frame; that more than a hundred of these muscles are employed every time we breathe; that there are thousands of veins and arteries distributed throughout every part of this wonderful system; that the whole mass of blood rushes with immense velocity through these vessels, and through the heart, fourteen times every hour; that respiration is nothing else than a species of *combustion*, in which the oxygen of the atmosphere is absorbed by the blood, and diffuses heat and vigour throughout the system; that the lungs are composed of an infinite number of membranous cells, or vesicles, variously figured, and full of air, communicating on all sides with one another, and that their number amounts to at least 1,700,000,000, that there are above three hundred thousand millions of pores in the glands of the skin which covers the body of a middle-sized man, through which the sweat and insensible perspiration are continually issuing; that thousands of lacteal and lymphatic tubes are absorbing and conveying nutriment to the blood; that the heart, in the centre of the system, is exerting an immense muscular force, and giving ninety-six thousand strokes every twenty-four hours: and that all this complicated system of mechanism, and hundreds of other functions of which we are ignorant, must be in constant action, in order to preserve us in existence, and secure our enjoyment.

This subject frequently engaged the attention of the pious Psalmist. With an eye of intelligence and devotion, he surveyed the curious organization of the human frame, from the rude embryo in the womb to the full developement of all its functions; and, struck with the wisdom and goodness displayed in its formation, he raised his thoughts to God in grateful adoration. "I will praise thee," he exclaims, "for I am fearfully and wonderfully made; marvellous are thy works! How precious are thy wonderful contrivances in relation to me, O God! How great is the sum of them! If I should count them, they are more in number than the sand." This body, however, wonderful as its structure is, is liable to decay, and must soon be dissolved in the grave. But we are assured that a period is approaching, when "all that are in their graves shall hear the voice of the Son of God, and shall come forth;" when this mortal frame "shall put on *immortality*," and when that which was sown in corruption "shall be raised in *glory*." If the human body, even in its present state of degradation, excited the pious admiration of the Psalmist, much more will it appear worthy of our highest admiration, when it emerges from darkness and corruption to participate in the glories of an *immortal* life. Its faculties will then be invigorated, its tendency to dissolution destroyed, every principle of disease annihilated, and every thing that is loathsome and deformed for ever prevented. Being "fashioned like unto Christ's glorious body," its beauty will be exquisite, its symmetry perfect, its aspect bright and refulgent, and its motions vigorous and nimble. Its sensitive organs will be refined and improved, and the sphere of their operation extended. Its auditory organs will be tuned to receive the most delightful sensations from the harmonies of celestial music, and its visual powers rendered capable of perceiving the minutest objects, and penetrating into the most distant regions. New senses and faculties of perception, and new powers of motion, fitted to transport it with rapidity from one portion of space to another, will, in all probability, be superadded to the powers with which it is now invested. And surely, the contrivances and adaptations which must enter into the structure of such an organical frame, cannot be less curious and exquisite, nor display less wisdom and intelligence, than those which we now perceive in our mortal bodies. On the contrary, we must necessarily suppose thousands of the most delicate contrivances and compensations, different from every thing we can now conceive, to be essentially requisite in the construction of an organized body intended for perpetual activity, and destined to an *immortal* duration. To investigate and to contemplate the contrivances of Divine wisdom, by which the elements of disease and death are for ever prevented from entering into this renovated frame, and by which it will be preserved in undecaying youth and vigour throughout the lapse of innumerable ages, we must necessarily conclude, will form a part of the studies of renovated man in the future world: nor can we help thinking, that the knowledge of the wonders of the human frame we now acquire, may be a preparatory qualification, for enabling us to form an enlightened and comprehensive conception of the powers, qualities, and peculiar organization of the bodies of the saints after the period of the resurrection.

HISTORY.

Another branch of study in which the saints in heaven will engage, is History. History contains a record of past facts and events; and makes us acquainted with transactions which happened hundreds or thousands of years before we were brought into existence. When viewed in its proper light, it may be considered as nothing else than a detail of the operations of Divine Providence in relation to the moral intelligences of this world. It illustrates the character of the human race, and the deep and universal depravity in which they are involved; and displays the rectitude of the character of God, and the equity of his moral administration.

History, therefore, will form a prominent object of study among the celestial inhabitants, as furnishing those materials which will illustrate the ways of Providence, and display the wisdom and righteousness of Jehovah in his government of the world. At present we can contemplate only a few scattered fragments of the history of mankind. Of the history of some nations we are altogether ignorant; and of the history of others we have only a few unconnected details, blended with fabulous narrations and extravagant fictions. Of no nation whatever have we an *entire* history composed of authentic materials; and, consequently, we perceive only some broken and detached links in the chain of the Divine dispensations, and are unable to survey the *whole* of God's procedure towards our race, in one unbroken series, from the creation to the present time. We know nothing decisively respecting the *period* during which man remained in a state of innocence, nor of the particular transactions and events that happened previous to his fall. And how little do we know of the state of mankind, of the events which befell them, and of the civil and religious arrangements which existed, during the period of sixteen hundred years which intervened between the creation and the deluge, though the world was then more fertile and populous than it has ever since been! How little do we know of the state of mankind immediately previous to the flood, of the scenes of consternation and terror which must have been displayed over all the earth, when the fountains of the great deep were broken up, and the cataracts of heaven opened, and of the dreadful concussion of the elements of nature, when the solid strata of the earth were rent asunder, when the foundations of the mountains were overturned, and the whole surface of the globe transformed into one boundless ocean! How little do we know of the circumstances which attended the gradual rise of idolatry, and of the origin of the great empires into which the world has been divided! How little do we know even of the history of the Jewish nation, posterior to the period of the Babylonish captivity! Whether were the ten tribes of Israel scattered among the nations, what events have befallen them, and in what countries are they now to be found? Of the history of all the nations in the world (the Jews only excepted) from the time of the deluge to the days of Hezekiah, a period of nearly two thousand years, we remain in profound ignorance. And yet, during that long period, God had not forsaken the earth; his dispensations towards his rational offspring were still going forward, empires were rising and declining, one generation passing away, and another generation coming, and thousands of millions of mankind ushered into the eternal world. Those chasms in the history of mankind, which hide from our view the greater portion of God's moral dispensations, will, doubtless, be filled up in the eternal state, so that we shall be enabled to take a full and comprehensive view of the whole of the Divine procedure, in all its connections and bearings towards every nation upon earth.

But the history of *man* is not the only topic in this department of knowledge, that will occupy the attention of the inhabitants of heaven. The history of *angels;* of their faculties, intercourses, and employments; of their modes of communication with each other; of their different embassies to distant worlds; of the transactions which have taken place in their society, and of the revolutions through which they may have passed; the history of *apostate* angels; the cause of their fall, and the circumstances with which it was attended; the plans they have been pursuing since that period, and the means by which they have endeavoured to accomplish their infernal devices; will doubtless form a portion of the history of Divine dispensations, which " the saints in light " will be permitted to contemplate. Over this part of the Divine economy a vail of darkness is spread, which, we have reason to believe, will be withdrawn, when that which is perfect is come, and " when we shall know even as also we are known." It is also probable, that the leading facts in relation to the history of other worlds will be disclosed to their view. The history of the different planets in the solar system, and of those which are connected with other systems in the universe; the periods of their creation, the character of their inhabitants, the changes through which they have passed, the peculiar dispensations of providence towards them, and many other particulars, may be gradually laid open to the "redeemed from among men," for enlarging their views of the Divine government. By means of such communications they will acquire a clearer and more distinct conception of the moral character and attributes of God, of the rectitude of his administrations, and of " his manifold wisdom" in the various modes by which he governs the different provinces of his vast empire. Under the impressions which such views will produce, they will rejoice in the Divine government, and join with rapture in the song of Moses, the servant of God, and the song of the Lamb, saying, " Great and marvellous are thy works, Lord God Almighty! *Just and true are thy ways, thou King of saints!*'

Thus I have briefly stated, in the preceding pages, some of those branches of science which will be recognised by the righteous in a future state. Several other departments of scientific knowledge might have been specified; but my intention simply was, to present to the view of the reader, a few specimens as illustrations of my general position, "that science must be considered as having a relation to a future world." If it be admitted that any one science will be cultivated in heaven, it will follow, that the greater part, if not the whole, of those sciences which bring to light the treasures of useful knowledge, will likewise be prosecuted by superior intelligences. For all the useful sciences have an intimate connection with each other; so that an acquaintance with one department of knowledge is essentially requisite to a clear and comprehensive view of another. Astronomy supposes a knowledge of arithmetic, geometry, trigonometry, conic sections, and other parts of mathematics; experimental philosophy supposes a previous acquaintance with natural history and physiology, and is intimately connected with chemistry, mineralogy, and botany; and anatomy and physiology suppose a knowledge of the leading principles of hydrostatics, pneumatics, and optics. The principles of one science run into another, and reflect a mutual lustre on each other, so that all the sciences, when properly conducted, and viewed in their true light, have but one object in view, namely, to ascertain the facts existing in the universe, their connections and relations, the laws by which they are governed, and the illustrations they afford of the power, wisdom, and benevolence of the Creator.

In order to elucidate this topic a little further, the following brief remarks may be stated: It is admitted, by every believer in Revelation,[1] that, at the close of the present arrangements respecting our world, "All that are in their graves shall be raised to life; and that, however different the constitution of these new-modelled bodies may be from their present state of

---

[1] The followers of Baron Swedenburg only excepted.

organization, they will still be *material* vehicles, furnished with organs of sensation as the medium of perception to the immaterial spirit. In what manner the disembodied spirit views material objects and relations, and applies the knowledge of them which it acquired while united to an organical structure, we can have no conception whatever, till we be actually ushered into the separate state; and, therefore, the observations already made, or which may yet be thrown out on this subject, are not intended to apply to the intermediate state of the spirits of good men. That state, what ever may be the *modus* of perception and enjoyment in it, is a state of imperfection, and, in some respects, an *unnatural* state, if we suppose that the spirit is not connected with any material vehicle. Now, if it be admitted that the spirits of the just, at the general resurrection, are to be reunited to *material* organical structures, it must also be admitted, that those structures must have some material *substratum* on which to rest, or, in other words, a material world or habitation in which they may reside. This last position is also as evident, from the declarations of Scripture, as the first. For, while we are informed that the elementary parts of our globe shall be dissolved, we are at the same time assured, that "*new heavens and a new earth*" shall be prepared, " wherein the righteous shall dwell;" that is, a world purified from physical and moral evil, and fitted to the renovated faculties of the redeemed, will be prepared in some part of the universe, for the residence of the just.

In reference to the *locality*, and the circumstances of our future destination, there appear to be only four or five suppositions that can be formed. Either, 1. The world we now inhabit will be new modelled, after the general conflagration, and furnished as a proper place of residence for its renovated inhabitants: or, 2. Some of the globes now existing in other regions of space, to which the holy inhabitants of our world will be transported, may be allotted as the more permanent habitation of the just: or, 3. Some new globe or world will be immediately created, adapted to the circumstances of redeemed men, and adorned with scenery fitted to call forth into exercise their renovated powers: or, 4. The redeemed inhabitants of heaven may be permitted to transport themselves from one region or world to another, and be furnished with faculties and vehicles for this purpose: or, 5. After remaining for a certain lapse of ages in that particular world to which they shall be introduced immediately after the resurrection, they may be transported to another region of the universe, to contemplate a new scene of creating power and intelligence, and afterwards pass, at distant intervals, through a successive series of transportations, in order to obtain more ample prospects of the riches and glory of God's universal kingdom.

In all these cases, whatever supposition we may adopt as most probable, the general laws which now govern the universe, and the general relations of the great bodies in the universe to each other, will remain, on the whole, unchanged; unless we adopt the unreasonable and extravagant supposition, that the whole frame of Jehovah's empire will be unhinged and overturned, for the sake of our world, which, when compared with the whole system of nature, is but an undistinguishable atom amidst the immensity of God's works. With equal reason might we suppose, that the conduct of the inhabitants of a planet which revolves around the star *Sirius*, or the catastrophe which may have befallen the planets Ceres, Pallas, Juno, and Vesta, must necessarily involve in them the destruction of the terraqueous globe.

Let us suppose, for a moment, that the globe we now inhabit, with its surrounding atmosphere, shall be cleared from the physical evils which now exist, and undergo a new arrangement to render it fit for being the abode of holy intelligences in a future state. On this supposition, would not the *general relation of things* in the universe remain materially the same as at present? The wide expanse of the firmament, and all the orbs it contains, would present the same general arrangement and relation to each other which they now do. Supposing this new modelled world to be of a spherical or spheroidal figure, which appears to be the general form of all the great bodies in the universe with which we are acquainted, there would then exist certain properties and relations between circles cutting each other at right angles, or in any other direction; or, in other words, between an equator and poles, parallels and meridians, etc., as at present. The direction of its motion, the inclination of its axis, the component parts of its surface and atmosphere, and other circumstances, might be changed, which would produce an immense variety of phenomena, different from what now takes place; but the same general principles of geography, astronomy, arithmetic, geometry, chemistry and mechanics, which apply to all the various relations of material objects where ever existing, would also be applicable in the present case; and, consequently, such sciences would be recognised and cultivated, and the principles on which they are built, reasoned and acted upon, though in a more perfect manner than at present, in this new world and new order of things. Such sciences, therefore, as flow from the natural and necessary relations of material objects, and which tend to direct us in our conceptions of the wisdom and power of the great Architect of nature, must be known and cultivated in a future world, where rational spirits are united to an organic structure, and related to a material system; and consequently, if the elementary and fundamental principles of such sciences be not acquired now, they will remain to be acquired hereafter.

The remarks now stated, with a few modifications, will apply to any of the other suppositions which may be made in reference to the place and circumstances of our future destination. Even although the relations of external objects and their various properties, in the future world, were altogether different from those which obtain in the present state of things, still it would be useful and highly gratifying to the mind, to be enabled to compare the one with the other, and to perceive how the Divine wisdom is displayed in every mode and variety of existence. No possible mode of material existence, however, can be conceived to exist, to which some of the elementary principles of scientific knowledge do not apply.

There are indeed, several arts and sciences which more immediately respect the present world, and our relations in it, which cannot be supposed to be subjects of investigation in a future state of happy existence. The study of *languages,* which forms a prominent object of attention with many of those who declaim on the vanity of human science; the study of medicine as a practical art; the study of civil and municipal law; the study of political economy, heraldry, and fortification; the arts of war, farriery, falconry, hunting, and fishing; the arts of the manufacturer, clothier, dyer, etc.: in short, all those arts and sciences which have their foundation in the moral depravity of our nature, will of course pass away, as exercises which were peculiar to the deranged state of our terrestrial habitation, and the degraded condition of its inhabitants; and which therefore can have no place in a scene of moral perfection. But the principles of the mathematics, and the axioms on which they are built, the truths of natural philosophy, astronomy, geography, mechanics, and similar sciences, will be recognised, and form the basis of reasoning and of action, so long as we are sentient beings, and have a relation to the material system of the universe. Many truths, indeed, which now require much study, and long and intricate trains of reasoning before they can be acquired, may be perceived by simple intuition, or at least be more easily and rapidly apprehended than at present. If a genius like Sir Isaac Newton could perceive at a glance the truth of Euclid's propositions in geometry, without attending to every part of the process requisite for ordinary minds, we may reasonably conclude, that in a world where the physical and moral obstructions to intellectual energy are removed, every science and every relation subsisting among corporeal and intellectual beings, will be more clearly, rapidly, and comprehensively perceived and understood.

Many striking instances have occasionally occurred, of the capacity and vigour of the human mind, even amidst the obscurities, and the obstructions to mental activity, which exist in the present state of things. The illustrious *Pascal*, no less celebrated for his piety than for his intellectual acquirements, when under the age of twelve years, and while immersed in the study of languages, without books, and without an instructor, discovered and demonstrated most of the propositions in the first book of Euclid, before he knew that such a book was in existence, to the astonishment of every mathematician; so that, at that early age, he was an inventor of geometrical science. He afterwards made some experiments and discoveries on the nature of sound, and on the weight of the air, and demonstrated the pressure of the atmosphere; and, at the age of sixteen, composed a treatise on *Conic Sections*, which, in the judgment of men of the greatest abilities, was viewed as an astonishing effort of the human mind. At nineteen years of age, he invented an arithmetical machine, by which calculations are made, not only without the help of a pen, but even without a person's knowing a single rule in arithmetic; and, by the age of twenty-four, he had acquired a proficiency in almost every branch of human knowledge, when his mind became entirely absorbed in the exercises of religion. The celebrated *Grotius*, at the age of thirteen, only a year after his arrival at the university of Leyden, maintained public theses in mathematics, philosophy, and law, with universal applause. At the age of fourteen, he ventured to form literary plans which required an amazing extent of knowledge; and he executed them in such perfection, that the literary world was struck with astonishment. At this early age, he published an edition of *Martianus Capella*, and acquitted himself of the task in a manner which would have done honour to the greatest scholars of the age. At the age of seventeen, he entered on the profession of an advocate, and pleaded his first cause at Delf, with the greatest reputation, having previously made an extraordinary progress in the knowledge of the sciences. The *Admirable Crichton*, who received his education at Perth and St. Andrews, by the time he had reached his twentieth year, was master of ten languages, and had gone through the whole circle of the sciences as they were then understood. At Paris, he one day engaged in a disputation, which lasted nine hours, in the presence of three thousand auditors, against four doctors of the church and fifty masters, on every subject they could propose, and, having silenced all his antagonists, he came off amidst the loudest acclamations, though he had spent no time in previous preparation for the contest. *Gassendi*, a celebrated philosopher of France, at the age of four, declaimed little sermons of his own composition; at the age of seven, spent whole nights in observing the motions of the heavenly bodies, of which he acquired a considerable knowledge; at sixteen, he was appointed professor of rhetoric at Digne, and at the age of nineteen, he was elected professor of philosophy in the university of Aix. His vast knowledge of philosophy and mathematics was ornamented by a sincere attachment to the Christian religion, and a life formed upon its principles and precepts. *Jeremiah Horrox*, a name celebrated in the annals of astronomy, before he attained the age of seventeen, had acquired, solely by his own industry, and the help of a few Latin authors, a most extensive and accurate knowledge of astronomy, and of the branches of mathematical learning connected with it. He composed astronomical tables for himself, and corrected the errors of the most celebrated astronomers of his time. He calculated a transit of the planet Venus across the sun's disk, and was the first of mortals who beheld this singular phenomenon, which is now considered of so much importance in astronomical science. Sir Isaac Newton, the fame of whose genius has extended over the whole civilized world, made his great discoveries in geometry and fluxions, and laid the foundation of his two celebrated Works, his "*Principia*" and "*Optics*," by the time he was twenty-four years of age; and yet these works contain so many abstract, profound, and sublime truths, that only the first-rate mathematicians are qualified to understand and appreciate them. In learning mathematics, he did not study the geometry of Euclid, who seemed to him too plain and simple, and unworthy of taking up his time. He understood him almost before he read him; and a cast of his eye upon the contents of his theorems, was sufficient to make him master of their demonstrations. Amidst all the sublime investigations of physical and mathematical science in which he engaged, and amidst the variety of books he had constantly before him, the Bible was that which he studied with the greatest application; and his meekness and *modesty* were no less admirable than the variety and extent of his intellectual acquirements. *J. Philip Baratier*, who died at Halle in 1740, in the twentieth year of his age, was endowed with extraordinary powers of memory and comprehension of mind. At the age of five, he understood the Greek, Latin, German, and French languages; at the age of nine he could translate any part of the Hebrew Scriptures into Latin, and could repeat the whole Hebrew Psalter; and, before he had completed his tenth year, he drew up a Hebrew lexicon of uncommon and difficult words, to which he added many curious critical remarks. In his thirteenth year he published, in two volumes octavo, a translation, from the

Hebrew, of Rabbi Benjamin's " Travels in Europe, Asia, and Africa," with historical and critical notes and dissertations; the whole of which he completed in four months. In the midst of these studies, he prosecuted philosophical and mathematical pursuits, and in his fourteenth year invented a method of discovering the longitude at sea, which exhibited the strongest marks of superior abilities. In one winter he read twenty great folios, with all the attention of a vast comprehensive mind.

Such rapid progress in intellectual acquirements strikingly evinces the vigour and comprehension of the human faculties; and if such varied and extensive acquisitions in knowledge can be attained, even amidst the frailties and physical impediments of this mortal state, it is easy to conceive, with what energy and rapidity the most sublime investigations may be prosecuted in the future world, when the spirit is connected with an incorruptible body, fitted to accompany it in all its movements; and when every moral obstruction which now impedes its activity shall be completely removed. The flights of the loftiest genius that ever appeared on earth, when compared with the rapid movements and comprehensive views of the heavenly inhabitants, may be no more than as the flutterings of a microscopic insect, to the sublime flights of the soaring eagle. When endowed with new and vigorous senses, and full scope is afforded for exerting all the energies of their renovated faculties, they may be enabled to trace out the hidden springs of nature's operations, to pursue the courses of the heavenly bodies, in their most distant and rapid career, and to survey the whole chain of moral dispensations, in reference, not only to the human race, but to the inhabitants of numerous worlds.

I shall conclude this part of my subject with an observation or two, which may tend to illustrate and corroborate the preceding remarks.

In the first place, it may be remarked, that our knowledge in the future world, will not be diminished, but increased to an indefinite extent. This is expressly declared in the Sacred Records. "Now we see through a glass darkly, but then face to face. Now we know in part, but then shall we know, even as also we are known," 1 Cor. xiii, 12. This passage intimates, not only that our knowledge in a future state shall be enlarged, but that it shall be increased to an extent to which we can, at present, affix no limits. And if our intellectual views shall be immensely expanded in the realms of light, we may rest assured, that all those branches of useful science which assist us in exploring the operations of the Almighty, will not only be cultivated, but carried to their highest pitch of perfection. For the faculties we now possess will not only remain in action, but will be strengthened and invigorated; and the range of objects on which they will be employed will be indefinitely extended. To suppose otherwise, would be to suppose man to be deprived of his intellectual powers, and of the faculty of reasoning, as soon as he entered the confines of the eternal world.[1] When we enter that world, we carry with us the moral and intellectual faculties, of which we are now conscious, and, along with them, all those ideas and all that knowledge which we acquired in the present state. To imagine that our present faculties will be *essentially* changed, and the ideas we have hitherto acquired totally lost, would be nearly the same as to suppose, that, on entering the invisible state, men will be transformed into a new order of beings, or be altogether annihilated. And, if our present knowledge shall not be destroyed at death, it must form the groundwork of all the future improvements we may make, and of all the discoveries that may be unfolded to our view in the eternal state.

Again, the superior intellectual views which some individuals shall possess beyond others, will constitute the principal distinction between redeemed men in the heavenly state. The principal preparation for heaven will consist in renewed dispositions of mind, in the full exercise of love to God, and love

[1] An old Welsh minister, while one day pursuing his studies, his wife being in the room, was suddenly interrupted by her asking him a question, which has not always been so satisfactorily answered: " John Evans, do you think we shall be known to each other in heaven?" Without hesitation he replied, " To be sure we shall; do you think we shall be *greater fools* there than we are here?" If the reader keep in mind that our knowledge in heaven will be *increased*, and not diminished, or, in other words, that we shall not be " greater fools there than we are here," he will be at no loss to appreciate all that I have hitherto stated on this subject.

to all subordinate holy intelligences, and in all the diversified ramifications of action into which these grand principles necessarily diverge. When arrived at that happy world, the saints will feel themselves to be all equal; as they were once "children of disobedience even as others," as they were all redeemed "by the precious blood of Christ," as they were renewed by the influence of the Spirit of grace; as they stand in the relation of brethren in Christ, and "sons and daughters of the Lord God Almighty," as they are the companions of angels, and kings and priests to the God and Father of all. Without the exercise of holy dispositions, heaven could not exist, although its inhabitants had reached the highest pitch of intellectual improvement: and all who shall ultimately be admitted into that happy state, will feel that they are eternally indebted for the privileges and the felicity they enjoy, "to Him that sits upon the throne, and to the Lamb who was slain, and redeemed them to God by his blood." But, notwithstanding, there will be a considerable difference, at least in the first instance, in regard to *the expansion of their intellectual views*. In this point of view, it is impossible to suppose that they can be all equal. Suppose a Negro slave, who had been recently converted to Christianity, and a profound Christian philosopher, to enter the eternal world at the same time, is it reasonable to believe, that there would be no difference in the amplitude of their intellectual views? They would both feel themselves delivered from sin and sorrow, they would be filled with admiration and wonder at the new scenes which opened to their view, and would be inspired with the most lively emotions of humility and reverence; but if each of them carried along with him that portion of knowledge which he acquired in the present life, there behoved to be a considerable difference in the comprehension of their views and the range of their intellectual faculties; unless we suppose that a change amounting to a miracle was effected in the mind of the Negro, whose mental views were previously circumscribed within the narrowest limits. And to suppose such a miracle wrought in every individual case, would not only be contrary to every thing we know of the general plan of the Divine procedure, but would destroy almost every motive that should now induce us to make progress "in the knowledge of our Lord and Saviour Jesus Christ," and in our views of the works and dispensations of the Almighty. In the course of ages, indeed, the negro may equal the philosopher in the extent of his intellectual acquisitions; but, in the first instance, both Scripture[1] and reason declare, that a difference must exist, unless the laws which govern the intellectual world be entirely subverted. Can we suppose, for a moment, that an ignorant profligate, who has been brought to repentance, and to the "knowledge of the truth," only a few hours before his entrance into the world of spirits, shall, at the moment he has arrived in the world of bliss, acquire those enlarged conceptions of Divine truth, which an Owen, a Watts, a Doddridge, or a Dwight, attained at the same stage of their existence? or that a Hottentot who had been brought to the knowledge of Christianity, only during the last month of his life, shall enter into heaven with the expansive views of a Newton or a Boyle? Such a supposition would involve a reflection on the *wisdom* of the Divine administration, and would lead us to conclude, that all the labour bestowed by the illustrious characters now alluded to, in order to improve in the knowledge of Divine subjects, was quite unnecessary, and even somewhat approaching to egregious trifling.

Not only will the views of the saints in heaven be different in point of expansion and extent, but their love to God, and the virtues and graces which flow from this principle, will be diminished or increased, or, at least, somewhat modified by the narrowness or expansion of their intellectual views. If it be admitted that, the more we know of God, the more ardently shall we love him, it will follow: that, in proportion as we acquire a comprehensive and enlightened view of the operations of God in the works of creation, in the scheme of Providence, and in the plan of redemption, in a similar proportion will our love and adoration of his excellences be ardent and expansive. In this point of view, "the saints in light" will make improvement in holiness throughout all the ages of eternity, though, at every stage of their existence, they will enjoy pure and unmingled bliss. Every science they cultivate, and

---

[1] See Dan. xii, 3. 1 Cor. xv, 41, 42. Matt. xxv, 14, etc.

every stage to which they advance in intellectual improvement, will enable them to discover new glories in the Divine character, which will raise their affections to God still higher, and render their conformity to his moral image more complete.

It has frequently been a subject of discussion among theologians, "Whether there shall be degrees of glory in heaven." This question may be easily settled, if there be any weight in the remarks and considerations now stated. In so far as there is a difference in the vigour and expansion of the intellectual powers, and in the amplitude of objects they are enabled to embrace, in so far may there be said to be "degrees of glory:" and a superiority, in this respect, may be considered as the natural reward which accompanies the diligent improvement of our time and faculties upon earth, though such a distinction can never be supposed to produce any disposition approaching to envy, as so frequently happens in the present state. On the contrary, it may be supposed to produce a holy emulation to improve every faculty, to cultivate every branch of celestial science, and to increase in the knowledge of God. In corroboration of these views, we are told in Scripture, that the reward bestowed on those servants to whom talents were intrusted, was in proportion to the improvement they had made; and that, at the close of time, the saints will present an appearance analogous to that of the spangled firmament; for "as one star differeth from another star in glory, so also is the resurrection from the dead." And the reason of this difference is intimated by the prophet Daniel, "They that excel in wisdom shall shine as the brightness of the firmament; and they that turn many to righteousness as the stars for ever and ever."

If the remarks now stated have any solid foundation, it will follow, that what is generally termed *human science*, ought not to be indiscriminately considered as having a relation merely to the present world. Such an idea would tend to damp our ardour in the prosecution of scientific knowledge, and immensely to lessen its value. He who prosecutes science as a subject of speculation merely in reference to the contracted span of human life, acts from very mean and narrow views, and may be considered, in some points of view, as little superior to the avaricious man whose mind is completely absorbed in the acquisition of the perishing treasures of this world. The Christian philosopher, who traces the perfections and the agency of God in every object of his investigation, ought to consider his present pursuits as the commencement of a course of improvement which will have no termination; as introductory to the employments and the pleasures of a higher state of existence; and as affording him a more advantageous outset into that better world than happens to those who are destitute of his enlarged views. For the more we know at present of the wonders of infinite power, wisdom, and goodness in the material works of the Almighty, it is obvious, that the better prepared we shall be for more enlarged contemplations of them at a future period, and the greater pleasure shall we feel in beholding those objects and operations, which are now hid in obscurity, unvailed to view.

In throwing out the preceding reflections, I am far from pretending to determine the particular arrangements which the Almighty has formed in relation to our future destination, or the particular circumstances which may exist in other worlds. These things lie altogether beyond the range of our investigation, and must, therefore, remain inscrutable in our present state. But there are certain general principles or relations which necessarily flow from the nature of things, which must be considered as included within any particular arrangements which may be formed; and it is such general principles only to which I refer. Nor should it be considered as presumption, to endeavour to ascertain these general principles or necessary relations of things. The Creator evidently intended we should know them; since he has exhibited such an immense variety of his works before us, and has bestowed upon us faculties adequate to explore their magnitude and arrangement, to investigate the laws which direct their motions, and to perceive their connection and dependency, and some of the grand designs for which they were intended.

To every thing that has just now been stated in relation to the prosecution of science in the celestial world, I am aware, it will be objected, by some, that such knowledge, if it be requisite in a future state, will be acquired by immediate intuition, or communicated in a direct manner by the Creator himself. For such an assumption, however, though frequently reiterated, there is no foundation in any passage of Scripture when rationally interpreted; and it is repugnant to the clearest dictates of reason. It is contrary to every regular mode with which we are acquainted, by which rational beings are conducted to knowledge and happiness; it would imply a continued miracle; it would supersede the use of the intellectual faculty; and it would ultimately detract from the felicity of intelligent agents. For, a great part of the happiness of finite intelligences arises from the gradual evolution of truth, in consequence of the exercise of their rational powers. Were all our knowledge in a future state to be acquired by immediate intuition, or by direct supernatural communications from the Deity, our rational faculties would, in many respects, be bestowed in vain. It appears to be one of the main designs for which these faculties were bestowed, that we might be directed in the prosecution of knowledge, and led to deduce, from the scenes of the visible universe, those conclusions which will gradually expand our views of the plans and perfections of its Almighty Author. Adam, when in a state of innocence, (and his condition in that state, as a moral agent, was precisely similar to the state of good men in a future world, except his liability to fall,) was not acquainted, in the first instance, with every object in the world in which he was placed, and their various relations to each other. He could not know, for example, the peculiar scenery of nature which existed on the side of the globe opposite to that on which he was placed. He must have exercised his senses, his locomotive faculties, and his reasoning powers, and made observations and experimental researches of various kinds, before he became thoroughly acquainted with the structure, the order, and beauty of his terrestrial habitation. For, to suppose man, in any state, a mere passive subject of intellectual and external impressions, would be to reduce him to something like a mere machine; and would imply a subversion of all the established laws which regulate the operations of matter and intellect throughout the universe.

We know, likewise, that truth is gradually developed even to superior intelligences. The manifold wisdom of **God** in reference to the Church, and the plans of his grace in relation to the Gentile world, were, in some measure, vailed to the angels, till the facts of the death and resurrection of Christ, and the preaching and miracles of the apostles were exhibited to their **view**;[1] and hence they are represented as "desiring to look into," or prying with avidity into the mysteries of redemption; which evidently implies, the active exertion of their powers of reason and intelligence, and their gradual advancement in the knowledge of the purposes and plans of the Almighty. **And,** if beings far superior to man in intellectual capacity, acquire their knowledge in a *gradual* manner, by reflection on the Divine dispensations, and the exercise of their mental powers, it is unreasonable to suppose, that man, even in a higher sphere **of** existence, will acquire all his knowledge at once, or without **the** exertion of those intellectual energies with which he is **endowed.**

In short, were the saints in heaven to acquire all their knowledge as soon as they entered on that scene of happiness, we must suppose them endowed with capacities, not only superior to the most exalted seraphim, but even approximating to the infinite comprehension of the Deity himself. For the range of investigation presented to intelligent beings is boundless, extending to all the objects and moral dispensations of God, throughout the immensity of his empire. And could we suppose finite minds capable of embracing the whole of this range of objects at one comprehensive grasp, their mental energy would soon be destroyed, and their felicity terminate; for they could look forward to no further expansion of their views, nor to a succession of a new range of objects and operations through all the future ages of eternity.

[1] Ephesians, iii, 5–11.

PART III.

ON THE AIDS WHICH THE DISCOVERIES OF SCIENCE AFFORD FOR ENABLING US TO FORM A CONCEPTION OF THE PERPETUAL IMPROVEMENT OF THE CELESTIAL INHABITANTS IN KNOWLEDGE AND FELICITY.

On the subject of a future world, and the exercises and enjoyments of its inhabitants, many foolish and inaccurate conceptions have prevailed even in the Christian world. We are assured, that the foundation of the felicity to be enjoyed in that world, rests on the absence of every evil, and the attainment of moral perfection; that the principle of depravity must be destroyed, and the affections purified and refined, before we can enjoy "the inheritance of the saints in light." These are principles which are clearly exhibited in the Scriptures, which are accordant to the dictates of sound reason, and which are generally recognised by the various sections of the religious world. But the greater part of Christians rest contented with the most vague and incorrect ideas of the felicity of heaven, and talk and write about it in so loose and figurative a manner, as can convey no rational nor definite conception of the sublime contemplations and employments of celestial intelligences. Instead of eliciting, from the metaphorical language of Scripture, the *ideas* intended to be conveyed, they endeavour to expand and ramify the figures employed by the Sacred writers still further, heaping metaphor upon metaphor, and epithet upon epithet, and blending a number of discordant ideas, till the image or picture presented to the mind assumes the semblance of a splendid chaotic mass, or of a dazzling but undefined meteor. The term *glory,* and its kindred epithets, have been reiterated a thousand times in descriptions of the heavenly state; the redeemed have been represented as assembled in one vast crowd above the visible concave of the sky, adorned with "starry crowns," drinking at "crystal fountains," and making "the vault of heaven ring" with their loud acclamations. The Redeemer himself has been exhibited as suspended like a statue in the heavens above this immense crowd, crowned with diadems, and encircled with a refulgent splendour, while the assembly of the heavenly inhabitants were *incessantly* gazing on this object, like a crowd of spectators gazing at the motion of an air balloon, or of a splendid meteor. Such representations are repugnant to the *ideas intended to be conveyed* by the metaphorical language of Inspiration, when stripped of its drapery. They can convey nothing but a meagre and distorted conception of the employments of the celestial state, and tend only to bewilder the imagination, and to "darken counsel by words without knowledge."

Hence it has happened, that certain infidel scoffers have been led to conclude, that the Christian heaven is not an object to be desired; and have frequently declared, that "they could feel no pleasure in being suspended for ever in an ethereal region, and perpetually singing psalms and hymns to the Eternal:" an idea of heaven which is too frequently conveyed by the vague and distorted descriptions which have been given of the exercises and entertainments of the future world.

There is an intimate connection between the word and the works of God: they reflect a mutual lustre on each other, and the discoveries made in the latter are calculated to expand our conceptions, and to direct our views, of the revelations contained in the former. Without taking into account the sublime manifestations of the Deity exhibited in his visible creation, our ideas of celestial bliss must be very vague and confused, and our hopes of full and *perpetual* enjoyment in the future state extremely feeble and languid. From the very constitution of the human mind, it appears, that in order to enjoy uninterrupted happiness, without satiety or disgust, it is requisite that *new* objects and new trains of thought be continually opening to view. A perpetual recurrence of the same objects and perceptions, however sublime in themselves, and however interesting and delightful they may have been felt at one period, cannot afford uninterrupted gratification to minds endowed with capacious powers, and capable of ranging through the depths of immensity. But all the objects in this sublunary world and its environs, and all the events recorded in sacred and profane history, are not sufficient to occupy the expansive minds of renovated intelligences for a million of ages, much less throughout an endless duration of existence. A series of objects and of moral dispensations, more extensive than those immediately connected with the globe we inhabit, must, therefore be supposed to engage the attention of "the spirits of just men made perfect," during the revolutions of eternal ages; in order that their faculties may be gratified and expanded, that new views of the Divine character may be unfolded; and that, in the contemplation of his perfections, they may enjoy a perpetuity of bliss.

It has been, indeed, asserted by some, that "the mysteries of redemption will be sufficient to afford scope for the delightful investigation of the saints to all eternity." It is readily admitted, that contemplations of the Divine perfections, as displayed in human redemption, and of the stupendous facts which relate to that economy, will blend themselves with all the other exercises of redeemed intelligences. While their intellectual faculties are taking the most extensive range through the dominions of Him who sits upon the throne of universal nature, they will never forget that love "which brought them from darkness to light," and from the depths of misery to the splendours of eternal day. Their grateful and triumphant praises will ascend to the Father of glory, and to the Lamb who was slain, *for ever and ever*. But, at the same time, the range of objects comprised within the scheme of redemption, in its reference to human beings, cannot be supposed, without the aid of other objects of contemplation, to afford full and uninterrupted scope to the faculties of the saints in heaven, throughout an unlimited duration. This will appear, if we endeavour to analyze some of the objects presented to our view in the economy of redemption.

In the first place, it may be noticed, that a vail of mystery surrounds several parts of the plan of redemption. "God manifested in the flesh," the intimate union of the eternal self-existent Deity with "the man Christ Jesus," is a mystery impenetrable to finite minds. But the eternity, the omnipresence, and the omniscience of the Deity, are equally mysterious; for they are equally incomprehensible, and must **for** ever remain incomprehensible to all limited intelligences. It is equally incomprehensible that a sensitive being should exist, furnished with all the organs and functions requisite for animal life, and yet of a size ten thousand times less than a mite. These **are** facts which must be admitted on the evidence of sense and of reason, but they lie altogether beyond the sphere of our comprehension. Now, an object which involves a mystery cannot be supposed to exercise and entertain the mind through eternity, considered simply as *incomprehensible*, without being associated with other objects which lie within the **range of** finite comprehension; otherwise, reflections on the eternity **and** omnipresence of God, considered purely as abstractions of the mind, might gratify the intellectual faculties, in the future world, in as high a degree as any thing that is mysterious in the scheme of redemption. But it is quite evident, that perpetual reflections **on** infinite space and eternal duration, abstractly considered, **cannot** produce a very high degree of mental enjoyment, unless **when** considered in their relation to objects more definite and comprehensible. **Such** contemplations, however, will doubtless be mingled with all the other views and investigations of the saints in the heavenly world. In proportion as they advance through myriads of ages in the course of unlimited duration, and in proportion to the enlarged views they will acquire, of the distances and magnitudes of the numerous bodies which diversify **the** regions of the universe, their ideas of infinite space, and of eternal duration, will be greatly expanded. For **we** can acquire ideas of the extent of space, only by comparing the distances and bulks of material objects with one another; and of **duration, by** the trains of thought derived from sensible objects, which **pass** through our minds, and from the periodical revolutions **of** material objects around us. The same things may be **affirmed in** relation to all that is mysterious in the economy of human redemption: and, if what has been now said be admitted, it will follow, that such mysteries, considered merely **as** incomprehensible realities, could not afford a rapturous train **of** thought to entertain the mind throughout the ages of eternity. It is definite and tangible objects, and not abstract mysteries, that constitute the proper subject of contemplation to a rational mind. For, although we were to ponder on what is incomprehensible, such as the eternity of God, for millions of years, we should be as far from comprehending it, or acquiring any new ideas respecting it, at the end of such a period, as at the present moment.

In the next place, redemption may be considered in reference to the important *facts* connected with it, in which point of view, chiefly, it becomes a tangible object for the exercise of the moral and intellectual powers of man. These facts relate either to the "man Christ Jesus, the Mediator between God and man," or to the saints whose redemption he procured. The general facts which relate to Christ, while he sojourned in our world, are recorded in the New Testament by the Evangelists. These comprehend his miraculous conception, and the circumstances which attended his birth; his private residence in Nazareth; his journeys as a public teacher through the land of Judea; his miracles, sufferings, crucifixion, resurrection, and ascension to heaven. There is doubtless a variety of interesting facts, besides those recorded in the Gospels, with which it would be highly gratifying to become acquainted: such as, the manner in which he spent his life, from the period of the first dawnings of reason, to the time of his commencing his public ministrations; the various trains of thought that passed through his mind; the mental and corporeal exercises in which he engaged; the social intercourses in which he mingled; the topics of conversation he suggested; the amusements (if any) in which he indulged; the pious exercises and sublime contemplations in which he engaged, when retired from the haunts and the society of men: and particularly those grand and important transactions in which he has been employed, since that moment when a cloud interposed between his glorified body and the eyes of his disciples, after his ascent from Mount Olivet; what regions of the material universe he passed through in his triumphant ascent; what intelligence of his achievements he conveyed to other worlds; what portion of the immensity of space, or what globe or material fabric, is the scene of his more immediate residence; what are the external splendours and peculiarities of that glorious world; what intercourse he has with the spirits of just men made perfect, with Enoch and Elijah, who are already furnished with bodies, and with other orders of celestial intelligences; what scenes and movements will take place in that world, when he is about to return to our terrestrial sphere, to summon all the tribes of men to the general judgment? The facts in relation to these, and similar circumstances, still remain to be disclosed, and the future details which may be given of such interesting particulars, cannot fail to be highly gratifying to every one of the "redeemed from among men." But still, it must be admitted, that although the details respecting each of the facts to which I allude, were to occupy the period of a thousand years, the subject would soon be exhausted, if other events and circumstances, and another train of Divine dispensations, were not at the same time presented to view; and the future periods of eternal duration would be destitute of that *variety* and *novelty* of prospect which are requisite to secure perpetual enjoyment.

The other class of facts relates to the redeemed themselves, and comprehends those diversified circumstances in the course of providence, by means of which they were brought to the knowledge of salvation, and conducted through the scenes of mortality to the enjoyment of endless felicity. These will, no doubt, afford topics of interesting discourse, to diversify and enliven the exercises of the saints in heaven. But the remark now made in reference to the other facts alluded to above, is equally applicable here. The series of Divine dispensations towards every individual, though different in a few subordinate particulars, partakes of the same character, and wears the same general aspect. But although the dispensations of Providence towards every one of the redeemed were as different from another as it is possible to conceive, and although a hundred years were devoted to the details furnished by every saint, eternity would not be exhausted by such themes alone.

Again, it has been frequently asserted, that the saints in heaven will enjoy perpetual rapture in continually gazing on the glorified humanity of Christ Jesus. The descriptions sometimes given of this circumstance, convey the idea of a vast concourse of spectators gazing upon a resplendent figure placed upon an eminence in the midst of them; which, surely, must convey a very imperfect and distorted idea of the sublime employments of the saints in light. The august splendours of the "man Christ Jesus," the exalted station he holds in the upper world, the occasional intercourse which all his saints will hold with him, the lectures on the plans and operations of Deity with which he may entertain them, the resplendent scenes to which he may guide them, and many other circumstances, will excite the most rapturous admiration of Him who is "the brightness of the Father's glory." But, since the glorified body of Christ is *a material substance*, and, consequently, limited to a certain portion of space, it cannot be supposed to be at all times within the view of every inhabitant of heaven; and, although it were, the material splendours of that body, however august and astonishing, cannot be supposed to afford new and varied gratification throughout an endless succession of duration. He will be chiefly recognised as the *Head* of the redeemed family of man, " in whom are hid all the treasures of wisdom and knowledge," who will gradually reveal the secret counsels of God, and direct his saints to those displays of Divine glory which will enlighten and entertain their mental powers. This seems to be intimated in such representations as the following: "The Lamb that is in the midst of the throne shall feed them, and shall lead them to living fountains of water." By directing their attention to those objects in which they may behold the most august displays of Divine perfection, and teaching them in what points of view they ought to be contemplated, and what conclusions they ought to deduce from them, " he will feed" the minds of his people with Divine knowledge, and " lead them" to those sublime and transporting trains of thought, which will fill them with " joy unspeakable and full of glory."

Thus it appears, that neither the mysteries, nor the leading facts connected with the plan of redemption, when considered merely in relation to human beings, can be supposed to be the principal subjects of contemplation in the heavenly state, nor sufficient to produce those diversified gratifications which are requisite to ensure perpetual enjoyment to the expanded intellects of redeemed men in the future world, though such contemplations will undoubtedly be intermingled with all the other intellectual surveys of the saints in glory.

I now proceed to the principal object in view, namely, to inquire what other objects will employ the attention of good men in the world to come, and what light the material works of God, which have been unfolded to our view, tend to throw upon this subject.

The foundation of the happiness of heavenly intelligences being laid in the destruction of every principle of moral evil, in the enjoyment of moral perfection, and in the removal of every physical impediment to the exercise of their intellectual powers, they will be fitted for the most profound investigations, and for the most enlarged contemplations. And one of their chief employments, of course, will be, to investigate, contemplate, and admire the glory of the Divine perfections. Hence it is declared in Scripture as one of the privileges of the saints in light, that *"they shall see God as he is,"* that "they shall see his face," and that "they shall behold his glory;" which expressions, and others of similar import, plainly intimate, that they shall enjoy a clearer vision of the Divine glory than in the present state. But how is this vision to be obtained? The Deity, being a spiritual uncompounded substance, having no visible form, nor sensible quantities, "inhabiting eternity," and filling immensity with his presence, his essential glory cannot form an object for the *direct contemplation* of any finite intelligence. His glory, or, in other words, the grandeur of his perfections, can be traced only in the external manifestation which he gives of himself in the material creation which his power has brought into existence; in the various orders of intelligences with which he has peopled it; and in his moral dispensations towards all worlds and beings which now exist, or may hereafter exist, throughout his boundless empire.

It is in this point of view, that our knowledge of the material universe assists our conceptions of the scenes of a future state, and throws a refulgence of light on the employments, and the uninterrupted pleasures, of the redeemed in heaven. By the discoveries of modern science, in the distant regions of space, we are fully assured, that the attributes of the Deity have not been exercised solely in the construction of our sublunary sphere, and of the aerial heavens with which it is encompassed, nor his providential regards confined to the transactions of the frail beings that dwell upon its surface, but extend to the remotest spaces of the universe. We know, that far beyond the limits of our terrestrial abode, the Almighty has displayed his omnipotence in framing worlds, which, in magnitude and in splendour of accompaniments, far surpass this globe on which we dwell. The eleven planetary bodies which, in common with the earth, revolve about the sun, contain a mass of matter two thousand five hundred times greater, and an extent of surface sufficient to support an assemblage of inhabitants three hundred times more numerous, than in the world which we inhabit. The Divine *wisdom* is also displayed in reference to these vast globes; in directing their motions, so as to produce a *diversity of seasons*, and a regular succession of *day and night;* in surrounding some of them with *moons*, and with luminous rings of a magnificent size, to adorn their nocturnal heavens, and to reflect a mild radiance in the absence of the sun; in encompassing them with *atmospheres*, and diversifying their surface with *mountains and plains*. These and other arrangements, which indicate special contrivance and design, show that those bodies are destined by the Creator to be the abodes of intellectual beings, who partake of his bounty, and offer to him a tribute of adoration and praise.

Although no other objects were presented to our view, except those to which I now allude, and which are contained within the limits of our system; yet even here, within this small province of the kingdom of Jehovah, a grand and diversified scene is displayed for the future contemplation of heavenly intelligences. But it is a fact which cannot be disputed, that the sun and all his attendant planets form but a small speck in the map of the universe. How great soever this earth, with its vast continents and mighty oceans, may appear to our eye; how stupendous soever the great globe of Jupiter, which would contain within its bowels a thousand worlds as large as ours; and overwhelming as the conception is, that the sun is more than a thousand times larger than both; yet, were they this moment detached from their spheres, and blotted out of existence, there are worlds within the range of the Almighty's empire where such an awful catastrophe would be altogether unknown. Nay, were the whole cubical space occupied by the solar system, a space 3,600,000,000 miles in diameter, to be formed into a solid globe, containing 24,000,000,000,000,000,000,000,000 cubical miles, and overspread with a brilliancy superior to that of the sun, to continue during the space of a thousand years in this splendid state, and then to be extinguished and **annihilated; there** are beings, **who** reside in spaces within the range of **telescopes,** to whom **its** creation and destruction would be equally **unknown;** and to an eye which could take in the whole compass of nature, it might be altogether unheeded, or, at most, be regarded as the appearance **and** disappearance **of** a lucid point in an obscure corner **of** the universe; just as the detachment of a drop of water from **the** ocean, or a grain of sand from the sea-shore is unheeded by **a common** observer.

At immeasurable distances from our earth and system, immense assemblages of shining orbs display their radiance. The amazing extent of that space which intervenes between our habitation and these resplendent globes, proves their immense magnitude, and that they shine not with borrowed but with native splendour. From what we know of the wisdom and intelligence of the Divine Being, we may safely conclude, that he **has** created nothing in **vain; and,** consequently, that these enormous globes of light were not dispersed through the universe, merely as so many splendid tapers to illuminate the voids of infinite space. To admit, for a moment, such a sup**position, would** be inconsistent with the marks of intelligence **and design** which are displayed in all the other scenes of na**ture** which lie within the sphere of our investigation. It would represent the Almighty as amusing himself with splendid toys, an idea altogether incompatible with the adorable Majesty of Heaven, and which would tend to lessen our reverence of his character, as the only wise God. If every part of nature in **our** sublunary system is destined to some particular use in reference to sentient beings; if even the muddy waters of a stagnant pool are replenished with myriads of inhabitants; should we for a moment doubt that so many thousands of magnificent globes have a relation to the accommodation and happiness of intelligent beings: since in every part of the material system which lies open to our minute inspection, it appears, that matter exists solely for the purpose of sentient and intelligent creatures. As the Creator is consistent in all his plans and operations, it is beyond dispute, that those great globes which are suspended throughout the vast spaces of the universe are destined to some noble purposes, worthy of the infinite power, wisdom, and intelligence which produced them. And what may these purposes be? Since most of these bodies are of a size equal, if not superior, to our sun, and shine by their own native light, we are led by analogy to conclude, that they are destined to subserve a similar purpose in the system of nature; to pour a flood of radiance on surrounding worlds, and to regulate their motions by their attractive influence. So that each of these luminaries may be considered, not merely as a world, but as the centre of thirty, sixty, or a hundred worlds, among which they distribute light, and heat, and comfort.[1]

If, now, we attend to the *vast number* of those stupendous globes, we shall perceive what an extensive field of sublime investigation lies open to all the holy intelligences that exist in creation. When we lift our eyes to the nocturnal sky, we behold several hundreds of these majestic orbs, arranged in a kind of magnificent confusion, glimmering from afar on this obscure corner of the universe. But the number of stars, visible to the vulgar eye, is extremely small compared with the number which has been descried by means of optical instruments. In a small portion of the sky, not larger than the

---

[1] The Author has had the opportunity of illustrating this subject, in minute detail, in his Work entitled "THE SCENERY OF THE HEAVENS DISPLAYED, with the view of proving and illustrating the doctrine of a PLURALITY OF WORLDS;" in which the positions here assumed are shown to have the force of a moral demonstration, on the same general principles by which we prove the being of a God, and the immortality of man. In this Work, all the known facts in relation to *Descriptive Astronomy*, and the structure of the Heavens, are particularly detailed, and accompanied with original remarks and moral and religious reflections, forming a comprehensive Compend of Popular Astronomy.

apparent breadth of the moon, a greater number of stars has been discovered than the naked eye can discern throughout the whole vault of heaven. In proportion as the magnifying powers of the telescope are increased, in a similar proportion do the stars increase upon our view. They seem ranged behind one another in boundless perspective, as far as the assisted eye can reach, leaving us no room to doubt, that were the powers of our telescopes increased a thousand times more than they now are, millions beyond millions, in addition to what we now behold, would start up before the astonished sight. Sir William Herschel informs us, that, when viewing a certain portion of the *Milky Way*, in the course of seven minutes, more than fifty thousand stars passed across the field of his telescope; and it has been calculated, that within the range of such an instrument, applied to all the different portions of the firmament, more than *eighty millions* of stars would be rendered visible.

Here, then, within the limits of that circle which human vision has explored, the mind perceives, not merely eighty millions of worlds, but, at least *thirty* times that number; for every star, considered as a sun, may be conceived to be surrounded by at least thirty planetary globes;[1] so that the *visible system* of the universe may be stated, at the lowest computation, as comprehending within its vast circumference, 2,400,000,000 of worlds! This celestial scene presents an idea so august and overwhelming, that the mind is confounded, and shrinks back at the attempt of forming any definite conception of a multitude and a magnitude so far beyond the limits of its ordinary excursions. If we can form no adequate idea of the magnitude, the variety, and economy of *one* world, how can we form a just conception of *thousands*? If a *single million* of objects of any description present an image too vast and complex to be taken in at one grasp, how shall we ever attempt to comprehend an object so vast as two thousand four hundred millions of worlds! None but that Eternal Mind which counts the number of the

---

[1] The solar system consists of eleven primary and eighteen secondary planets; in all, twenty-nine, besides more than a hundred comets; and it is probable that several planetary bodies exist within the limits of our system which ha not yet been discovered. Other systems may probably contain a more numerous retinue of worlds, and perhaps of a larger size than those belonging to the system of the Sun.

stars, which called them from nothing into existence, and arranged them in the respective stations they occupy, and whose eyes run to and fro through the unlimited extent of creation, can form a clear and comprehensive conception of the number, the order, and the economy of this vast portion of the system of nature.

But here, even the very feebleness and obscurity of our conceptions tend to throw a radiance on the subject we are attempting to illustrate. The magnitude and incomprehensibility of the object, show us, how many diversified views of the Divine glory remain to be displayed; what an infinite variety of sublime scenes may be afforded for the mind to expatiate upon; and what rapturous trains of thought, ever various, and ever new, may succeed each other without interruption, through out an unlimited duration.

Let us now endeavour to analyze some of the objects presented to our mental sight, in this vast assemblage of systems and worlds which lie within the sphere of human vision.

The first idea that suggests itself, is, that they are all *material structures*, in the formation of which, infinite wisdom and goodness have been employed; and consequently, they must exhibit scenes of sublimity and of exquisite contrivance worthy of the contemplation of every rational being. If this earth, which is an abode of apostate men, and a scene of moral depravity, and which, here and there, has the appearance of being the ruins of a former world, presents the variegated prospect of lofty mountains, romantic dells, and fertile plains; meandering rivers, transparent lakes, and spacious oceans; verdant landscapes, adorned with fruits and flowers, and a rich variety of the finest colours, and a thousand other beauties and sublimities that are strewed over the face of nature; how grand and magnificent a scenery may we suppose, must be presented to the view, in those worlds where moral evil has never entered to derange the harmony of the Creator's works, where love to the Supreme, and to one another, fires the bosoms of all their inhabitants, and produces a rapturous exultation, and an incessant adoration of the Source of happiness! In such worlds, we may justly conceive, that the sensitive enjoyments, and the objects of beauty and grandeur which are displayed to their view, as far exceed the scenery and enjoyments of this world, as their moral and intellectual qualities excel those of the sons of men.

In the next place, it is highly reasonable to believe, that *an infinite diversity of scenery exists* throughout all the worlds which compose the universe; that no one of all the millions of systems to which I have now adverted, exactly resembles another in its construction, motions, **order,** and decorations. There appear, indeed, to be certain laws and phenomena which are common to all the systems which exist within the limits of human vision. It is highly probable, that the **laws of** gravitation extend their influence through every region of **space** occupied by material substances; and it is beyond a doubt, that the phenomena of vision, and the laws by which light is reflected and refracted, exist in the remotest regions which the telescope has explored. For the light which radiates from the most distant stars (as formerly stated) is found to be of the same nature, to move with **the** same velocity, to be refracted by the same laws, and to exhibit the same colours, as the light which proceeds from the sun, and is reflected from surrounding objects. The medium of vision must, therefore, be acted upon, and the organs of sight perform their functions, in those distant regions, in the same manner as takes place in the system of which we form a part, or, at least, in a manner somewhat analogous to it. And this circumstance shows, that the Creator evidently intended we should form some faint ideas, at least, of the general procedure of nature in distant worlds, in order to direct our conceptions of the sublime scenery of the universe, even while we remain in this obscure corner of creation. But, although the visible systems of the universe appear to be connected by certain general principles and **laws** which operate throughout the whole, yet the indefinite modifications which these laws may receive in each particular system, may produce an almost infinite diversity of phenomena in different worlds, so that no one department of the material universe may resemble another. Nor is it difficult to conceive how such a diversity of scenery may be produced. With regard to the terraqueous globe: were its axis to be shifted, so as to point to a different quarter of the heavens, or were the angle which it forms with the ecliptic to be greater or less than it now is, the general appearance of the firmament would be changed, the apparent motions of the sun and stars, the days and nights, the seasons of the year, and an immense variety of phenomena in the earth and heavens would assume a very different aspect from what they now wear. Were the component parts of the atmosphere materially altered, were its refractive power much increased, or were a greater portion of *caloric* or of *electricity* introduced into its constitution, the objects which diversify the landscape of the earth, and the luminaries of heaven, would assume such a variety of new and uncommon appearances, as would warrant the application of the Scripture expression, " a new heaven and a new earth." It is, therefore, easy to conceive, that when infinite power and wisdom are exerted for this purpose, every globe in the universe, with its appendages, may be constructed and arranged in such a manner as to present a variety of beauties and sublimities peculiar to itself.

That the Creator has actually produced this effect, is rendered in the highest degree probable, from the infinite variety presented to our view in those departments of nature which lie open to our particular investigation. In the *animal kingdom* we find more than a hundred thousand different species of living creatures, and about the same variety in the productions of *vegetable* nature; the *mineral* kingdom presents to us an immense variety of earths, stones, rocks, metals, fossils, gems, and precious stones, which are strewed in rich profusion along the surface, and throughout the interior parts of the globe. Of the individuals which compose every distinct species of animated beings, there is no one which bears an exact resemblance to another. Although the eight hundred millions of men that now people the globe, and all the other millions that have existed since the world began, were to be compared, no two individuals would be found to present exactly the same aspect in every point of view in which they might be contemplated. In like manner, no two horses, cows, dogs, lions, elephants, or other terrestrial animals, will be found bearing a perfect resemblance. The same observation will apply to the scenery of lakes, rivers, grottoes, and mountains, and to all the diversified landscapes which the surface of the earth and waters presents to the traveller and the student of nature.

If, from the earth we direct our views to the other bodies which compose our planetary system, we shall find a smaller diversity, so far as our observations extend. From the surface of one of the planets, the sun will appear seven times *larger*, and from the surface of another, three hundred and sixty times *smaller* than he does to us. One of these bodies is destitute of a moon; but from its ruddy aspect, either its surface or its atmosphere appears to be endowed with a phosphorescent quality, to supply it with light in the absence of the sun. Another is surrounded by *four* resplendent moons, much larger than ours; a third is supplied with *six*, and a fourth, with *seven* moons and two magnificent rings to reflect the light of the sun, and diversify the scenery of its sky. One of these globes revolves round its axis in *ten* and another in *twenty-three* hours and a half. One of them revolves round the sun in eighty-eight, another in two hundred and twenty-four days; a third in twelve years, a fourth in thirty, and a fifth in eighty-two years. From all which, and many other circumstances that have been observed, an admirable *variety* of phenomena is produced, of which each planetary globe has its own peculiarity. Even our moon, which is among the smallest of the celestial bodies which is nearest to us, and which accompanies the earth during its revolution round the sun, exhibits a curious variety of aspect, different from what is found on the terraqueous globe. The altitude of its mountains, the depth of its vales, the conical form of its insulated rocks, the circular ridges of hills which encompass its plains, and the celestial phenomena which are displayed in its firmament; present a scenery which, though in some points resembling our own, is yet remarkably different on the whole, from the general aspect of nature in our terrestrial habitation.

If, therefore, the Author of nature acts on the same general principles in other systems, as he has done in ours, (which there is every reason to believe, when we consider his infinite wisdom and intelligence,) we may rest assured, that every one of the two thousand four hundred millions of worlds which are comprehended within the range of human vision, has a magnificence and glory peculiar to itself, by which it is distinguished from all the surrounding provinces of Jehovah's empire. In this view, we may consider the language of the apostle Paul as expressing not only an *apparent* but a *real* fact, "There is one glory of the sun, and another glory of the moon, and another glory of the stars: *for one star differeth from another star in glory.*" To suppose that the Almighty has exhausted his omnipotent energies, and exhibited all the manifestations of his glory which his perfections can produce, in one system, or even in one million of systems, would be to set limits to the resources of his wisdom and intelligence, which are infinite and incomprehensible. Hence we find the sacred writers, when contemplating the numerous objects which creation exhibits, breaking out into such exclamations as these, "*How manifold*, O Jehovah, are thy works! In wisdom hast thou made them all."

In the next place: Besides the magnificence and variety of the material structures which exist throughout the universe, *the organized and intelligent beings with which they are peopled*, present a vast field of delightful contemplation. On this general topic, the following ideas may be taken into consideration:

1. The *gradations of intellect*, or the *various orders* of intelligences which may people the universal system. That there is a vast diversity in the scale of intellectual existence, may be proved by considerations similar to those I have already stated. Among sentient beings, in this world, we find a regular gradation of intellect, from the mussel, through all the orders of the aquatic and insect tribes, till we arrive at the dog, the monkey, the beaver, and the elephant, and last of all, to *man*, who stands at the top of the intellectual scale, as the lord of this lower world. We perceive, too, in the individuals which compose the human species, a wonderful diversity in their powers and capacities of intellect, arising partly from their original constitution of mind, partly from the conformation of their corporeal organs, and partly from the degree of cultivation they have received. But it would be highly unreasonable to admit, that the most accomplished genius that ever adorned our race, was placed at the summit of intellectual perfection.

On the other hand, we have reason to believe, that man, with all his noble powers, stands nearly at the bottom of the scale of the intelligent creation. For a being much inferior to man, in the powers of abstraction, conception, and reasoning, could scarcely be denominated a rational creature, or supposed capable of being qualified for the high destination to which man is appointed. As to the number of species which diversify the ranks of superior intellectual natures, and the degrees of perfection which distinguish their different orders, we have no *data* afforded by the contemplation of the visible universe, sufficient to enable us to form a definite conception. The intellectual faculties, even of finite beings, may be carried to so high a pitch of perfection, as to baffle all our conceptions and powers of description. The following description, in the words of a celebrated Swiss naturalist, may perhaps convey some faint idea of the powers of some of the highest order of intelligences.

"To convey oneself from one place to another with a swiftness equal or superior to that of light; to preserve oneself by the mere force of nature, and without the assistance of any other created being; to be absolutely exempted from every kind of change; to be endowed with the most exquisite and extensive senses; to have distinct perceptions of all the attributes of matter, and of all its modifications; to discover effects in their causes; to raise oneself by a most rapid flight to the most general principles; to see in the twinkling of an eye these principles; to have at the same time, without confusion, an almost infinite number of ideas; to see the past as distinctly as the present, and to penetrate into the remotest futurity; to be able to exercise all these faculties without weariness: these are the various outlines from which we may now draw a portrait of the perfections of superior natures."[1]

A being possessed of faculties such as these, is raised as far above the limited powers of man, as man is raised above the

---

[1] This writer, in addition to these, states the following properties: "To be invested with a power capable of displacing the heavenly bodies, or of changing the course of nature; and to be possessed of a power and skill capable of organizing matter, of forming a plant, an animal, a world." But I can scarcely think that such perfections are competent to any being but the Supreme.

insect tribes. The Scriptures assure us, that beings, approximating in their powers and perfections to those now stated, actually exist and perform important offices under the government of the Almighty. The perfections of the angelic tribes, as represented in Scripture, are incomparably superior to those of men. They are represented as possessed of powers capable of enabling them to wing their flight with amazing rapidity from world to world. For the angel Gabriel, being commanded to fly swiftly, while the prophet Daniel was engaged in supplication, approached to him, before he had made an end of presenting his requests. During the few minutes employed in uttering his prayer, this angelic messenger descended from the celestial regions to the country of Babylonia. This was a rapidity of motion surpassing the comprehension of the most vigorous imagination, and far exceeding even the amazing velocity of *light*. They have power over the objects of inanimate nature; for one of them "rolled away the stone from the door of the sepulchre," at the time of Christ's resurrection. They are intimately acquainted with the springs of life, and the avenues by which they may be interrupted; for an angel slew, in one night, 185,000 of the Assyrian army. They are perfectly acquainted with all the relations which subsist among mankind, and can distinguish the age and character of every individual throughout all the families of the earth. For one of these powerful beings recognised all the first-born in the land of Egypt, distinguished the Egyptians from the children of Israel, and exerted his powers in their destruction. And, as they are "ministering spirits to the heirs of salvation," they must have a clear perception of the persons and characters of those who are the objects of the Divine favour, and to whom they are occasionally sent on embassies of mercy. They are endowed with great physical powers and energies; hence they are said "*to excel in strength;*" and the phrases, "*strong* angel," and "a *mighty* angel," which are sometimes applied to them, are expressive of the same perfection. Hence they are represented, in the book of the Revelation, as "holding the four winds of heaven," as executing the judgments of God upon the proud despisers of his government, as "throwing mountains into the sea," and binding the prince of darkness with chains, and casting "him into the bottomless pit."

They are endowed with unfading and immortal youth, and experience no decay in the vigour of their powers. For the angels who appeared to Mary at the tomb of our Saviour, appeared as *young men*, though they were then more than four thousand years old. During the long succession of ages that had passed since their creation, their vigour and animation had suffered no diminution or decay. **They are** possessed of *vast powers of intelligence*. Hence they are exhibited in the book of Revelation, as being "*full of eyes*," that is, endowed with "all sense, all intellect, all consciousness; turning their attention every way; beholding at once all things within the reach of their understandings; and discerning them with the utmost clearness of conception." The various other qualities now stated, necessarily suppose a vast comprehension of intellect; and the place of their residence, and the offices in which they have been employed, have afforded full scope to their superior powers. They dwell in a world where *truth* reigns triumphant, where moral evil has never entered, where substantial knowledge irradiates the mind of every inhabitant, where the mysteries which envelop the character of the Eternal are continually disclosing, and where the plans of his providence are rapidly unfolded. They have ranged through the innumerable regions of the heavens, and visited distant worlds for thousands of years; they have beheld the unceasing variety, and the endless multitude of the works of creation and providence, and are, doubtless, enabled to compare systems of worlds, with more accuracy and comprehension than we are capable of surveying villages, cities, and provinces. Thus, their original powers and capacities have been expanded, and their vigour and activity strengthened; and consequently, in the progress of duration, their acquisitions of wisdom and knowledge must indefinitely surpass every thing that the mind of man can conceive. We have likewise certain intimations, that among these celestial beings there are *gradations of nature and of office;* since there are among them, "seraphim and cherubim, archangels, thrones, dominions, principalities, and powers," which designations are evidently expressive of their respective endowments, of the stations they occupy, and of the employments for which they are qualified.

Hence it appears, that although we know but little in the mean time of the nature of that diversity of intellect which prevails among the higher orders of created beings, the intimations given in the sacred volume, and the general analogy of nature, lead us to form the most exalted ideas of that amazing progression and variety which reign throughout the intellectual universe.

2. Not only is there a gradation of intellect among superior beings, but it is highly probable, that a similar gradation or variety obtains, in the form, the organization, and the movements of their corporeal vehicles.

The human form, especially in the vigour of youth, is the most beautiful and symmetrical of all the forms of organized beings with which we are acquainted; and in these respects, may probably bear some analogy to the organical structures of other intelligences. But, in other words, there may exist an indefinite variety, as to the general form of the body or vehicle with which their inhabitants are invested, the size, the number, and quality of their organs, the functions they perform, the splendour and beauty of their aspect, and particularly in the number and perfection of their senses. Though there are more than a hundred thousand species of sensitive beings which traverse the earth, the waters, and the air, yet they all exhibit a marked difference in their corporeal forms and organization. Quadrupeds exhibit a very different structure from fishes, and birds from reptiles; and every distinct species of quadrupeds, birds, fishes, and insects, differs from another in its conformations and functions. It is highly probable, that a similar variety exists, in regard to the corporeal vehicles of superior intelligences, accommodated to the regions in which they respectively reside, the functions they have to perform, and the employments in which they are engaged; and this we find to be actually the case, so far as our information extends. When any of the angelic tribes were sent on embassies to our world, we find that, though they generally appeared in a shape somewhat resembling a beautiful human form, yet in every instance there appeared a marked difference between them and human beings. The angel who appeared at the tomb of our Saviour, exhibited a bright and resplendent form: "His countenance was like the brightness of lightning, and his raiment as white as snow," glittering with an extraordinary lustre, beyond what mortal eyes could bear. The angel who delivered Peter from the prison, to which he had been confined by the tyranny of Herod, was arrayed in such splendour, that a glorious light shone through the whole apartment where the apostle was bound, dark and gloomy as it was. That these beings have organs of speech, capable of forming articulate sounds and of joining in musical strains, appears from the words they uttered on these and other occasions, and from the song they sung in the plains of Bethlehem, when they announced the birth of the Saviour. They appear to possess the property of rendering themselves *invisible* at pleasure: for the angel that appeared to Zacharias in the sanctuary of the temple, was invisible to the surrounding multitudes without, both at the time of his entrance into, and his exit from, the "holy place." To what is here stated respecting angels, it will doubtless be objected, "that these intelligences are *pure spirits*, and assume corporeal forms only on particular occasions." This is an opinion almost universally prevalent; but it is a mere assumption, destitute of any rational or Scriptural argument to substantiate its truth. There is no passage in Scripture, with which I am acquainted, that makes such an assertion. The passage in Psalm civ, 4, "Who maketh his angels spirits, and his ministers a flaming fire," has been frequently quoted for this purpose; but it has no reference to any opinion that may be formed on this point; as the passage should be rendered, "Who maketh the winds his messengers, and a flaming fire his ministers." Even although the passage were taken as it stands in our translation, and considered as referring to the angels, it would not prove, that they are pure immaterial substances; for, while they are designated *spirits*, which is equally applicable to *men*, as well as to angels, they are also said to be a "flaming fire," which is a *material* substance. This passage seems to have no particular reference to either opinion; but, if considered as expressing the attributes of angels, its meaning plainly is, that they are endowed with *wonderful activity;* that they move with the swiftness of the winds, and operate with the force and energy of flaming fire; or, in other words, that He, in whose service they are, and who directs their movements, employs them "with the strength of winds, and with the rapidity of lightnings."

In every instance in which angels have been sent on embassies to mankind, they have displayed *sensible* qualities. They exhibited a *definite form* somewhat analogous to that of man, and *colour and splendour,* which were perceptible by the organs of vision; they emitted *sounds* which struck the organ of hearing; they produced the harmonies of *music* and sung sublime sentiments which were uttered in articulate words; they were distinctly heard and recognised by the persons to whom they were sent, Luke ii, 14; and they exerted their power over the sense of *feeling;* for the angel who appeared to Peter in the prison, "*smote* him on the side, and *raised him up.*" In these instances, angels manifested themselves to men through the medium of three principal senses by which we recognise the properties of material objects; and why, then, should we consider them as purely immaterial substances, having no connection with the visible universe? We have no knowledge of angels but from revelation; and all the descriptions it gives of these beings lead us to conclude, that they are connected with the world of matter as well as with the world of mind, and are furnished with organical vehicles, composed of some refined material substance suitable to their nature and employments.

When Christ shall appear the second time, we are told that he is to come, not only in the glory of his Father, but also in "the glory of his holy angels," who will minister to him, and increase the splendour of his appearance. Now, the glory which the angels will display must be *visible,* and consequently, material; otherwise, it could not be contemplated by the assembled inhabitants of our world, and could present no glory or lustre to their view. An assemblage of purely spiritual beings, however numerous and however exalted in point of intelligence, would be a mere inanity, in a scene intended to exhibit a *visible* display of the divine supremacy and grandeur. The vehicles or bodies of angels are doubtless of a much finer mould than the bodies of men; but, although they were at all times invisible through such organs of vision as we possess, it would form no proof that they were destitute of such corporeal frames. The air we breathe is a *material* substance, yet it is *invisible;* and there are substances whose rarity is more than ten times greater than that of the air of our atmosphere. Hydrogen gas is more **than** twelve times lighter than common atmospheric air. If, therefore, an organized body were formed of a material substance similar to air, or to hydrogen gas, it would in general be invisible; but, in certain circumstances, might reflect the rays of light, and become visible, as certain of the lighter gaseous bodies are found to do. **This is,** in some measure, exemplified in the case of the *animalculæ*, **whose** bodies are imperceptible to the naked eye, and yet, are regularly organized material substances, endowed with all the functions requisite to life, motion, and enjoyment.

In particular, there is every reason to conclude, that there is a wonderful variety in the number and acuteness of their organs of sensation. **We** find a considerable variety, in these respects, among the sensitive beings which inhabit our globe. Some animals appear to have only *one* sense, as the *mussel*, **and** the *zoophytes;* many have but *two* senses; some have *three;* and man, the most perfect animal, has only *five*. These senses, too, in different species, differ very considerably in point of vigour and acuteness. The dog has a keener scent, the stag a quicker perception of sounds, and the eagle and the lynx more acute visual organs, than mankind. The same diversity is observable in the form, and the number of sensitive organs. In man, the ear is short and erect, and scarcely susceptible of motion; in the horse and the ass, it is long and flexible; and in the mole, it consists simply of a hole which perforates the skull. In man there are *two* eyes; in the scorpion and spider *eight;* and in a fly, more than *five thousand*.

That superior beings, connected with other worlds, have additional senses to those which we possess, is highly probable, especially when we consider the general analogy of nature, and the gradations which exist among organized beings in our world. It forms no reason why we should deny that such senses exist, because we can form no distinct conceptions of any senses besides those which we possess. If we had been deprived of the senses of *sight* and *hearing*, and left to derive all our information merely through the medium of feeling, tasting, and smelling, we could have had no more conception of articulate language, of musical harmony and melody, of the beauties of the earth, and of the glories of the sky, than a mussel, a vegetable, or a stone. To limit the number of senses which intelligent organized beings may possess, to the five which have been bestowed upon man, would be to set bounds to the infinite wisdom and skill of the Creator, who, in all his works, has displayed an endless variety in the manner of accomplishing his designs. While, in the terrestrial sphere in which we move, our views are limited to the *external* aspects of plants and animals, organized beings, in other spheres, may have the faculty of penetrating into their *internal* (and to us, invisible) movements; of tracing an animal from its embryo state, through all its gradations and evolutions, till it arrive at maturity; of perceiving, at a glance, and, as it were, through a transparent medium, the interior structure of an animal, the complicated movements of its curious machinery, the minute and diversified ramifications of its vessels, and the mode in which its several functions are performed; of discerning the fine and delicate machinery which enters into the construction, and produces the various motions of a microscopic animalculum, and the curious vessels, and the circulation of juices, which exist in the body of a plant; of tracing the secret processes which are going on in the mineral kingdom, and the operation of chemical affinities among the minute particles of matter, which produced the diversified phenomena of the universe. And, in fine, those senses which the inhabitants of other worlds enjoy in common with us, may be possessed by them in a state of greater acuteness and perfection. While our visual organs can perceive objects distinctly, only within the limits of a few yards or miles around us, *their* organs may be so modified and adjusted, as to enable them to perceive objects with the same distinctness, at the distance of a hundred miles, or even to descry the scenery of distant worlds. If our powers of vision had been confined within the range to which a worm or a mite is circumscribed, we could have formed no conception of the amplitude of our present range of view; and it **is by** no means improbable, that organized beings exist, whose extent of vision as far exceeds ours, as ours exceeds that of the smallest insect, and that they may be able to perceive the diversified landscapes which exist in other worlds, and the movements of their inhabitants, as distinctly as we perceive the objects on the opposite side of a river, or of a narrow **arm of** the sea.

After Stephen had delivered his **defence** before the Sanhedrim, **we are** told "he looked up steadfastly into heaven, and **saw the** glory of God, and Jesus standing at **the** right hand of God; and said, Behold, I see the heavens opened, and **the** Son **of** man standing on the right hand of God." **Some have** supposed that the eyes of Stephen, on this occasion, **were so** modified or strengthened, that he was enabled to penetrate **into that** particular region where the glorified body of Christ more immediately resides. But whether this opinion be tenable or not, certain it is, that angels are endowed with senses or faculties which enable them to take a minute survey of the solar system, **and of** the greater part of our globe, even when at a vast distance from our terrestrial **sphere**; otherwise, they could not distinguish the particular position of our earth in its annual course round the sun, in their descent from more distant regions, nor direct their course to that particular country, city, or village, whither they are sent on any special embassy.

What has been now said in reference to the organs of vision, is equally applicable to the organs of *hearing*, and to several of the other senses; and since faculties or senses, such as those I have now supposed, would tend to unvail more extensively the wonderful operations of the Almighty, **and** to excite incessant admiration of his wisdom and beneficence, it is reasonable to believe that he has bestowed them on various orders of his creatures for this purpose, and that man may be endowed with similar senses, when he arrives at moral perfection, and is placed in a higher sphere of existence.

Besides the topics to which I have now adverted, namely, the gradation of intellect, and the diversity of corporeal organization, **a** still more ample and interesting field of contemplation will be opened in the *history* of the numerous worlds dispersed throughout the universe; including the grand and delightful, or the awful and disastrous events which have taken place in the several regions of intellectual existence.

The particulars under this head which may be supposed to gratify the enlightened curiosity of holy intelligences, are such as the following: the different periods in duration at which the various habitable globes emerged from nothing into existence; the changes and previous arrangements through which they passed before they were replenished with inhabitants; the distinguishing characteristic features of every species of intellectual beings; their modes of existence, of improvement, and of social intercourse; the solemn forms of worship and adoration that prevail among them; the laws of social and of moral order peculiar to each province of the Divine Empire;[1] the progress they have made in knowledge, and the discoveries they have brought to light, respecting the works and the ways of God; the peculiar manifestations of himself which the Divine Being may have made to them, "at sundry times and in divers manners;" the most remarkable civil and moral events which have happened since the period of their creation; the visible emblems of the Divine Presence and glory which are displayed before them; the information they have obtained respecting the transactions and the moral government of other worlds; the

[1] There are certain general laws which are common to all the orders of intellectual beings throughout the universe. The two principles which form the basis of our *moral law* are of this nature: "Thou shalt love the Lord thy God with all thine heart, and with all thine understanding," and "thou shalt love thy neighbour as thyself." For we cannot suppose the Deity, in consistency with the sanctity and rectitude of his nature, *to reverse these laws*, in relation to any class of intelligences, or to exempt them from an obligation to obey them; and, therefore, they may be considered as the two grand moral principles which direct the affections and conduct of all holy beings throughout the immensity of God's empire, and which unite them to one another, and to their common Creator. But, in subordination to these principles or laws, there may be a variety of special moral laws, adapted to the peculiar economy, circumstances, and relations which exist in each distinct world. As we have certain special laws in the moral code, such as the *fifth* and *seventh* precepts of the Decalogue, which, in all probability, do not apply to the inhabitants of some other worlds, so they may have various specific regulations or laws, which cannot apply to us in our present state. The reader will find a particular illustration of the two fundamental laws to which I have now adverted, and of their application to the inhabitants of all worlds, in a work which I lately published, entitled, "*The Philosophy of Religion, or, an Illustration of the Moral Laws of the Universe.*"

various stages of improvement through which they are appointed to pass; the different regions of the universe to which they may be transported, and the final destination to which they are appointed.

In particular, the facts connected with their *moral history*, in so far as they may be unfolded, will form an interesting subject of discourse and of contemplation. It is highly probable, when we consider the general benignity of the Divine Nature, and the numerous evidences of it which appear throughout the whole kingdom of animated nature, that the inhabitants of the greatest portion of the universal system, have retained the moral rectitude in which they were created, and are, consequently, in a state of perfect happiness. But, since we know, from painful experience, that *one* world has swerved from its allegiance to the Creator, and been plunged into the depths of physical and moral evil, it is not at all improbable, that the inhabitants of several other worlds have been permitted to fall into a similar calamity: for this purpose among others, that the importance of moral order might be demonstrated, that the awful consequences of a violation of the eternal laws of Heaven might be clearly manifested, and that a field might be laid open for the display of the rectitude and mercy of God as the moral Governor of the universe. In reference to such cases (if any exist) the points of inquiry would naturally be, What is the ultimate destination of those beings who, in other regions of creation, have acted the part of rebellious man? Has their Creator interposed for their deliverance in a manner analagous to that in which he has accomplished the redemption of mankind? If so, wherein do such schemes of mercy differ, and wherein do they agree with the plan of salvation by Jesus Christ? What scenes of moral evil have been displayed, and how have the moral disorders in those worlds been overruled and counteracted by the providential dispensations of the Almighty? Here, a thousand questions would crowd upon the mind, a variety of emotions of opposite kinds would be excited, and a most interesting field of investigation would be laid open to the contemplation of the redeemed inhabitants of such a world as ours. And, it is easy to conceive with what kindred emotions and sympathetic feelings, and with what transporting gratulations, the renovated inhabitants of such worlds would recognise each other, should they ever be brought into contact, and permitted to mingle their ascriptions of praise to the Creator and Redeemer of worlds.

Even in those worlds where the inhabitants have retained their primeval innocence, there may be an almost infinite variety in the Divine dispensations, both in a moral and intellectual point of view. As finite intelligences, from their very nature, are *progressive* beings, and, therefore, cannot be supposed to acquire all the treasures of wisdom and knowledge, and to comprehend all the multifarious displays of Divine perfection, during the first stages of their existence; there may be an admirable diversity of modes, corresponding to their peculiar circumstances and stages of improvement, by which the Creator may gradually unfold to them the glory of his nature, and enable them to take a more extensive survey of the magnitude and order of his dominions. Some may be only emerging from the first principles of science, like Adam soon after his creation, and may have arrived but a few degrees beyond the sphere of knowledge which bounds the view of man; others may have arrived at a point where they can take a more expansive survey of the order, economy, and relations, of material and intellectual existences; while others, after having contemplated, for ages, a wide extent of creation, in *one* district of the empire of God, may be transported to a new and a distant province of the universe, to contemplate the perfections of Deity in another point of view, and to investigate and admire a new scene of wonders. If every individual of the human race, from his birth to his death, passes through a train of providences peculiar to himself, it appears at least highly probable, reasoning from the analogies to which we have already adverted, and from the variety that every where appears in the natural and moral world, that the Divine dispensations towards every distinct class of intelligent beings, have some striking peculiarities, which do not exactly coincide with those of any other.

That some portion, at least, of the natural and moral history of other worlds will be laid open to the inspection of redeemed men in the future world, may be argued from this consideration: that such views will tend *to unfold the moral character of the Deity*, and to display more fully his intelligence, wisdom, and rectitude, in the diversified modes of his administration, as the Governor of the universe. We have reason to believe that the material creation exists solely for the sake of sentient and intelligent beings; and that it has been arranged into distinct departments, and peopled with various ranks of intellectual natures, chiefly for the purpose of giving a display of the moral attributes of God, and of demonstrating the indispensable necessity and the eternal obligation of the moral laws he has enacted, in order to secure the happiness of the whole intelligent system. And, if so, we may reasonably conclude, that a certain portion of the Divine dispensations towards other classes of the intelligent creation will ultimately be displayed to our view. This position may likewise be argued from the fact, that other intelligences have been made acquainted with the affairs of our world, and the tenor of the dispensations of God towards our race. The angelic tribes have been frequently sent on embassages to our terrestrial sphere. On such occasions they have indicated an intimate acquaintance with the most interesting transactions which have taken place among us; and we are informed, that they still "desire to pry into" the scheme of redemption, and "to learn," from the Divine dispensations toward the Church "the manifold wisdom of God."[1] Some notices of the history, the employments, and the destination, of these celestial beings have likewise been conveyed to us. We know that they hold an elevated station in the kingdom of Providence; that they are possessed of great power and wisdom, of wonderful activity, of superior intellectual faculties, and of consummate holiness and rectitude of nature; that they are employed on certain occasions as ambassadors from God to man, in executing his judgments upon the wicked, and ministering to the heirs of salvation; and that a certain number of them fell from the high station in which they were originally placed, and plunged themselves into a state of sin and perdition. We have therefore reason to believe, that it is one part of the plan of the government of God, to disclose the history of one species

---

[1] See Ephesians, iii, 10; 1 Peter, i, 12.

of intellectual beings to another, in such portions, and at such seasons, as may seem most proper to Infinite Wisdom, and best suited to the state and character, and the gradual improvement, of his intellectual offspring.

In conformity to what has now been advanced, we find the saints in heaven represented as uttering a song of praise to God, in consequence of the survey they have taken of his moral administration, and of the admiration it excited. "They sing the song of Moses, and the song of the Lamb, saying, *Just and true are thy ways, thou King of Saints.*" And, in proportion as the dispensations of Providence towards other worlds are unfolded, in the same proportion will their views of Jehovah's "eternal righteousness" be expanded, and a new note of admiration and rapture added to their song of praise. The knowledge of the saints in heaven is represented as being very accurate and comprehensive. Hence it is declared, that, in that state of perfection, "they shall know, even as also they are known." This expression certainly denotes a very high degree of knowledge respecting the works and the ways of God; and, therefore, most commentators explain it as consisting in such an intuitive and comprehensive knowledge "as shall bear some fair resemblance to that of the Divine Being, which penetrates to the very centre of every object, and sees through the soul, and all things, as at one single glance:" or, at least, that "their knowledge of heavenly objects shall be as certain, immediate, and familiar, as any of their immediate friends and acquaintances now have of them."[1] And, if such interpretations be admitted, this knowledge must include a minute and comprehensive view of the dispensations of the Creator towards other worlds, and other orders of moral and intelligent agents.

In regard to the *manner* in which information respecting the structure, the inhabitants, and the history of other worlds may be communicated, our limited knowledge affords no certain *data* on which to ground a definite opinion. We may, however, reasonably suppose, that an intercourse and correspondence will be occasionally opened up, by means of celestial

---

See Doddridge's and Guyse's paraphrase on 1 Cor. xiii, 12.

beings endowed with faculties of rapid motion, who may communicate particular details of the intelligence they acquire in the regions they are accustomed to visit. Such correspondence has already partially taken place in our world, by means of those beings termed, in Scripture, "the angels," or "the *messengers* of Jehovah;" and, it is highly probable, had man continued in his state of original integrity, that such angelic embassies would have been much more frequent than they have ever been, and we might have been made acquainted, in this way, with some outlines of the physical and moral scenery of other worlds, particularly of those which belong to our own system; of which we must now be contented to remain in ignorance, and must have recourse to the aids of reason, and science, and observation, in order to trace some very general outlines of their physical economy. This is, doubtless, one deplorable effect, among others, of the apostacy of man, that intelligences endowed with moral perfection can no longer hold familiar intercourse with the race of Adam, but in so far as they are employed by their Creator in communicating occasional messages, which have a respect merely to their moral renovation.[1] We may, likewise, with some degree of probability, suppose, that every distinct order of holy intelligences, after having resided for a certain number of ages in one region of the universe, may be conveyed to another province of creation, to investigate the new scenes of wisdom and omnipotence there unfolded; and so on, in a continued series of transportations, throughout the ages of eternity. We know that man is destined to undergo such a change of locality; and although sin has made the passage from one world to another assume a gloomy and alarming aspect, it may nevertheless be an example, (though in a different manner) of those removals which take place with respect to other beings, from one province of creation to another. Nor have we any reason to believe, that the locality in which we shall be placed, after the general

---

[1] It is probable that the celestial beings who have occasionally held a communication with our race, are not all of the same species, or inhabit the same regions; since they are distinguished in Scripture by different names, as Seraphim, Cherubim, Thrones, Dominions, Angels, Archangels, etc.

resurrection, will form our permanent and everlasting abode; otherwise, we should be eternally chained down, as we are at present, to a small corner of creation.

In regard to the redeemed inhabitants of our world, there is every reason to believe that the *Redeemer* himself, he, "in whom dwell all the treasures of wisdom and knowledge," will be one grand medium through which information will be communicated respecting the distant glories of Jehovah's empire. This seems to be directly intimated, though in metaphorical language, in the following passage from the book of Revelation: "The Lamb who is in the midst of the throne shall feed them, and shall lead them to fountains of living water." Knowledge is the food of the mind; and in this sense the term is frequently applied in the Scriptures: "I will give them pastors (saith God) after mine own heart, who shall *feed them* with *knowledge* and *understanding*." "Feed the Church of God," says the apostle Peter, that is, instruct them in the knowledge of the truths of religion. Therefore, by imparting to his saints a knowledge of the plans and operations of God, and information respecting the magnificence of his works, in the regions around, "the Lamb in the midst of the throne *will feed them*," by gratifying their intellectual powers, and their desires after knowledge; and the noble and transporting trains of thought which such discoveries will inspire, (and which may be aptly compared to the effect produced by "fountains of living water" on a parched traveller,) will arrest all the faculties of their souls, and fill them "with joy unspeakable and full of glory."

Perhaps, it may not be beyond the bounds of probability to suppose, that, at certain seasons, during a grand convocation of the redeemed, with Jesus their exalted Head president among them, that glorious personage may impart knowledge to them of the most exalted kind, direct their views to some bright manifestations of Deity, and deliver most interesting lectures on the works and ways of God. This would be quite accordant with his office as the "Mediator between God and man," and to his character as the "Messenger of Jehovah," and the "Revealer" of the Divine dispensations.

Pointing to some distant world (which, even to the acute

visual organs of heavenly beings, may appear only as a small lucid speck in their sky,) we may suppose him giving such a descant as the following: "That world presents a very different aspect from what yours once did, owing chiefly to the moral purity and perfection of its inhabitants. *There*, the most grand and variegated objects adorn their celestial canopy; and the scenes around their habitations are intermingled with every thing that is beautiful to the eye, and gratifying to the senses and the imagination. Neither scorching heats, nor piercing colds, nor raging storms, ever disturb the tranquillity of those happy mansions. The fine ethereal fluid which they breathe produces a perpetual flow of pleasing emotions, and sharpens and invigorates their intellectual powers for every investigation. The peculiar refractive and reflective powers possessed by the atmospheric fluid which surrounds them, produce a variety of grand and beautiful effects, sometimes exhibiting aerial landscapes, and scenes emblematical of moral harmony and perfection; sometimes a magnificent display of the richest and most variegated colouring, and sometimes reflecting the images of the celestial orbs in various aspects and degrees of magnitude. Their vegetable kingdom is enriched with a variety of productions unknown in your former world, diversified with thousands of different forms, shades, colours, and perfumes, which shed a delicious fragrance all around. The inferior sentient beings are likewise different, and exhibit such ingenious, mild, and affectionate dispositions, as contribute in no inconsiderable degree, to the pleasure and entertainment of the more intelligent order of the inhabitants. The organs of vision of these intelligences are so acute, that they are enabled to perceive, as through a transparent medium, the various chemical and mechanical processes that are incessantly going on in the numberless ramifications of the vegetable tribes, and in the more curious and complicated structure of animal bodies; for the Creator has ordained, as one part of their mental enjoyments, that they shall be furnished with the means of tracing the mode of his operations, and the designs they are intended to accomplish in the different departments of nature.

"They are likewise extensively acquainted with moral science, with the moral relations of intelligent beings to their

Creator, and to one another, and with the outlines of the history of several other worlds; for the leading facts in the history of your world, respecting the fall of man, its dismal consequences, and your subsequent redemption and renovation, have been communicated to them, for the purpose of enlarging their views of God's moral dispensations, and illustrating the rectitude and benevolence of his government. In their intercourses and associations, no discordant voice is ever heard, no symptom of disaffection ever appears, no boisterous passions ever disturb their tranquillity; but all is harmony and order, peace and love. Their progress in the knowledge of God, and of his works, is rapid and sure, for they see clearly the first principles of all reasoning and science; and, without once making a false step, or deducing an erroneous conclusion, they trace them with rapidity and certainty, to all their legitimate consequences. Their acquaintance with natural and moral facts is extensive and minute. For the most sacred regard is attached to truth, which was never once violated in that happy society; and, therefore, every discovery, every new doctrine and fact, which is brought to light by any individual, is regarded by all other* as an established truth, which is never called in question, and which serves to direct and facilitate all their other researches. Unlike the exaggerations and falsehoods which were once propagated by lying travellers and sceptical philosophers, in your former world, which tended to bewilder the anxious inquirer, and to obscure the radiance of truth; in yonder world truth is regarded as a most sacred and invaluable treasure, as the basis of the happiness of the moral universe, and the foundation on which rests the throne of the Eternal; and, therefore, being never violated by any individual, every testimony and assertion is received with unhesitating confidence. By a rapid mode of communication which has been established, their intercourses with each other are frequent and delightful, and the discoveries which are made of the operations of infinite wisdom and benevolence, are quickly circulated through all the intelligent ranks of that abode of felicity and love. Beings from other worlds occasionally visit them, and convey interesting intelligence, and affectionate congratulations from the regions whence they came; and a glorious symbol of the Divine Majesty was lately displayed in their firmament, from which was announced, in majestic but mild and transporting language, the approbation of their Creator, and his purpose of translating them, as a reward of their obedience, to another region of his empire, to behold new displays of his beneficence and power.

"This is a specimen of the moral order and happiness which prevail among the greater part of those worlds which shine from afar in yonder firmament, but which are distinguished by a variety of peculiar circumstances, which shall be unfolded on another occasion."

Directing their view to another distant orb, which appears like a dim ruddy speck in an obscure quarter of the firmament, he may thus proceed: "That too is a world, on a different scale, and in a different condition. It is a thousand times larger than the globe you once inhabited, and was originally arrayed with all that magnificence and beauty which characterise the works of the Creator. During a considerable period its inhabitants retained their allegiance to their Maker, and their affection for each other. But certain individuals, whom a principle of pride and ambition had led to desire stations of pre-eminence, having dared to violate some of the fundamental laws of their Creator; the moral turpitude which this disposition and conduct produced, gradually spread from one rank to another, till the whole mass of its inhabitants was completely contaminated, and plunged into a gulph of misery. To such a dreadful length has this depravity proceeded, that even the external aspect of that world, which was once as fair as Eden, has assumed the appearance of a gloomy waste, and a barren wilderness. The rivers have been turned out of their course, by these infatuated beings, that they might overflow and change into a marsh the once fertile plains. The earth has been dug into immense pits and chasms, and the vegetable tribes have been torn from their roots and stripped of their verdure, in order to deface the primeval beauty of creation. By these, and other horrible devastations, the ethereal fluid in which they breathed, which formerly diffused a delightful fragrance, has now become the receptacle of noisome exhalations, which nauseate and irritate every species of sensitive existence. Its brillancy has thereby become obscured, so that their sun appears louring through its dense vapours, like a dusky ball; and their nocturnal sky, which once presented a splendid assemblage of shining orbs, is now covered with blackness, and darkness, and tempest, through which no celestial orb ever transmits the least glimmering ray. For the almighty Contriver of all worlds has so arranged, proportioned, and adjusted, every circumstance in the constitution of nature, that the smallest derangement by malevolent beings, of the order he has established, is always productive of disastrous effects.

"Instead of being animated with love to their Creator, and to one another, which is the first duty of all intelligent creatures, they hate their Maker, and curse him on account of the existence he has given them: and they hate each other, with a perfect hatred. There exists among them no peace, justice, sympathy, friendship, or confidence. Every one beholds and recognises another with the countenance of a fiend, and is ever intent upon annoying him to the utmost of his power. And, were it not that their bodies are constructed on an *immortal* principle, so that no power less than infinite can completely destroy them, their ferocious passions would, long ere now, have effected the utter extermination of every individual in that populous but miserable world. Their bodies, which were once fair and glorious, are now covered with every mark of vileness and deformity. They have no delight in contemplating the glories of their Creator's workmanship, for they have defaced every beauty which creation displayed, when it came fresh and fair from the hand of its Maker; and the intelligence and wisdom they formerly possessed, are now obliterated, and changed into ignorance and folly.

"At the commencement of this affecting scene of depravity, a messenger was despatched by their Almighty Sovereign, to warn them of their danger, and to urge them to reformation; but, as they had not then felt the full effects of that wretchedness into which they were plunging, after a few temporary pangs of remorse, 'they returned every one to his evil ways.' Holy intelligences, from other worlds, have occasionally been sent to contemplate the gloomy aspect, and the sad desolations of this wretched world; in order that they might bring back intelligence to the worlds with which they are more immediately connected, of the dismal effects produced by the violation of those eternal laws of rectitude which the Governor of the universe has ordained. The Creator has, for many ages, permitted those physical and moral disorders to exist; not because he delights in the misery of any of his creatures, but because he has a regard to the ultimate happiness of the whole intelligent system. He leaves them in the mean time, 'to eat of the fruit of their own ways,' that they may feel the full effects of their apostacy and wickedness. He has permitted them to proceed thus far in their rebellion and depravity, in order that surrounding worlds may be fully apprised of the dismal effects that must inevitably ensue on every infringement of moral order. This desolated world and its wretched inhabitants are doomed to remain in their present deplorable state, for ages yet to come, till an extensive and indelible impression be made on the inhabitants of every province of God's empire, of their eternal obligation to conform to those laws and principles of moral order, which his infinite wisdom has established for the regulation of the intelligent universe; and also, that those miserable beings themselves may be aroused to consideration, led to humble themselves in his presence, and made to feel some emotions of contrition for their impiety and ingratitude. When these ends are accomplished, a bright effulgence shall suddenly illume the darkness of their night, their atmosphere shall be cleared of its vapours, and the glorious orbs of heaven shall once more burst upon their view; the astonished inhabitants shall lift up their eyes with amazement at the wondrous and unlooked-for spectacle, and a divine messenger, arrayed in splendid majesty, shall proclaim, 'Peace from heaven, Good will from Jehovah to this guilty world.' In both hemispheres of this globe, shall the joyful message be proclaimed. This sudden and unexpected announcement will arrest the attention of every inhabitant, and rekindle in his breast those sparks of gratitude, which had been so long extinguished. To prove the sincerity of this annunciation, the 'Power of the Highest' will be interposed to purify the atmosphere, to restore the desolations which had been produced, and to renew the face of nature. A series of moral instructions will commence, and be carried on with vigour, till all be fully convinced of the folly and impiety of their conduct. Order will be gradually re-established; affectionate intercourses will commence; an indelible impression of their ingratitude and wickedness, and of the justice and benevolence of God, will be for ever fixed in their minds, which will secure them, at all future periods, from a similar apostacy; and peace, truth, and happiness, shall finally reign triumphant."

On such topics as these, may we suppose our Redeemer, in the character of Mediator, occasionally to expatiate, with irresistible eloquence, when presiding in the assemblies of his redeemed; and the emotions produced by such communications, will doubtless excite them to join in unison in celebrating the Divine character and administration, in such strains as these: "Halleluia! the Lord God omnipotent reigneth. True and righteous are his judgments. Salvation, and glory, and honour, and power, unto the Lord our God. Thou art worthy to receive glory, honour, and power; for thou hast created all things, and for thy pleasure they are and were created." [1]

Thus I have endeavoured to show, that even that portion of the universe which lies within the reach of our assisted vision, comprehends within its capacious sphere, at least two thousand

---

[1] I hope none of my readers will consider the supposition of the Redeemer occasionally delivering lectures on Divine subjects to an assembly of his saints, as either improbable, extravagant, or romantic. Since writing the above, I find, that the pious and philosophic *Dr. I. Watts* entertained a similar opinion. In his sermon, "On the happiness of separate spirits," when describing the employments of the upper world he thus expresses his sentiments on this topic: "Perhaps you will suppose there is no such service as hearing sermons, that there is no attendance upon the word of God, there. But are we sure there are no such entertainments? Are there no lectures of Divine wisdom and grace given to the younger spirits there, by spirits of a more exalted station? Or, may not our Lord Jesus Christ himself be the everlasting Teacher of his Church? May he not at solemn seasons summon all heaven to hear him publish some new and surprising discoveries which have never yet been made known to the ages of nature or of grace, and are reserved to entertain the attention, and to exalt the pleasure, of spirits advanced to glory? Must we learn all by the mere contemplation of Christ's person? Does he never make use of speech to the instruction and joy of saints above? Or, it may be, that our blessed Lord (even as he is man) has some noble and unknown way communicating a long discourse, or a long train of ideas and discoveries, to millions of blessed spirits at once, without the formalities of voice and language, and at some peculiar seasons he may thus instruct and delight his saints in heaven."

four hundred millions of worlds; that each of these worlds, being constructed by infinite wisdom, must exhibit, even in its external aspect, a scene worthy of the contemplation of every rational being; that it is highly probable, from ascertained facts, from analogy, and from revelation, that each of these worlds has a peculiarity of scenery, and of appendages, which distinguish it from every other; that there is a gradation of intellect, and beings of different orders, among the inhabitants of these worlds; that it is probable their corporeal forms and their organs of sensation are likewise wonderfully diversified; and that the natural and moral history of each present scenes and transactions different from those which are found in any other world. So that, when the mind endeavours to grasp the immense number of worlds here presented to our mental view, and considers the variety of aspect in which each of them requires to be contemplated, there appears, to such limited intellects as ours, no prospect of a termination to the survey of a scene so extensive and overwhelming; but, on the contrary, a rational presumption, that one scene of glory will be followed by another, in perpetual succession, while ages roll away.

If it would require, even to beings endowed with mental powers superior to those of man, several hundreds of years, to survey the diversified landscapes which our globe displays, to investigate the numerous chemical processes going on in the animal, the vegetable, and the mineral kingdoms throughout the surface of the earth, the recesses of the ocean and the subterraneous regions, and to trace the history of every tribe of its inhabitants during a period of six thousand years; if it would require thousands of years to explore the planetary system, which presents a field of inquiry two thousand times more extensive; how many hundreds of thousands of millions of years would be requisite to study and investigate the visible universe in all that variety of aspect to which I have now adverted! To explore the diversified structure and arrangements of the bodies which compose the solar system, and the moral events which have taken place among its inhabitants would require a long series of ages. The system of bodies connected with the planet Saturn, would, of itself, require several hundreds of years of study and research, in order to acquire a *general* view of its physical, moral, and intellectual aspects and relations. Here, we have presented to view: 1. A globe of vast dimensions, capable of containing a population of sentient and intelligent beings more than a hundred times greater than that of the earth. 2. Two immense rings, the one of them containing, on both its sides, an area of *eight thousand millions* of square miles, and the other an area of *twenty thousand millions* of miles, and sufficient to contain a population, *one hundred and forty times* larger than that of our globe, although they were as thinly peopled as the earth is at present. 3. Seven satellites, or moons, each of which is undoubtedly as large as the globe on which we live, and some of them, probably, of much greater dimensions. The magnificent and astonishing scenery displayed in this planet, so very different from any thing that is beheld in our terrestrial sphere; the stupendous luminous arches which stretch across its firmament, like pillars of cloud by day and pillars of fire by night; the diversified shadows they occasionally cast on the surrounding landscape; the appearance and disappearance of its moons, their eclipses, and diversified aspects in respect to each other, and to the inhabitants of the planet itself; the novel scenes which would appear in the animal, vegetable, and mineral kingdoms; the customs, manners, and employments of the inhabitants; the series of events which have happened among them, and the tenor of the Divine dispensations in relation to their past history and their future destination: these, and a thousand other particulars, of which we can form no distinct conception, could not fail to afford a sublime and delightful gratification to a rational intelligence for a series of ages.

It is probable, too, that even within the boundaries of the solar system, important physical and moral revolutions have happened since its creation, besides those which have agitated the world in which we dwell. On the surface of the planet Jupiter, changes are occasionally taking place, visible at the remote distance at which we are placed. The diversity of appearance which has been observed in the substances termed its *belts*, in whatever they may consist, or from whatever cause this diversity may originate, indicates changes as great, as if the whole mass of clouds which overhang **Europe**, and the northern parts of Asia and America, were to be completely swept away, and suspended in dense strata over the Pacific and the Indian oceans; **or, as** if the waters of the Atlantic ocean were to overflow the continent of America, and leave its deepest caverns exposed to view. **There were** lately discovered, between the orbits of Mars and **Jupiter, four** small planetary bodies; and, on grounds which are highly probable, astronomers have concluded, that they once formed a larger body, which moved in the same region, and which had burst asunder by some immense eruptive force proceeding from its central parts. This probable circumstance, together with a variety of singular phenomena exhibited by these planets, naturally lead us to conclude, that some important moral revolutions had taken place, in relation to the beings with which it was peopled; and suggest to the mind a variety of sublime and interesting reflections respecting scenes either of joy or of terror, which may hereafter be disclosed. The planet Mars, in several respects, bears a striking resemblance to our earth. Its rotation round its axis is accomplished in nearly the same time as the earth, namely, in 24 hours and 40 minutes. The inclination of its axis to the plane of its orbit is 28 degrees 42 minutes, that of the earth being 23 degrees 28 minutes. Consequently, it experiences a diversity of seasons and different lengths of days and nights, as we do in our sublunary sphere. Hence Sir William Herschel informs us, that he observed a luminous zone about the poles of this planet, which is subject to periodical changes, and is of opinion that this phenomenon is produced by the reflection of the sun's light upon its polar regions, and that the variation in the magnitude and appearance of this zone is owing to the melting of these masses of polar ice. Its atmosphere is likewise found to be very dense and obscure; which is the cause of that *ruddy* appearance which this orb uniformly exhibits. These circumstances indicate a striking similarity, in its *physical* constitution, to that of the earth. Whether the *moral* state of its inhabitants bears any resemblance to the present condition of mankind, is a question which naturally suggests itself, and which may possibly be solved in the future state to which we are destined. **Frost and** snow, the accumulation and melting of vast masses of polar ice, long nights, and wintry storms, scenes of darkness and desolation, stormy clouds, and a dense hazy atmosphere surcharged with wintry exhalations, do not appear to be the characteristics of a world where perfect happiness is enjoyed. The Sun which is the centre of our system, and which enlightens surrounding worlds with his beams, is five hundred times larger than all the planets and moons taken together. And, since we perceive frequent changes taking place in his surface and luminous atmosphere, there is doubtless a variety of astonishing processes and transformations going on, both in the exterior and interior parts of th's immense luminary, on a scale of magnitude and grandeur, which it would be highly gratifying to behold and investigate, and which would raise to the highest pitch, our conceptions of the magnificence and glory of Him "who dwells in light unapproachable."

If, then, the planetary system, which occupies no larger a portion of space than one of the smallest stars that twinkle in our sky, would afford such a vast multiplicity of objects for the contemplation of intelligent beings, during a lapse of ages; what an immense assemblage of august objects and astonishing events is presented before us in the physical arrangements, and the moral history, of the myriads of systems and worlds to which I have alluded, and what an immense duration would be requisite for finite minds to survey the wondrous scene! This consideration suggests an idea of duration, which, to limited intellects such as ours, seems to approximate to the idea of eternity itself. Even although it could be shown, that creation extended no farther than the utmost bounds which the ingenuity of man has enabled him to penetrate; still the vast assemblage of glorious objects contained within the range of our assisted vision, shows what an infinite variety of mental gratification the Creator may bestow on his intelligent offspring; and we are assured, that "no good thing will he withhold from them that walk uprightly."

But, would it be reasonable to admit, that the dominions of the universal Sovereign terminate at the boundaries of human vision? Can we believe, that puny man, who occupies so diminutive a speck among the works of God has penetrated to the utmost limits of the empire of Him who fills the immensity of space with his presence? As soon might we suppose, that a snail could penetrate to the utmost extremity of the ocean, and with one glance, survey its deepest caverns; or, that a microscopic animalcule, which is confined to a drop of water, in the crevice of a small stone, could explore, at one comprehensive view, the regions of Europe, Asia, Africa, and America. Shall we consider the *visible* system of nature, magnificent and extensive as it is, a palace sufficient for the habitation of the Deity? No: this would be, to circumscribe the Almighty within the limits of our imperfect vision, and within the sphere of our comprehension. "Behold, the heavens, and the heaven of heavens, cannot contain Him!" This declaration implies, that, beyond all that the inhabitants of this world can explore in the visible firmament, there is a "*heaven of heavens;*" a region which contains unnumbered firmaments, as glorious and extensive as that which we behold; throughout the vast extent of which, the Deity is eternally and essentially present. With regard to all that is visible by the unassisted eye, or by the telescope, in the vault of heaven, we may say with the poet:

"Vast concave! ample dome! wast thou design'd
A meet apartment for the Deity?
Not so: that thought alone thy state impairs,
Thy *lofty* sinks, and shallows thy *profound*,
And straitens thy diffusive; dwarfs the whole,
And makes a universe an *orrery.*"

Beyond the wide circumference of that sphere which terminates the view of mortals, a boundless region exists, which no human eye can penetrate, and which no finite intelligence can explore. To suppose that the infinitely extended region which surrounds all that is visible in creation, is a mere void, would be as unreasonable, as to have affirmed, prior to the invention of the telescope, that no stars existed beyond those which are visible to the naked eye. When we consider the limited faculties of man, and the infinite attributes of the Eternal Mind, we have the highest reason to conclude, that it is but a very small portion of the works of God which has been disclosed to our view. "Could you soar beyond the moon," says a well known writer, "and pass through all the planetary choir; could you wing your way to the highest apparent star, and take your stand on one of those loftiest pinnacles of heaven, you would there see other skies expanded, another sun distributing his beams by day, other stars that gild the alternate night, and other, perhaps nobler, systems established in unknown profusion through the boundless dimensions of space. Nor would the dominion of the universal Sovereign terminate *there*. Even at the end of this vast tour, you would find yourself advanced no farther than the suburbs of creation; arrived only at the frontiers of the great Jehovah's kingdom."

It is highly probable, that, were all the two thousand four hundred millions of worlds to which we have adverted, with all the eighty millions of suns around which they revolve, to be suddenly extinguished and annihilated, it would not cause so great a blank in creation, to an eye that could take in the whole immensity of nature, as the extinction of the *pleiades*, or seven stars, would cause in our visible firmament. The range of material existence may, indeed, have certain limits assigned to it; but such limits can be perceived only by that *Eye* which beholds, at one glance, the whole of infinite space. To the view of every *finite* mind, it must always appear boundless and incomprehensible. Were it possible that we could ever arrive at the outskirts of creation, after having surveyed all that exists in the material universe, we might be said, in some measure, to comprehend the Creator himself; having perceived the utmost limits to which his power and intelligence have been extended. For, although we admit, that the perfections of the Creator are *infinite*; yet we have no tangible measure of these perfections, but what appears in the immense variety and extent of material and intellectual existence. And we may hence conclude, that the highest order of created intellects, after spending myriads of ages in their research, will never come to a period in their investigations of the works and the ways of God.

Even although we could conceive certain limits to the material universe, and that, after the lapse of millions of ages, a holy intelligence had finished his excursions, and made the tour of the universal system which now exists; yet, who can set bounds to the active energies of the eternal Mind, or say, that new systems of creation, different from all that have hitherto been constructed, shall not be perpetually emerging into existence? By the time a finite being had explored every object which now exists, and acquired a knowledge of all the moral and physical revolutions which have happened among the worlds which, at present, diversify the voids of space, a new region of infinite space might be replenished with new orders of material and intellectual existence: and, were he to return to the point from which he at first set out, after numerous ages had elapsed, he would, doubtless, behold new changes and revolutions in many provinces of the Creator's dominions, new heavens and new earths, and new species of sentient and intellectual beings, different from all those he at first contemplated.

That such is the plan of the Creator's operations, is not a mere conjecture or surmise, but is warranted from observations which have been made on the phenomena of the celestial bodies. New stars have, at different periods, appeared in the heavens; which are plain indications of the continued exertion of creating power. Some planets have burst asunder into different fragments, and stars which had shone for ages have disappeared, and their existence, in their former state, cannot now be traced.[1] Such facts evidently show, that some important revolutions have taken place in relation to the bodies which have thus been withdrawn from our view. Having for ages run their destined course, either their constitution has undergone an essential change, or they have been removed to another region of immensity, to subserve other purposes in the magnificent arrangements of the Sovereign Intelligence. The observations made by Sir William Herschel on the *nebulous* appearances in the heavens, and on the changes and modifications which they undergo, lead to the conclusion, that new systems are gradually forming in the distant regions of the universe. And,

---

[1] Stars which are marked in ancient catalogues are not now to be found, and others are now visible which were not known to the ancients. Some have gradually increased in brilliancy. Some that were formerly *variable*, now shine with a steady lustre, while others have been constantly diminishing in brightness.

if the creating energy of the Omnipotent is at present in constant operation, and has been so for ages past, who shall dare to affirm, that it shall ever cease its exertion through all the ages of eternity?

Here, then, we have presented to our contemplation, an assemblage of material and intellectual existence, to which the human mind can affix no boundaries; which is continually increasing, and still an infinity of space remaining for perpetual accessions, during the lapse of endless ages; an assemblage of beings, which, in point of number, of magnitude, and of extent, seems to correspond with a boundless duration. So that, we have no reason to doubt that "the saints in light" will be perpetually acquiring new discoveries of the Divine glory, new prospects into the immensity of God's operations, new views of the rectitude and grandeur of his moral government, new accessions to their felicity, and new and transporting trains of thought, without the least interruption, as long as eternity endures.

THRONE OF GOD.

There is just one idea more that may be suggested, in addition to the several views exhibited above, in order to raise to a higher pitch of sublimity our views of the grandeur of the Divine Being, and of the magnificence of his works.

The Scriptures frequently refer to a particular place, circumstance, or manifestation, termed *the throne of God;* as in the following passages: "Heaven is my *throne*, and the earth is my footstool." "The Lord hath prepared *his throne in the heavens*." "A *glorious high throne*, from the beginning, is the place of thy sanctuary." "Therefore are they before the throne of God, and serve him day and night in his temple." "Blessing and honour, and glory, and power, be unto Him that sits upon the throne." These, and similar expressions and representations, must be considered either as merely metaphorical, or as referring to some particular region of the universe, where the Divine glory is reflected, in some peculiarly magnificent manner, from material objects, and where the manifestations of the Divine character are most illustriously displayed. If there be a reference to the splendour and magnitude of a particular portion of creation, there is an astronomical idea, which may help us to form some conception of this "glorious high throne," which is the peculiar residence of the Eternal. It is now considered by astronomers as highly probable, if not certain, from late observations, from the nature of gravitation, and other circumstances, that all the systems of the universe revolve round one common centre; and that this centre may bear as great a proportion, in point of magnitude, to the universal assemblage of systems, as the sun does to his surrounding planets. And, since our sun is five hundred times larger than the earth, and all the other planets and their satellites taken together; on the same scale, such a central body would be five hundred times larger than all the systems and worlds in the universe. Here, then, may be a vast universe of itself; an example of material creation, exceeding all the rest in magnitude and splendour, and in which are blended the glories of every other system. If this is in reality the case, it may, with the most emphatic propriety, be termed *the throne of God.*

This is the most sublime and magnificent idea that can possibly enter into the mind of man. We feel oppressed and overwhelmed in endeavouring to form even a faint representation of it. But however much it may overpower our feeble conceptions, we ought not to revolt at the idea of so glorious an extension of the works of God; since nothing less magnificent seems suitable to a Being of infinite perfections. This grand central body may be considered as the *Capital* of the universe. From this glorious centre, embassies may be occasionally despatched to all surrounding worlds, in every region of space. Here, too, deputations from all the different provinces of creation, may occasionally assemble, and the inhabitants of different worlds mingle with each other, and learn the grand outlines of those physical operations and moral transactions, which have taken place in their respective spheres. Here, may be exhibited to the view of unnumbered multitudes, objects of sublimity and glory, which are no where else to be found within the wide extent of creation. Here, intelligences of the highest order, who have attained the most sublime heights of knowledge and virtue, may form the principal part of the population of this magnificent region. Here, the glorified body of the Redeemer may have taken its principal station, as " the head of all principalities and powers:" and here, likewise, Enoch and Elijah may reside, in the mean time, in order to learn the history of the magnificent plans and operations of Deity, that they may be enabled to communicate intelligence respecting them to their brethren of the race of Adam, when they shall again mingle with them in the world allotted for their abode, after the general resurrection. Here, the *grandeur* of the Deity, the glory of his physical and moral perfections, and the immensity of his empire, may strike the mind with more bright effulgence, and excite more elevated emotions of admiration and rapture, than in any other province of universal nature. In fine, this vast and splendid central universe may constitute that august mansion referred to in the Scripture, under the designation of the *third heavens, the throne of the Eternal, the heaven of heavens, the high and holy place, and the light that is inaccessible and full of glory.*

Within the limits of the last 150 years, it has been found, that the principal fixed stars have a certain apparent motion, which is nearly uniform and regular, and is quite perceptible in the course of thirty or forty years. The star *Arcturus*, for example, has been observed to move three minutes and three seconds in the course of seventy-eight years. Most of the stars have moved toward the south. The stars in the northern quarter of the heavens seem to widen their relative positions, while those in the southern appear to contract their distances. These motions seem evidently to indicate, that the earth, and all the other bodies of the solar system, are moving in a direction from the stars, in the southern part of the sky, toward those in the northern. Dr. Herschel thinks, that a comparison of the changes now alluded to, indicates a motion of our sun with his attending planets towards the constellation *Hercules*. This progressive movement which our system makes in absolute space, is justly supposed to be a portion of that curve, which the sun describes around the *centre* of that *nebula* to which he belongs; and, that all the other stars belonging to the same nebula, describe similar curves. And since the universe appears to be composed of thousands of *nebulæ*, or starry systems, detached from each other, it is reasonable to conclude, that all the starry systems of the universe revolve round one common centre, whose **bulk** and attractive influence are proportionable to the size **and** the number of the bodies which perform their revolutions around it. We know, that the law of gravitation extends its influence from the sun to the planet *Herschel*, at the distance of eighteen hundred millions of miles, and to the remotest parts of the orbits of the comets, which stretch far beyond this limit: and there is the strongest reason to believe, that it forms a connecting bond between all the bodies of the universe, however distant from each other. **This being** admitted; the *motion* of the different systems now alluded to, and the *immensity* of the central body, from which motion of every kind originates, to produce the order and harmony of the universe, appear to be necessary, in order to preserve the balance of the universal system, **and to** prevent the numerous globes in **the universe from** gradually approaching each other, in the **course of** ages, **and** becoming **one** universal wreck. We are mechanically connected **with** the most distant stars visible through our telescopes, by means of *light*, which radiates from those distant luminaries, mingles with the solar rays, penetrates our atmosphere, and affects our optic nerves with the sensation of colours, similar to those produced by the rays of the sun. And we have equal reason to conclude, that we are likewise mechanically connected with these bodies by the law of gravitation. So that the idea thrown out here, however grand and overwhelming to our feeble powers, is not a mere conjecture, but is founded on observation, and on the general analogies of the universe.

Perhaps **some** whose minds are not accustomed to such bold excursions through the regions of material existence, may be apt to consider the grand idea which has now been suggested, and many of the preceding details, as too improbable and extravagant to claim our serious attention. In reply to such an insinuation, let it be considered, in the *first place*, that nothing has been stated but what corresponds to the whole analogy of nature, and to several sublime intimations contained in **the** system of Divine Revelation. It is a fact, which, in the present day, cannot be denied by any one acquainted with the subject, that the material universe, as far as our eye and our glasses can carry us, consists of a countless multitude of vast bodies, which completely baffle our feeble powers in attempting to form any adequate conception of them. This amazing fact, placed within the evidence of our senses, shows us, that it is impossible for the human mind to form too extensive ideas of the universe, or to conceive its structure to be more glorious and magnificent than it really is.[1]

Again, nothing short of such sublime and magnificent conceptions seems at all suitable to the idea of *a Being of infinite perfection and of eternal duration.* If we admit, that the Divine Being is *infinite,* pervading the immensity of space with his presence, why should we be reluctant to admit the idea, that his *Almighty energy is exerted* throughout the boundless regions of space? for it is just such a conclusion as the notion of an infinite intelligence should naturally lead us to deduce. Whether does it appear to correspond more with the notion of an infinite Being, to believe, that his creative power has been confined to this small globe of earth, and a few sparkling studs fixed in the canopy of the sky; or to admit, on the ground of observation and analogy, that he has launched into existence millions of worlds; that all the millions of systems within the reach of our vision, are but as a particle of vapour to the ocean, when compared with the myriads which exist in the unexplored regions of immensity; that the whole of this vast assemblage of suns and worlds revolves around the grand centre of the universe; and that this centre, where the throne of God is placed, is superior to all the other provinces of creation in

---

[1] In descending to the minute parts of nature, we obtain *ocular demonstration* of facts which overpower our faculties, and which would be altogether incredible, were they not placed within the evidence of the senses. In a drop of water, in which certain vegetable substances have been infused, *millions* of living creatures have been seen; and, in some instances, where the animalcules are transparent, their eyes, and the peristaltic motion of their bowels have been perceived. The *minuteness* of the blood-vessels and other parts of the structure of such creatures, is as wonderful and as incomprehensible, on the one hand, as the magnitude and immensity of the universe are on the other; demonstrating that, in the works of the Creator, there is an infinity on either hand, which limited intellects will never be able fully to comprehend.

magnitude, beauty, and magnificence? Who would dare to *prove* that such conceptions are erroneous, or impossible, or unworthy of that *Being* who sits on the throne of the universe? To attempt such a proof would be nothing less than to set bounds to Omnipotence; to prescribe limits to the operations of Him " whose ways are past finding out."

> " Can man *conceive beyond* what God *can do?*
> Nothing but *quite impossible* is *hard.*
> He summons into being with like ease
> A *whole creation,* and a *single grain.*
> Speaks he the word—a thousand worlds are born.
> A thousand worlds! There's space for millions **more;**
> And in what space can his great Fiat fail?
> Condemn me not, cold critic! but indulge
> The warm imagination; why condemn?
> Why not *indulge* such thoughts as swell our hearts
> With fuller admiration of that *Power*
> Which gives our hearts with such high thoughts to swell?
> Why not indulge in his augmented praise?
> Darts not his glory a still brighter ray,
> And the less left to Chaos, and the realms
> Of hideous Night?"

These views and reasonings are fully corroborated by the sublime descriptions of Deity contained in the Holy Scriptures. " Canst thou by searching find out God? canst thou find out the Almighty to perfection?" " He is the High and lofty One who inhabiteth eternity." " He is glorious in power." " He dwells in light unapproachable and full of glory." " Great is our Lord and of great power, his greatness is unsearchable; his understanding is infinite." " Can any thing be too hard for Jehovah?" " The everlasting God, the Lord, the Creator of the ends of the earth, fainteth not, neither is weary; there is no searching of his understanding." " He doeth great things, past finding out, and wonders without number." " He meteth out the heavens with a span, and comprehendeth the dust of the earth in a measure." " By the word of the Lord **were** the heavens made, and all the host of them by the Spirit of **his** mouth." " He spake, and it was done; He commanded, and it stood fast." " He stretched forth **the** heavens alone, **and** bringeth forth their hosts by number." " Lo, these are *parts* of his ways, but how little a portion **is heard** of him! and the thunder of his power who can understand? Behold, the heaven, and the heaven of heavens cannot contain him!" "The heavens declare the glory of God, and the firmament showeth forth his handywork." "Thine, O Lord! is the greatness, and the glory, and the majesty, for all in heaven and earth is thine, and thou art exalted above all." "Behold, the heaven and the heaven of heavens is the Lord's." "Jehovah *hath prepared his throne in the heavens*, and his kingdom ruleth over all." "I will speak of *the glorious honour of thy majesty*, and of *thy wondrous works.*" "Blessed be thy glorious name, who art exalted above all blessing and praise." "Thou, even thou, art Lord alone; thou hast made heaven, the heaven of heavens, with all their host, thou preservest them all, and the host of heaven worshippeth thee." "Who can utter the mighty acts of the Lord? who can show forth *all* his praise?" "Touching the Almighty, we cannot find him out." "He is excellent in power, and his glory is above the earth and heavens."

Such sublime descriptions of the Divine Being, which are interspersed throughout various parts of Revelation, lead us to form the most august conceptions of his creative energy, and plainly indicate, that it is impossible for the highest created intellect to form a more magnificent idea of his designs and operations than what in reality exists.

In short, though some of the preceding views may not precisely correspond to the facts which shall ultimately be found to exist in the universe, they ought, nevertheless, to be entertained and rendered familiar to the mind, since they open a sublime and interesting train of thinking; and since they cannot go beyond the magnificence of Jehovah's kingdom, nor be very different from what actually exists in the universe. They form a kind of sensible *substratum* of thought for the mind to fix upon, when it attempts to frame the loftiest conceptions of the object of our adoration. It may be laid down as a principle which ought never to be overlooked in Theology, that *our conceptions of the grandeur of God are precisely, or, at least, nearly commensurate with our conceptions of the grandeur and extent of his operations throughout the universe.* We all admit, that the Deity is infinite both in respect of space

and of duration. But an infinity of empty space, and an infinity of duration, abstractly considered, convey no precise or tangible ideas to the mind, to guide it in forming distinct conceptions of the Deity or of any other beings. It is only when the immensity of space is considered **as** diversified with an immense variety and multiplicity of objects, and when eternal duration is contemplated as **connected with** a constant succession of glorious scenes and transactions, that the soul of man can expand its views and elevate its conceptions of the incomprehensible Jehovah.

If these sentiments be admitted, it will follow, that the man whose ideas are confined within the limits **of a few** hundred miles, or even within the range of the globe we **inhabit**, must have his views of Deity confined within nearly the same **sphere**. For we have no sensible measures of the attributes of God, but those which are derived from the number and extent of his actual operations. When we attempt to think of Him, without the **assistance** of **his visible works, our** thoughts instantly run into confusion, and sink into **inanity**. And since we find, that the material works of God are so "great above **all** measure," so widely extended, and so magnificent in the scale **of** their operation, it is of the utmost importance, in a religious point of view, **that** the mind accustom itself to range at large through the wide extent of creation; to trace, by analogy, from what is known, the probable magnitude, arrangement, and grandeur of what is removed beyond the limits of our vision; to add magnitude to magnitude, system to system, and motion to motion, till our thoughts are overwhelmed with the mighty idea. And, though we may occasionally frame some erroneous or inadequate notions, when forming our conceptions of certain subordinate particulars, yet we need not fear, that, in point of number, magnitude, and variety, our conceptions can ever go beyond the realities which exist within the range of universal nature, unless we suppose, that "man can conceive beyond what God can do." **Such** trains of thought will tend to expand and elevate **the** mind, and give it a sublime turn of thinking; and will naturally produce an ardent desire of beholding a brighter display of the magnificence of the Creator in the eternal world.

From what has now been detailed respecting the numerous and august objects that may be presented to the contemplation of celestial intelligences we may conclude, that the chief subjects of study in the heavenly world will be *History* and *Philosophy*. Under the department of history, may be comprehended all the details which will be exhibited to them respecting the origin, progress, and consummation of the redemption of man, and the information they may receive respecting the natural and moral scenery, and the prominent providential occurrences and arrangements of other worlds.

As it is evident, that matter exists chiefly for the sake of sensitive and intelligent beings, so, it is highly probable, if not demonstratively certain, that the peopling of worlds with rational creatures is intended chiefly to display the *moral character* of the Creator in his providential dispensations, and in the whole series of his moral administration towards the numerous worlds and orders of creatures which exist throughout his dominions. All his other perfections, particularly his power and intelligence, appear to be exerted in subserviency to this grand object, and to the distribution of happiness throughout the universe. In so far, then, as the facts respecting his moral government, in other worlds, are made known to the redeemed in heaven, in so far will their views of his moral attributes, and of the principles of his administration in the universe, be enlarged and expanded. In the disclosures which, in the course of ages, may be made on this subject, displays of the *eternal righteousness* of Jehovah, of his *retributive justice*, of his " *tender mercy*," and of his *boundless benevolence*, may be exhibited, which will astonish and enrapture the mind more highly than even the magnificence and grandeur of his physical operations, and fill it with admiration of the amiable and adorable excellences of the Sovereign Ruler of the universe. If we account it a pleasant study to investigate the habits and economy of some of the insect tribes; if we should reckon it highly gratifying to learn the history of all the events which have befallen every nation and tribe of mankind since the world began, particularly those which relate to our first parents in paradise, and after their expulsion from it, to the antediluvians, to the ten tribes of Israel, to the Christians in the first centuries, to the Waldenses, to the Assyrians, Babylonians, and American Indians; how delightful and gratifying must it be, to learn the history of angels, principalities, and powers, and to become acquainted with the leading transactions which have occurred among beings of a higher order and of different species, dispersed among ten thousands of worlds! Great and marvellous as the history of our world, and of human redemption, appears, it may be far surpassed by the events which eternity will unfold. "The day is coming," (to use the words of a celebrated modern writer,[1]) "when the whole of this wondrous history shall be looked back upon by the eye of remembrance, and be regarded, as one incident in the extended annals of creation; and with all the illustration, and all the glory it has thrown on the character of the Deity, will it be seen as a single step in the evolution of his designs; and long as the time may appear, from the first act of our redemption to its final accomplishment, and close and exclusive as we may think the attentions of God upon it, it will be found that it has left him room enough for all his concerns, and that on the high scale of eternity, it is but one of those passing and ephemeral transactions, which crowd the history of a never-ending administration."

Under the department of *Philosophy* may be included all those magnificent displays which will be exhibited of the extent, the magnitude, the motions, the mechanism, the scenery, the inhabitants, and the general constitution of other systems, and the general arrangement and order of the universal system comprehended under the government of the Almighty. On these topics, with all their subordinate and infinitely diversified ramifications, the minds of redeemed intelligences from this world will find ample scope for the exercise of all their powers, and will derive from their investigations of them perpetual and uninterrupted enjoyment, throughout an endless existence.

That the subjects of contemplation now stated, will, in reality, form the chief employments of renovated men and other intellectual beings, in a future state, may also be proved from the representations given in the Word of God of the present

---

[1] Dr. Chalmers.

exercises of these intelligences. In the book of Revelation, the angels, under the figure of "living creatures full of eyes," and the "elders," or representatives of the Church of the redeemed, are represented as falling down before the throne of the Eternal, saying, "Thou art worthy, O Lord, to receive glory, honour, and power, *for thou hast created all things, and for thy pleasure they are and were created.*" Here, the material works of God are represented as the *foundation* or *reason* of the thanksgiving and adorations of the heavenly host; and the language evidently implies, that these works are the subject of their contemplation; that they have beheld a bright display of Divine perfection in their structure and arrangement; that they are enraptured with the enlarged views of the Divine glory which these works exhibit; and that their hearts, full of gratitude and admiration, are ever ready to burst forth in ascriptions of "glory, honour, and power," to Him who called the vast assemblage of created beings into existence. In another scene, exhibited in the same book, the saints who had come out of great tribulation, and had gotten the victory over all enemies, are represented with the harps of God in their hands, celebrating the Divine praises in this triumphant song, "Great and marvellous are thy works, Lord God Almighty; just and true are thy ways, thou King of saints." The first part of this song may be considered as the result of their contemplations of the magnificent fabric of the universe, and the omnipotent energies which its movements display; and the last part of it as the result of their study and investigation of the moral government of God in his providential arrangements towards men and angels, and towards all the worlds whose moral economy may be opened to their view. For the words of the song plainly imply, that they have acquired such an expansive view of the works of God as constrains them to declare, that they are "great and marvellous;" and that they have attained such an intimate knowledge of the Divine dispensation towards the intelligent universe, as enables them to perceive that all the ways of the King of heaven are "righteous and true."

From the preceding details we may also learn, what will form one constituent part of the misery of the wicked in the future world. As one part of the happiness of the righteous will consist in "seeing God as he is," that is, in beholding the Divine glory as displayed in the physical and moral economy of the universe; so it will, in all probability, form one bitter ingredient in the future lot of the unrighteous, that they shall be deprived of the transporting view of the Creator's glory, as displayed in the magnificent arrangements he has made in the system of nature. Confined to one dreary corner of the universe, surrounded by a dense atmosphere, or a congeries of sable clouds, they will be cut off from all intercourse with the regions of moral perfection, and prevented from contemplating the sublime scenery of the Creator's empire. This idea is corroborated by the declarations of Scripture, where they are represented as "banished from the new Jerusalem," "thrust out into outer darkness," and reserved for "the blackness of darkness for ages of ages." And, nothing can be more tormenting to minds endowed with capacious powers, than the thought of being for ever deprived of the opportunity of exercising them on the glorious objects which they know to exist, but which they can never contemplate, and about which they never expect to hear any transporting information.

If it be one end of future punishment to make wicked men sensible of their folly and ingratitude, and of the mercy and favours they have abused, it is probable that, in that future world or region to which they shall be confined, every thing will be so arranged as to bring to their recollection the comforts they had abused, and the Divine goodness they had despised, and to make them feel sensations opposite to those which were produced by the benevolent arrangements which exist in the present state. For example, in the present economy of nature, every one of our senses, every part of our bodily structure, every movement of which our animal frame is susceptible, and the influence which the sun, the atmosphere, and other parts of nature, produce on our structure and feelings, have a direct tendency to communicate pleasing sensations. But, in that world, every agency of this kind may be reversed, as to the effect it may produce upon percipient beings. Our sense of *touch* is at present accompanied with a thousand modifications of feelings which are accompanied with pleasure: but *there*, every thing that comes in contact with the organs of feeling may produce the most *painful* sensations. *Here*, the variety of colours which adorn the face of nature, delights the eye and the imagination; *there*, the most gloomy and haggard objects may at all times produce a dismal and alarming aspect over every part of the surrounding scene. *Here*, the most enchanting *music* frequently cheers and enraptures the human heart; *there*, nothing is heard but the dismal sounds " of weeping, and wailing, and gnashing of teeth." Ungrateful for the manifold blessings they received in this world from the bountiful Giver of all good, the inhabitants of that dreary region will behold their sin in their punishment, in being deprived of every thing which can administer to their sensitive enjoyment.

With regard to their *moral state*, similar effects will be produced. *Here*, they hated the society of the righteous, and loved to mingle with evil doers in their follies and their crimes; *there*, they will be for ever banished from the company of the wise and the benevolent, and will feel the bitter effects of being perpetually chained to the society of those malignant associates who will be their everlasting tormentors. *Here*, they delighted to give full scope to their depraved appetites and passions; *there*, they will feel the bitter and horrible effects of the full operation of such lusts and passions, when unrestrained by the dictates of reason, and the authority of the Divine law. If, to these sources of sorrow and bitter deprivations, be added the consideration, that in such minds, the principles of malice, envy, hatred, revenge, and every other element of evil, which pervaded their souls while in this life, will rage without control, we may form such a conception of future misery as will warrant all the metaphorical descriptions of it which are given in Divine Revelation, without supposing any further interposition of the Deity, in the *direct* infliction of punishment. While he leaves them simply to "*eat of the fruit of their own ways, and to be filled with their own devices*," their punishment must be dreadful, and far surpassing every species of misery connected with the present state of the moral world.

On the other hand, a consideration of the infinitely diversified sources of bliss to which our attention has been directed, has a powerful tendency to impress the minds of the saints with a lively perception of the *unbounded* nature of Divine benignity, and of "the love of God which is in Christ Jesus our Lord." It is chiefly in connection with such expansive views of the attributes and the government of the Deity, that the love of God towards the Redeemed appears "boundless," and "passing comprehension;" for it introduces them into a scene which is not only commensurate with infinite duration, but is boundless in its prospects of knowledge, of felicity, and of glory. And, therefore, amidst all the other employments of the heavenly state, they will never forget their obligation to that unmerited grace and mercy which rescued their souls from destruction; but will mingle with all their sublime investigations, ascriptions of "blessing, and honour, and glory, and power, to Him that sits upon the throne, and to the Lamb, for ever and ever."

The substance of what has been detailed in this department of my subject may be now briefly stated in the following summary:

The redeemed in heaven will enjoy perpetual and uninterrupted felicity: the foundation of this felicity will be laid in their complete freedom from sin, and their attainment of moral perfection; their renovated faculties will be employed in contemplating the Divine glory; the Divine glory consists in the manifestation of the Divine perfections; the sensible display of these perfections will be given (and can only be given) in the works of creation, in the intelligences which people the material world, their orders, gradations, history, and present state; in the variety of scenery which the abodes of intelligence exhibit; in the economy and moral order which prevail among them; and in the various dispensations of Divine providence in reference to all worlds and orders of beings.

With regard to the happiness of heaven, the Scriptures convey to us, in general propositions, certain intimations of its nature, qualities and objects, and of the qualifications which are requisite in order to its enjoyment. The discoveries which science has made in the visible creation form so many illustrations of the Scriptural declarations on this subject; and it is undoubtedly our duty to direct our trains of thought, and to expand our conceptions of the felicities of the future world, by every illustrative circumstance which can be traced in the scene of nature which the Almighty has presented to our view. For the word and the works of God must always harmonize, and reflect a mutual lustre on each other. What we find to be actually existing within the visible scene of the universe, can never contradict any of the statements of Revelation; but, on the contrary, must tend to elucidate some one or other of its interesting communications. And, since we find, in our survey of the system of nature, an assemblage of astonishing objects, which tends to raise our conceptions of the Supreme Being, and of the sublime and diversified nature of future felicity; it becomes us to prosecute those trains of thought which the analogies of Nature and of Revelation suggest, in order to enlarge the capacities of our minds, to exalt our ideas of celestial bliss, and to prepare us for more expansive and sublime contemplations, in that world where the physical and moral obstructions which now impede our progress, and obscure our intellectual views, shall be completely and for ever removed.

From the whole of what we have stated on this department of our subject, we may learn the value of the human soul, and the importance which ought to be attached to our immortal destination. What a shadow does human life appear when contrasted with the scenes of futurity! What a small point in duration do the revolutions of time present when compared with a boundless eternity! What a limited scene does this world, with all its glories, exhibit, when set in competition with the extent and the splendours of that empire which stretches out into immensity, and shall endure for ever! And is man to be transported to other regions of the universe, to mingle with the inhabitants of other worlds, and to exist throughout an endless duration? What a noble principle does the human mind appear, when we consider it as qualified to prosecute so many diversified trains of thought, to engage in so sublime investigations, to attain the summit of moral perfection, and to expatiate at large, through the unlimited dominions of the Almighty, while eternal ages are rolling on! How important, then, ought every thing to be considered which is connected with the scene of our eternal destination! If these truths be admitted, reason and common sense declare, that a more interesting and momentous subject cannot possibly occupy the mind of man. It is so profoundly interesting, and connected with so many awful and glorious consequences, that we must be utterly **dead** to every noble and refined feeling, if we be altogether indifferent about it.

If there **were only a** bare *probability* for the opinion, that man is immortal, and that the scenes to which I have alluded might possibly be realized, it ought to stimulate the most anxious inquiries, and awaken all the powers and energies of **our** souls. For it is both our duty and **our highest** interest to obtain light and satisfaction, on a point on which our present comfort and our ultimate happiness must depend. But, if the Light of Nature, and the dictates of revelation **both** conspire to *demonstrate* the eternal destiny of mankind, **nothing can** exceed the folly and the infatuation of those who trifle with their everlasting interests, **and** even try every scheme, and prosecute every trivial object, that may have a tendency to turn **aside their thoughts** from this important subject. Yet, how **often** do we find, **in the conduct** of the various classes of mankind, the merest trifles set in competition with the scenes of happiness or of misery that lie beyond the grave. The groveling pleasures derived from hounding **and** horse-racing, balls, masquerades, and theatrical amusements; the acquisition of a few paltry pounds **or** shillings, the rattling of dice, or the shuffling of a pack of cards, will absorb the minds of thousands who profess to be rational beings, while they refuse to spend *one serious hour* in reflecting on the fate of their immortal spirits, **when** their bodies shall have dropped into the tomb. Nay, such is the indifference, and even *antipathy*, with which **this** subject is treated by certain classes of society, that it is considered as unfashionable, and in certain cases, would be regarded **as a** species of insult, to introduce, in conversation, a sentiment **or a** reflection on the eternal destiny of man. "The carelessness **which** they betray in a **matter** which involves their existence, **their** eternity, their **all**," says an energetic French writer, "awakes my indignation, rather than my pity. It is astonishing. It is horrifying. It is monstrous. I speak not this from the pious zeal of a blind devotion. On the **contrary, I** affirm, that self-love, that self-interest, that **the** simplest light of reason, should inspire these sentiments; and, in fact, for this we need but the perfections of ordinary men. It requires but little elevation of soul to discover, that here there is no substantial delight; that our pleasures are but vanity; that the ills of life are innumerable; and that, after all, death, which threatens us every moment, must, in a few years, perhaps in a few days, place us in the eternal condition of happiness, or misery, or nothingness."

It is, therefore, the imperative duty of every man who makes any pretentions to prudence and rationality, to endeavour to have his mind impressed with a conviction of the reality of a future and invisible world, to consider its importance, and to contemplate, in the light of reason and of revelation, the grand and solemn scenes which it displays. While the least doubt hovers upon his mind in relation to this subject, he should give himself no rest till it be dispelled. He should explore every avenue where light and information may be obtained; he should prosecute his researches with the same earnestness and avidity as the miser digs for hidden treasures; and above all things, he should study, with deep attention and humility, the revelation contained in the Holy Scriptures, with earnest prayer to God for light and direction. And if such inquiries be conducted with reverence, with a devotional and contrite spirit, and with perseverance, every doubt and difficulty that may have formerly brooded over his mind, will gradually evanish, as the shades of night before the orient sun. "If thou criest after knowledge, and liftest up thy voice for understanding; if thou seekest her as silver, and searchest for her as for hid treasures: then shalt thou understand the fear of the Lord, and find the knowledge of God. For the Lord giveth wisdom, out of his mouth cometh knowledge and understanding. In all thy ways acknowledge him and he shall direct thy paths. Then shall thy light break forth in obscurity, and thy darkness shall be as the noonday."

In fine, if we are thoroughly convinced of our relation to an eternal world, it will be our constant endeavour to cultivate those heavenly dispositions and virtues, and to prosecute that course of action, which will prepare us for enjoyments of the heavenly state. "For, without holiness no man can see the Lord;" and we are assured that "no unclean thing can enter the gates of the New Jerusalem," and that neither "thieves, nor extortioners, nor the covetous, nor the effeminate, nor drunkards, nor revilers, nor idolaters, shall inherit the kingdom of God."

PART IV

ON THE MORAL QUALIFICATIONS REQUISITE TO THE ENJOYMENT OF THE FELICITY OF THE FUTURE WORLD.

THERE is scarcely an individual who admits the doctrine of the immortality of man, who does not indulge a certain degree of hope, that he shall be admitted into a happier world, when his spirit wings its way from this earthly scene. Even the man of the world, the profligate, and the debauchee, notwithstanding their consciousness of guilt, and of the opposition of their affections to the Divine Law, and the duties of the Christian life, are frequently found buoying themselves up, in the midst of their unhallowed courses, with the vain expectation, that an All-Merciful Creator will not suffer them ultimately to sink into perdition, but pity their weaknesses and follies, and receive them, when they die, into the joys of heaven. Such hopes arise from ignorance of the Divine character, and of that in which true happiness consists, and from fallacious views of the exercises of a future state, and the nature of its enjoyments. For, in order to enjoy happiness, in any state, or in any region of the universe, the mind must be embued with a relish for the society, the contemplations, and the employments peculiar to that region or state, and feel an ardent desire to participate in its enjoyments.

What pleasure would a miser, whose mind is wholly absorbed in the acquisition of riches, feel in a world where neither gold nor silver, nor any other object of avarice is to be found? What entertainment would a man, whose chief enjoyment consists in hounding, horse-racing, routs, and masquerades, derive in a scene where such amusements are for ever abolished? Could it be supposed that those who now find their highest intellectual pleasures in Novels and Romances, and in listening to tales of scandal, would experience any high degree of enjoyment in a world where there is nothing but substantial realities, and where the inhabitants are united in bonds of purest affection? or that those whose minds never rise beyond the pleasures of gambling, card-playing, and gossiping chit-chat, would feel any relish for the refined enjoyments, the sublime contemplations, and the enraptured praises, of the heavenly inhabitants? All the arrangements of the celestial state behoved to be changed and overturned, and angels, archangels, and redeemed men banished from its abodes, before such characters could find entertainments agreeable to their former habits and desires. Although they were admitted into the mansions of bliss, they would be miserably disappointed; and would feel themselves in a situation similar to that of a rude savage or a Russian boor, were he to be introduced into an assembly of princes and nobles. They would perceive nothing congenial in their former pursuits; they would feel an inward reluctance to the pure and holy exercises of the place, and they would anxiously desire to flee away to regions and to companions more adapted to their groveling views and affections. For, it is the decree of Heaven, a decree founded on the moral laws which govern the intelligent universe, and which, like the law of the Medes and Persians, cannot be changed, that, "*Without holiness no man can see the Lord*," and that "no impure person that worketh abomination, or maketh a lie, can enter within the gates of the Heavenly Jerusalem."

The foundation of felicity in the future state, is substantially the same as that which forms the basis of happiness in the present world. However elevated the station in which an individual may be placed, however much wealth he may possess, and however splendid his rank and equipage, he can enjoy no *substantial felicity*, while he remains the slave of groveling appetites and affections, and while pride and envy, ambition and revenge, exercise a sovereign control over his mind. While destitute of supreme love to God, and benevolent affection towards man, and of the Christian virtues which flow from these fundamental principles of moral action, the mind must remain a stranger to true happiness, and to all those expansive views, and delightful feelings, which raise the soul above the pleasures of sense, and the trivial vexations and disappointments of the present life.

These positions could be demonstrated, were it necessary, by numerous facts connected with the moral scenery of human society. Whence proceeds that *ennui*, which is felt in the fashionable world, in the absence of balls, parties, operas, and theatrical entertainments? Whence arise those domestic broils, those family feuds and contentions, which are so common in the higher, as well as in the lower ranks of life, and which embitter every enjoyment? Whence does it happen, that, in order to obtain gratification, and to render existence tolerable, so many thousands of rational beings condescend to indulge in the most childish, foolish, and brutal diversions? Even in the most polished circles of society, many who pride themselves on their superiority to the vulgar throng, are found deriving their chief gratification, not only in scattering destruction among the brutal and the feathered tribes, but in mingling among the motley rabble of a *cockpit*, and in witnessing a couple of *boxers* encountering like furious fiends, and covering each other with wounds and gore. Whence arise the torments that are felt from wounded pride and disappointed ambition? and how does it happen that social parties cannot enjoy themselves for a couple of hours, without resorting to cards and dice, gambling and gossiping, and the circulation of tales of scandal! How is it to be accounted for, that suicide is so frequently committed by persons in the higher circles, who are surrounded with luxuries and splendour; and that murmuring discontentment and ingratitude, mark the dispositions and conduct of the lower ranks of society? All these effects proceed from the absence of Christian principles and dispositions, and from the narrow range of objects to which the intellectual powers are confined. The man who is actuated by Christian views and affections, looks down with indifference and contempt on the degrading pursuits to which I have alluded; his soul aspires after objects more congenial to his rational and immortal nature; and in the pursuit of these, and the exercise of the virtues which religion inculcates, he enjoys a refined pleasure which the smiles of the world cannot produce, and which its frowns cannot destroy.

As in the present life there are certain mental endowments necessary for securing substantial happiness, so, there are certain *moral* qualifications *indispensably* requisite in order to prepare us for relishing the entertainments and the employments of the life to come. The foundation of future felicity must be laid in "repentance towards God, and faith towards our Lord Jesus Christ." We must be convinced of our sin and depravity as descendants of the first Adam, of the demerit of our offences, of the spotless purity and eternal rectitude of that Being whom we have offended, and of the danger to which we are exposed as the violators of his law. We must receive, with humility and gratitude, the Salvation exhibited in the Gospel, and "behold," with the eye of faith, "the Lamb of God who taketh away the sins of the world." We must depend on the aid of the Spirit of God to enable us to counteract the evil propensities of our nature, to renew our souls after the Divine image, and to inspire us with ardent desires to abound in all those "fruits of righteousness which are to the praise and glory of God." We must "add to our faith, fortitude and resolution; and to fortitude, knowledge; and to knowledge, temperance; and to temperance, patience; and to patience, godliness; and to godliness, brotherly kindness and charity. For, if these things be in us and abound, they will permit us to be neither barren nor unfruitful in the knowledge of our Lord Jesus Christ; and so an entrance shall be abundantly administered unto us into the everlasting kingdom of our Lord and Saviour."[1]

The foundation of religion being thus laid in the exercise of such Christian graces, the following dispositions and virtues, among many others, will be cherished and cultivated, and will form substantial qualifications for enabling us to participate in "the inheritance of the saints in light."

1. Supreme Love to God, the original source of happiness. This is the first duty of every rational creature, and the most sublime affection that can pervade the human mind. It glows in the breasts of angels and archangels, of cherubim and seraphim; yea, there is not an inhabitant of any world in the uni-

---

[1] 2 Peter, i, 5, 6, 7, 8, 11.—Doddridge's Translation.

verse, who has retained his primitive integrity, in whose heart it does not reign triumphant. It unites all holy intelligences to the Creator and to one another; and, consequently, it must qualify us for holding a delightful intercourse with such beings, wherever they exist, and in whatever region of the universe our future residence may be appointed. It enlivens the adoration of the angelic tribes, when they exclaim, "Thou art worthy, O Lord, to receive glory, and honour, and thanksgiving, and power." It animates them in all their celestial services: it inspires them with a noble ardour in executing the commands of their Sovereign, and it qualifies its possessor, to whatever world he may belong, for co-operating with them, in carrying forward that scheme of Universal Benevolence, towards the accomplishment of which all the arrangements of the Creator ultimately tend.

This holy affection is congenial to every view we can take of the character and operations of the Deity, and its obligation is deduced from the clearest principles of *reason*, as well as from the dictates of Revelation. It is founded on every attribute of the Divinity, and on every part of his physical and moral administration. His Omnipotence is every moment exerted in supporting the frame of the universe, in bringing about the alternate succession of day and night, summer and winter, seed time and harvest, and in directing the operation of the elements of nature, in such a way as to contribute to the happiness of man. His Wisdom and Intelligence are displayed in proportionating and arranging every object in the system of Nature, in such a manner, that every thing is preserved in order and harmony; and in organizing the bodies of men and other creatures, so as to prevent pain, and to produce a combination of pleasurable sensations. His goodness extends over all his works, and is displayed towards every rank of sensitive and intelligent existence. It appears in the splendours of the sun, in the radiance of the moon, in the glories of the starry firmament, in the beautiful assemblage of colours which diversify the face of Nature, in the plants and flowers which adorn the fields, in the gentle zephyrs, in the rains and dews that fertilize the soil, in the provision made for the sustenance of the innumerable beings that inhabit the air, the waters, and the earth, and "in filling the hearts of men with food and gladness." His mercy and forbearance are exercised towards all men, even to the most profligate and abandoned, in supporting them in existence and loading them with his benefits, even when they are engaged in acts of rebellion against him. For he commandeth the sun to arise on the evil as well as on the good, and sendeth rain both on the just and the *unjust*. He displays his long-suffering for many years, towards the thoughtless prodigal, and the violators of his law, to demonstrate, that "he desires not that any should perish, but that all should come to repentance."

A Being possessed of such attributes, and incessantly displaying such beneficence throughout creation, demands the highest affection and veneration of all his intelligent offspring; so that it is the dictate of enlightened reason, as well as of revelation, "Thou shalt love the Lord thy God with all thy heart, with all thy soul, and with all thy strength." For it is from him, as the original source of felicity, that all our sensitive and intellectual enjoyments proceed, and on him we depend for all the blessings that shall accompany us in every future stage of our existence. Love to God is, therefore, the most reasonable and amiable affection that can glow in the human heart, and the spring of every virtuous action, and of every pleasing and rapturous emotion. If we are possessed of this divine principle, we shall delight in his worship, and bow with reverence at his footstool; we shall feel complacency in his character and administration; we shall contemplate with *admiration* the incomprehensible knowledge, the omnipotent power, and the boundless beneficence, displayed in the mighty movements of Creation and Providence; we shall feel the most lively emotions of gratitude for the numerous blessings he bestows; we shall be resigned to his will under every providential arrangement, and we shall long for that happy world, where the glories of his nature and the "kindness of his love" shall be more illustriously displayed. But the man who is destitute of this amiable affection, is incapable of those sublime and rapturous emotions which animate the minds of celestial intelligences, and altogether unqualified for mingling in their society. He is a rebel against the Divine government, a nuisance in the universe of God, the slave of grovelling appetites and passions, and consequently, unfit for participating in the exercises and enjoyments of the saints in glory.

2. *Love to mankind* is another affection which is indispensably requisite to qualify us for participating in the joys of heaven. This distinguishing characteristic of the saints naturally and necessarily flows from love to the Supreme Being. "For," says the apostle John, "every one that loveth him who begat, loveth them also who are begotten of him. If God loveth us, we ought also to love one another. If a man say, I love God, and hateth his brother, he is a liar; for he who loveth not his brother, whom he hath seen, how can he love God, whom he hath not seen?" As the spring flows from the fountain, and partakes of its qualities, and as the shadow always accompanies the substance, and is produced by it, so love to man uniformly accompanies the love of God, and is produced by the powerful influence which this governing principle exerts over the mind.

This affection is accordant with the dictates of reason, and congenial to the best feelings of the human heart. When we consider that our fellow-men derived their origin from the same Almighty Being who brought *us* into existence; that they are endowed with the same physical functions as ourselves, and the same moral and intellectual powers; that they relish the same pleasures and enjoyments, possess the same feelings, and are subjected to the same wants and afflictions; that they are involved in the same general depravity, and liable to the same temptations and disasters; that they are journeying along with us to the tomb, and that our dust must soon mingle with theirs: when we consider the numerous relations in which we stand to our brethren around us, and to all the inhabitants of the globe; our dependence upon all ranks and descriptions of men, and upon almost every nation under heaven, for our sensitive and intellectual enjoyments; and that thousands of them are traversing sea and land, and exposing themselves to innumerable dangers, in order to supply us with the comforts and the luxuries of life: when we consider, that they are all destined to an immortal existence, and shall survive the dissolution of this globe, and bear a part in the solemn scenes which shall open to view when time shall be no more: in short, when we consider that the Great Father of all, without respect of persons, makes the same vital air to give play to their lungs, the same water to cleanse and refresh them, the same rains and dews to fructify their fields, the same sun to enlighten their day, and the same moon to cheer the darkness of their night; we must be convinced, that love to our brethren of mankind is the law of the Creator, and the most rational and amiable affection that can animate the human heart in relation to subordinate intelligences. He who is destitute of this affection is a pest in society, a rebel and a nuisance in the kingdom of God, and of course, unqualified for the enjoyment of celestial bliss. "For he who hateth his brother is a *murderer;* and we know that no murderer hath eternal life abiding in him."[1]

But, our love is not to be confined to our brethren of the race of Adam. It must take a loftier flight, and comprehend within its expansive grasp, all the holy intelligences in the universe, in so far as their nature and qualities have been made known to us. We must love the angelic tribes. They are beings who stand near the summit of the scale of intellectual existence; they are endowed with faculties superior to man, they dwell in the glorious presence of God, and are employed as his ministers in superintending the affairs of his government. They are possessed of wonderful activity, invested with powers of rapid motion, and flourish in immortal youth. They are adorned with consummate holiness and rectitude, and with peculiar loveliness of character. Pride and vanity, envy and malice, wrath and revenge, never rankle in their breasts. They never indulge in impiety, never insult the Redeemer, nor bring a railing accusation against their brethren. They glow with an intense and immortal flame of love to their Creator; they are incessantly employed in acts of benevolence; they occasionally descend to our world on embassies of mercy, and are ministering spirits to the heirs of salvation. On all these accounts they demand our esteem, our approbation, and our affectionate regard. And, although they are at present placed beyond the reach of our beneficence, and we have no opportunity of expressing our benevolent wishes, yet we may after-

[1] 1 John, iii, 15.

wards be joined to their society, and co-operate with them in their labours of love.

The indispensable necessity of love to mankind, and to every class of holy intelligences, as a preparation for heaven, will appear when we consider, that we shall mingle in their society, and hold intimate fellowship with them in the eternal world. For the inhabitants of our world, who are admitted into heaven, are represented in Scripture, as joining "the general assembly and Church of the first-born, the spirits of just men made perfect, and the innumerable company of angels;" and hence they are exhibited, in the book of Revelation, as joining with one heart and one mind in contemplating the Divine operations, and in celebrating the praises of their common Lord. In the society of that blessed world, love pervades every bosom, it reigns for ever triumphant; and therefore, every exercise and intercourse is conducted with affection, harmony, and peace. Among the other evils which shall be banished from the New Jerusalem, it is declared in the book of Revelation, that "there shall be no more *crying*," or, as the word should be rendered "there shall be no more *clamour, broils,* or *contentions,*" arising from the operation of malignant principles. No jarring affection is ever felt, no malevolent wish is ever uttered, and no discordant voice is ever heard, among all the myriads of those exalted intelligences. Kindness and benignity, expansive benevolence, condescension and humility, are the characteristics of all the inhabitants of heaven. Without these qualities the celestial world would become a scene of eternal confusion, and happiness would be banished from its abodes. If, therefore, we would be qualified to associate with these glorious beings, and to participate in their enjoyments, we must cultivate the same virtues and be animated by similar dispositions, otherwise, we could experience no delight in the society of angels, and of "the spirits of the just made perfect." Were an individual whose heart is full of rancour and envy, who delights in broils and contentions, and in the exercise of revenge, to be admitted into that society, he would find no associates actuated by congenial feelings, he would disturb the harmony of the celestial choir, and would be instantly expelled, with every mark of indignation and horror, from those blessed abodes. "For what fellowship hath righteousness with unrighteousness? what communion hath light with darkness? and what concord hath Christ with Belial?" By a law which pervades the whole moral universe wherever it extends, which can never be rescinded, and which, like the law of gravitation in the material world, connects all the individuals of which it is composed in one harmonious system; such characters must, of necessity, be for ever excluded from the mansions of the blessed. On the other hand, the man whose heart glows with love to his Creator, and with expansive affection to mankind and towards all holy beings, is secured of eternal happiness, as *the necessary result* of the possession of such divine principles; and must enjoy felicity, while such principles remain in exercise, during all the future periods of his existence, and in every region of the universe to which he may be transported.

3. *Humility* is another essential qualification for enjoying the felicity of the future world. There is nothing that appears more prominent in the character of the bulk of mankind, than *pride*, which displays itself in a thousand different modes in the intercourses of society. It is uniformly accompanied with haughtiness of demeanour, self-conceit, obstinacy, arrogance, and a whole train of malignant passions and affections. It is the pest of general society, the source of domestic broils and contentions, and the greatest curse that can fall on a Christian church, when it insinuates itself into the minds of those who "love to have the pre-eminence." It is a source of torment to its possessor, and to all around him; and of all the malignant passions which rankle in the human breast, it is the most inconsistent with the present character and condition of man. It is peculiar to fallen and depraved intelligences; for it is certain, from the very constitution of the moral system, that no emotions of pride or haughtiness are ever felt in the breasts of angels, or any other holy beings; because such affections are incompatible with the principle of love to God and to our fellow-creatures.

In opposition to this principle, which predominates in the minds of fallen man, and apostate angels, *humility* is a distinguishing characteristic of the sons of God, whether on earth or in heaven. Hence, we are told, that "God resisteth the proud, but giveth grace to the humble;" that even "a proud look is an abomination in his sight," while he beholds with complacency "the humble and the contrite spirit." Hence we are exhorted "to clothe ourselves with humility;" and "to forbear one another in all lowliness and meekness of mind, and to esteem others better than ourselves." Humility consists in a just sense of our character and condition, both as dependent beings and as apostate creatures, accompanied with a correspondent train of dispositions and affections. However much this disposition has been disrelished by Hume and other infidels, who consider it as both vicious and contemptible, when viewed in its true light, it appears congenial to the best feelings of our nature, and to the plainest deductions of reason. When we consider our condition as *creatures*, dependent every moment on a Superior Being "for life, and breath, and all things;" when we reflect on the curious organization of our corporeal frame, the thousands of veins, arteries, muscles, bones, lacteals, and lymphatics, which are interwoven through its constitution; the incessant pulsation of the heart in the centre of the system, and the numerous other functions and movements over which we have no control; when we reflect on our *character* as guilty and depraved creatures, in the presence of Him "who is of purer eyes than to behold iniquity;" and on the numerous diseases, pains, sorrows, and physical evils, from the war of the elements, to which we are subjected: when we consider, that, ere long, our bodies must crumble into dust, and become the prey of noisome reptiles: when we reflect on *the low station in which we are placed in the scale of intelligent existence;* that we are only like so many atoms, or microscopic animalcules, when contrasted with the innumerable myriads of bright intelligences that people the empire of God, and that the globe on which we dwell is but as "the drop of a bucket," when compared with the millions of more resplendent worlds that roll through the vast spaces of creation: and, in short, when we consider the grandeur of that Omnipotent Being whose presence pervades every region of immensity, and in whose sight "all the inhabitants of the world are as grasshoppers, and are counted to him as less than nothing and vanity," there is no disposition that appears more conformable to the character and condition of man, than "lowliness of mind" and none more unreasonable and inconsistent with the rank and circumstances in which he is placed, than pride, haughtiness, and arrogance.

This amiable disposition forms a peculiar trait in the character of angels and other pure intelligences. It is poor, puny, sinful man, alone, who dares to be proud and arrogant. It is that rebellious worm of the dust *alone*, (if we except the angels of darkness,) that looks down with supercilious contempt on his fellow-creatures, and attempts to exalt himself above the throne of God. No such affections are ever felt in the breasts of superior beings who have kept their first estate. In proportion to the enlarged capacity of their minds; in proportion to the expansive views they have acquired of the dominions of Jehovah; in proportion to the elevated conceptions they have attained of the character and attributes of their Creator; in a similar proportion are their minds inspired with *humility*, reverence, and lowly adoration. Having taken an extensive survey of the operations of Omnipotence, having winged their way to numerous worlds, and beheld scenes of wisdom and benevolence, which the eye of man hath not yet seen, nor his imagination conceived, and having contemplated displays of intelligence and power, which are beyond the reach even of their own superior faculties to comprehend; they see themselves as finite and imperfect creatures, and even, as it were, *fools*,[1] in the presence of Him whose glory is ineffable, and whose ways are past finding out. Hence, they are represented as "covering their faces with their wings," in the presence of their Sovereign;[2] and, in the book of Revelation, they are exhibited as "casting their crowns before the throne, and saying, Thou art worthy, O Lord, to receive glory, and honour, and power."[3] What a striking contrast does such a scene present to the haughty airs, and the arrogant conduct, of the proud beings

---

[1] In the book of Job, Eliphaz, when describing the perfections of the Almighty, declares, that "the heavens are not clean in his sight," and that even "his angels he chargeth with *folly*." Job, iv, 18; xv, 15.

[2] Isaiah, vi, 2.   [3] Rev. iv, 10, 11.

that dwell on this terrestrial ball, who are at the same time immersed in ignorance and folly, **immorality and crime!**

In their intercourses with the inhabitants of **our world, and** the offices they perform as ministering spirits to **the heirs of** salvation, the **same** humble and condescending demeanour is displayed. **One** of the highest order of these celestial messengers, "Gabriel, who stands in the presence of God," winged his flight from his heavenly mansions to our wretched world; and, directing his course to one of the most despicable villages of Galilee, entered into the hovel of a poor virgin, and delivered a message of joy, with the most affectionate and condescending gratulations. Another of these benevolent beings **entered** the dungeon in which Peter was bound with **chains, knocked off** his fetters, addressed him in the language of kindness, and delivered him from the hands of his furious persecutors. When Paul was tossing in a storm, on the billows of the Adriatic, a forlorn exile from his native land, and a poor despised prisoner, on whom the grandees of this world looked down with contempt; another of these angelic beings " stood by him," during the darkness of the night and the war of the elements, and consoled his mind with the assurance of the Divine favour and protection. Lazarus was a poor despised individual, in abject poverty and distress, and dependent on charity for his subsistence. He lay at the gate of a rich man, without friends or attendants, desiring to be fed with the crumbs which fell from his table. His body was covered with boils and ulcers, which were exposed without covering to the open air, for " the dogs came **and** licked his sores." What nobleman **or** grandee would have condescended to make a companion of a fellow-creature in such loathsome and abject circumstances? Who, even of the common people, would have received such a person into their houses, **or** desired his friendship? Who would have accounted it an honour, when he died, to attend his funeral? Celestial beings, however, view the circumstances, and the characters of men in a very different light from that in which they appear to "the children of pride." Poor and despised as Lazarus was, a choir of angels descended from their mansions of glory, attended him on his dying couch, and wafted his disembodied spirit to the **realms of bliss.**

Since, then, it appears, that angelic beings, notwithstanding **their** exalted stations, and the superior glories of their character, are "clothed with humility;" it must form a distinguishing trait in our moral characters, if we expect to be admitted into their society in the world to **come.** For how could we enter into harmonious fellowship with these pure intelligences, if **we were** actuated with dispositions diametrically opposite to theirs, **and what** happiness would result from such an association, were it possible to be effected? A proud man, were he admitted into heaven, could feel no permanent enjoyment. The external glory of the place might dazzle **his** eyes for a little, but he would feel no relish for the society and **the** employments of that world. The peculiar honour conferred on patriarchs, prophets, and apostles, and the noble army of martyrs, and the exalted stations of the cherubim and seraphim, would excite his envy and ambition, and, ere long, he would attempt to sow the seeds of discord, and to introduce anarchy and confusion among the hosts of heaven. So that the passion of pride, when cherished in the soul as the governing principle of action, is utterly incompatible with our admission into the regions of harmony and love.

Let me ask the man in whose heart pride and haughtiness predominate, if he really imagines that he can be a candidate for a glorious and immortal existence? Does he not at once perceive the inconsistency of such a thought with the dictates of reason and the nature of future felicity? Of what has he any reason to be proud? Is he proud of his *birth?* of his *ancestors?* of his *wealth* or his *station?* of his *beauty?* of his per**sonal** *accomplishments?* of his *gallantry?* of his *debaucheries?* of his military *prowess?* or of *the thousands of human beings he has slain in battle?* **Is he** proud of his skill in music, in dancing, in fencing, in fox-hunting, and in gambling? of his knowledge in languages, in literature, in arts and sciences? Or is he proud that he is subjected to the asthma, the gravel, the dropsy, and the **gout; that** his funeral **will** be attended by a train of mourners, **and that a** monument of marble will be erected to his memory, when his carcase is putrifying with the reptiles of the dust? **Suppose** he were admitted into the celes**tial** mansions; **which of all these topics** would he choose for the theme of his conversation, and the ground of his boasting? Would he attempt to entertain the cherubim and the seraphim, by telling them how many rude chieftains he was descended from, how many ancient families he was connected with, and how many acres of land he possessed as a patrimony in that wretched world which is soon to be wrapt in flames? Would he tell them of his expertness as a marksman, of his dexterity as a horse-racer, of his adroitness as a boxer, of his skill in manœuvring an army, of the villages he had burned, of the towns he had pillaged, or of the thousands he had butchered in storming a city? He would be overwhelmed with shouts of indignation, and instantly hissed from their abodes. Would he boast of his skill in languages and antiquities, or of his knowledge in arts and sciences? What a poor *ignoramus* (if I may use the expression) would he appear in the presence of Gabriel, the angel of God, who has so frequently winged his way, in a few hours, from heaven to earth, and surveyed the regions of unnumbered worlds! Would a poor worm of the earth, whose view is confined within a few miles around it, boast of its knowledge in the presence of beings endowed with such capacious powers, and who have ranged over so vast a portion of the universe of God? And, if he has nothing else to boast of, why is he proud? What a pitiful figure he would make among the *intelligent* and adoring hosts of heaven! While such a disposition, therefore, predominates in the mind, its possessor can enjoy no substantial felicity either in this life or in the life to come.

On the other hand, the man who, like his Redeemer, is "meek and lowly in heart," has "the witness in himself," that he has obtained the approbation of his God, that he is assimilated to angelic beings in his temper and affections, that he has the principle of eternal life implanted in his soul, and that he is in some measure qualified for joining in the exercises, and enjoying the felicity, of the heavenly state. "For thus saith the High and Lofty One that inhabiteth eternity, whose name is Holy; I dwell in the high and holy place; *with him also that is of a contrite and humble spirit*, to revive the spirit of the humble, and to revive the heart of the contrite ones."

4. *Active beneficence*, with all its accompanying virtues, is **another** characteristic of the man who is training for **the** heavenly inheritance. Wherever the principle of love to God and man, and the grace of humility are in exercise, they will uniformly lead **the** individual who **is** under their influence to "abound in the fruits of righteousness," and to use every active endeavour to promote the comfort and happiness of mankind. He will endeavour, as far as his power and influence extend, to relieve the wants of the poor, the fatherless, and the widow, to soothe the disconsolate, to comfort the afflicted, to shelter the houseless and benighted traveller, to instruct the ignorant, and to meliorate the moral and physical condition of every rank of society. He will patronize every scheme which has for its object to remove the evils which exist in the social state; to increase the comforts of mankind; to improve the soil; to facilitate human labour; to clear away nuisances from the habitations of men; to promote order, cleanliness, and domestic enjoyment; to train the minds of the young to knowledge and virtue; to introduce useful improvements in the mechanical arts, and to diffuse useful science among all ranks. Above all things, he will endeavour, in so far as his station and opportunities permit, to promote the spiritual improvement and the *eternal happiness* of mankind, and will study to render all his other exertions subservient to the attainment of this most interesting and momentous object. In contributing to the accomplishment of this end, he will give his countenance and support to every institution, and to every rational scheme, which is calculated to promote the knowledge of the Scriptures of truth, throughout our own country and in other lands, and to make known "the salvation of God" over all the earth. In such benevolent exertions he will persevere, even in the face of every species of opposition, obloquy, and reproach, through the whole course of his existence in this world, till death transport him to a nobler sphere of action and enjoyment.

The necessity of acquiring habits of active beneficence, in order to our preparation for the felicity of the future world, **will** appear, if we consider that heaven is *a social state*, and that a considerable portion of its happiness will consist in the mutual interchange of benevolent affections, and beneficent actions. There will, indeed, be no poor and distressed objects to be relieved and comforted, no sorrows to be alleviated, and no physical nor moral evils to be counteracted; for, in the New Jerusalem "there shall be no more death, neither sorrow, nor crying, neither shall there be any more pain; for the former things shall have passed away, and God shall wipe away all tears from their eyes." But its inhabitants will be for ever employed in acts of beneficence towards each other, corresponding to their dignified stations, and the circumstances in which they are placed. This is evident from the very nature of *Love*, which pervades the heart of the whole of that "multitude which no man can number." Love can be manifested only by its *effects*, or by those external acts of kindness and benignity which tend to communicate happiness to others; and there can be no doubt, that, in a thousand ways incomprehensible to us, the inhabitants of the upper world will be the means of diffusing ecstatic delight through the bosoms of surrounding intelligences, which will form a part of that joy which is "unspeakable and full of glory." The sympathetic feelings they will express for each other, both in respect to their former and their present condition, the interest they will take in listening to each other's history, the scenes of felicity to which they will conduct each other, the noble and enrapturing subjects of conversation with which they will entertain one another, the objects of beauty and sublimity to which they will direct each other's attention, the lectures on divine subjects, which the more capacious and exalted spirits among them may deliver to their younger brethren of the Church of the first-born, and the intelligence from distant worlds which the seraphim may communicate on returning from their embassies of love to other regions, may form a part of those beneficent services, into which every inhabitant of that world will engage with peculiar pleasure. To communicate happiness in every possible mode, to make surrounding associates exult with joy, and to stimulate them to celebrate the praises of the "Giver of all good," will be their unceasing desire and their everlasting delight.

We have every reason to believe, that a vast system of universal Benevolence is going on throughout the universe of God, and that it is the grand object of his moral government, to distribute happiness among unnumbered worlds.[1] In prosecuting this object, he employs created intelligences as his ministers in accomplishing his designs, and for communicating enjoyment to each other. With respect to the angels, we are informed by Paul, that " they are all *ministering spirits*, sent forth to minister to them who shall be heirs of salvation." Hence we learn, from sacred history, that they delivered Peter from the fury of Herod and the Jewish rulers, Daniel from the ravenous lions, Lot from the destruction of Sodom, and Jacob from the hands of Esau; that they strengthened and refreshed Elijah in the wilderness, comforted Daniel when covered in sackcloth and ashes, directed Joseph and Mary in their journey to Egypt, and Cornelius to Peter, to receive the knowledge of salvation; that they communicated " good tidings of great joy," to Zacharias, the father of John the Baptist, to the Virgin Mary, and to the shepherds in the plains of Bethlehem, and consoled the hearts of the disconsolate disciples by proclaiming the resurrection of their Lord and Master: and we have reason to conclude, that such ministrations are appointed to be continued throughout all the periods of time.

It is not improbable, that the spirits of just men made perfect are likewise occasionally employed in similar services. When the vision of the New Jerusalem was exhibited to John by a celestial messenger, he " fell down to worship before the feet of the messenger who showed him these things." But the messenger forbade him, saying, " See thou do it not; for *I am thy fellow-servant, and of thy brethren the prophets*, and of them that keep (or are interested in) the sayings of this book." These words would naturally lead us to conclude, that this messenger was a departed saint, since he designates himself a *brother*, a *prophet*, and a *fellow-servant*. Perhaps it was the spirit of Moses, of David, of Isaiah, of Jeremiah, or of Daniel, who would account it an honour to be employed in such a service by their exalted Lord. But whether or not such a supposition may be admitted, certain it is that the saints will hereafter be employed in active beneficent services, in concert with other holy beings, so long as their existence endures. For

[1] See part I, pages 63–65.

they are constituted "Kings and Priests to the God and Father of our Lord Jesus Christ," and are "workers together with God," in carrying forward the plans of his government.

Since, then, it appears, that the inhabitants of heaven are incessantly employed in acts of beneficence, the habit of beneficence which is acquired in this world, along with its accompanying virtues, may be considered as a preparation and a qualification for that more extensive sphere of moral action into which the saints shall be introduced, when they wing their way from this earthly ball to the regions above. And consequently, those who never engage in "works of faith and labours of love," and who are governed by a principle of *selfishness* in the general tenor of their conduct, must be considered as unqualified for taking a part in the benevolent employments of the celestial world.[1]

Let us now consider for a little, the happiness which must flow from an association with intelligent beings, animated with the sublime principles and holy dispositions to which I have now adverted.

In the present world, one of the principal sources of misery arises from the malevolent dispositions, and immoral conduct, of its inhabitants. Pride, ambition, malignant passions, falsehood, deceit, envy, and revenge, which exercise a sovereign sway over the hearts of the majority of mankind, have produced more misery and devastation among the human race than the hurricane and the tempest, the earthquake and the volcano, and all the other concussions of the elements of nature. The lust of *ambition* has covered kingdoms with sackcloth and ashes, levelled cities with the ground, turned villages into heaps of smoking ruins, transformed fertile fields into a wilderness, polluted the earth with human gore, slaughtered thousands and millions of human beings, and filled the once

---

[1] This subject might have been illustrated at greater length; but as the Author has already had occasion to enter into a minute discussion of the principles of moral action, and their relation to the inhabitants of all worlds, in his Work on "The Philosophy of Religion," he refers his readers to that treatise, for a more ample elucidation of the several topics to which he has briefly adverted in the preceding pages, particularly to Chap. I, throughout Chap. II, Sects. 3, 4, 5, 6, 8. and the *General Conclusions* at the end.

cheerful abodes of domestic life with the sounds of weeping, lamentation, and woe. *Injustice* and violence have robbed society of its rights and privileges, and the widow and fatherless of their dearest enjoyments. Superstition and revenge have immolated their millions of victims, banished peace from the world and subverted the order of society. The violation of truth in contracts, affirmations, and promises, has involved nations in destruction, undermined the foundations of public prosperity, blasted the good name and the comfort of families, perplexed and agitated the minds of thousands and millions, and thrown contempt on the revelations of heaven, and the discoveries of science. Malice, envy, hatred, and similar affections, have stirred up strifes and contentions, which have invaded the peace of individuals, families, and societies, and embittered all their enjoyments. It is scarcely too much to affirm, that more than nine-tenths of all the evils, perplexities, and sorrows, which are the lot of suffering humanity, are owing to the wide and extensive operation of such diabolical principles and passions.

What a happiness, then, must it be, to mingle in a society where such malignant affections shall never more shed their baleful influence, and where love, peace, and harmony, mutual esteem, brotherly kindness and charity, are for ever triumphant! To depart from a world where selfishness and malignity, strife and dissensions, wars and devastations, so generally prevail, and to enter upon a scene of enjoyment where the smiles of benevolence beam from the countenances of unnumbered glorious intelligences, must raise in the soul the most ecstatic rapture, and be the groundwork of all those other "pleasures which are at God's right hand for evermore." Even in this world, amidst the physical evils which now exist, what a scene of felicity would be produced, were all the illustrious philanthropic characters now living, or which have adorned our race in the ages that are past, to be collected into one society, and to associate exclusively, without annoyance from "the world that lieth in wickedness!" Let us suppose a vast society composed of such characters as Moses, Elijah, Jeremiah, Daniel, Paul, James, and John, the Evangelists, men who accounted it their highest honour to glorify God and to promote the salvation of mankind; such philanthropists as **Howard, Clarkson, Venning,** and **Sharpe,** who displayed the most benignant affections, and spent their mortal existence in unwearied efforts to meliorate the condition of the prisoner, and relieve the distresses of the wretched, in every land, to deliver the captive from his oppressors, to loose the shackles of slavery, to pour light and vital air into the noisome dungeon, and to diffuse blessings among mankind where ever they were found; such profound philosophers as Locke, Newton, and Boyle, whose capacious intellects seemed to embrace the worlds both of matter and of mind, and who joined to their mental accomplishments, modesty, humility, equanimity of temper, and general benevolence; such amiable divines as Watts, Doddridge, Bates, Harvey, Edwards, Lardner, and Dwight, whose hearts burned with zeal to promote the glory of their Divine Master, and to advance the present and everlasting interest of their fellow-men. To associate perpetually with such characters, even with the imperfections and infirmities which cleaved to them in this sublunary region, would form something approaching to a paradise on earth.

But, let us suppose such characters divested of every moral and mental imperfection, endowed with every holy principle and virtue that can adorn a created intelligence, and with capacious intellectual powers in vigorous and incessant exercise, dwelling in a world where every natural evil is removed, where scenes of glory meet the eye at every step, and where boundless prospects stretch before the view of the enraptured mind. Let us further suppose intelligences invested with faculties far more energetic and sublime, who have ranged through the immensity of creation, who have mingled with the inhabitants of ten thousand worlds, who have learned the history of the Divine dispensations in relation to them all, and who are inspired with every amiable and benignant feeling, and with humility, love, and condescension; let us suppose ambassadors of this description, from numerous worlds, occasionally joining this celestial society, and "rehearsing the mighty acts of Jehovah," as displayed in the regions from whence they came; let us suppose "the man Christ Jesus" president among them, in the effulgence of his glory, and unfolding his peerless excellence to every eye: let us suppose these glorious beings engaged in conversations, contemplations, investigations, thanksgivings, adorations, and beneficent services, corresponding to the magnificence of the region in which they reside, and to the dignity of their natures, and we have a faint picture of the social enjoyments of the celestial world. This is the society of heaven, the general assembly of the Church triumphant, for which **we must now be** inspired with a divine relish, and for which we **must** now be prepared in the temper and disposition of our minds, if we expect to be hereafter admitted into that "house, **not** made with hands, which is eternal in the heavens."

O blessed and glorious society! where no contentions ever arise, where no malignant spirit interrupts **the universal** harmony, where no malevolent affection is ever displayed; where no provocation disturbs the serenity of the mind, where not one revengeful thought arises against the most depraved inhabitant of the universe; where **a** single falsehood is never uttered, where folly, impertinence, and error, never intrude; where no frown sits louring on the countenance, and no cloud ever intercepts the sunshine of benevolence; where "Holiness to the Lord" is inscribed on every heart, where every member is knit to another by the indissoluble bonds of affection and esteem; **where a** friendship is commenced which shall never be dissolved, where love glows in every bosom, and benignity beams from every countenance; where moral excellence is displayed in its most sublime, and diversified, and transporting forms; where "a multitude, which no man can number from all nations, and kindreds, and peoples, and tongues," join in unison with angels and archangels, principalities and powers, in swelling the song of salvation to Him that sits upon the throne, and to the Lamb that was slain, for ever and ever! Ye glorious hosts of heaven who minister to the heirs of salvation on earth! **ye** redeemed inhabitants from our world, "who came out of great tribulation, and are now before the throne of God, and serve him day and night in his temple!" we long to join your blessed society. You dwell amidst scenes of magnificence and the splendours of eternal day; you are for ever secure from sin and sorrow, and every evil annoyance; your joys are uninterrupted, ever increasing, and ever new; your prospects are boundless as the universe, and your duration permanent as the throne of the Eternal! We dwell "in houses of clay, whose foundation is in the dust;" we sojourn in "a land of pits and snares," and within "the region of the shaddow of Death;" we walk amidst scenes of sorrow and suffering, surrounded by "the tents of strife," and exposed to the malice of "lying lips and deceitful tongues!" From our earthly prison, to which we are now chained as prisoners of hope, we lift up our eyes to your happy mansions with longing desires, and exclaim, "O that we had the wings of a Seraph, that we might fly away to your blissful seats and be at rest!" We long to join "the general assembly and Church of the firstborn, which are written in heaven, the spirits of just men made perfect, the innumerable company of angels, Jesus the Mediator of the New Covenant, and God the Judge of all."

May the Father of all mercies, who hath begotten us to the lively hope of an incorruptible inheritance, grant that we may persevere in the Christian course, be kept from falling, be "guarded by his Almighty Power, through faith unto salvation," and that in due time "an entrance may be abundantly administered to us into the everlasting kingdom of our Lord and Saviour Jesus Christ." To whom be glory for ever and ever. Amen.

From the subject to which our attention has now been directed, we may learn what will constitute one bitter ingredient in the punishment which awaits the wicked in the future world. As the principle of love which pervades the minds of the inhabitants of heaven, with the diversified ramifications into which it diverges, forms the ground-work of all the other enjoyments of the celestial world; so the principle of malignity which predominates in the hearts of the wicked, will be the source of the greater part of that misery they are doomed to suffer in the eternal state. "We cannot form a more dreadful picture of future punishment, than by conceiving the principles of falsehood, deceit, and malignity, and the passions of pride, hatred, malice, and revenge, raging with uncontrolled and perpetual violence. **We** need represent to ourselves nothing more horrible in the place of punishment, than by supposing **the** Almighty simply permitting wicked men to give full scope to their malevolent dispositions; leaving them 'to eat the fruit of their own ways, and to be filled with their own devices.' The effects produced by **the** uncontrolled operation of such principles and passions, would be such as may be fitly represented by the emblems **of** the worm that never dies, of 'devouring fire,' and of their necessary concomitants, 'weeping and wailing, and gnashing of teeth.'"[1]

In order to illustrate this sentiment, **and to** impress it more deeply upon the mind of the reader, I shall select **two or** three facts in relation to certain characters whose names **stand conspicuous** in the annals of history.

Every reader of history is acquainted with the character and actions of *Antiochus Epiphanes*, whose name stands so high on the rolls of impiety and crime. Having besieged the city of Jerusalem, he took it by storm, and, during the three days it was abandoned **to** the fury of the soldiers, he caused forty thousand [2] **men to** be inhumanly butchered; he exercised every species of cruelty upon the citizens, and unmercifully put to death all those who fell into his hands, and whom he considered **as** his enemies. He despatched Appollonius at the head of 22,000 men, with orders to plunder *all the cities of Judea* to murder **all** the men, and sell the **women** and children for slaves. He accordingly came with his **army, and, to** outward appearance, with a peaceable intention; neither was he suspected by the Jews, as he was superintendent of the tribute in Palestine. He kept himself inactive till the next Sabbath, when they were all in a profound quiet, and then, on a sudden, began the work of slaughter. He sent a portion of his men to the temples and synagogues, with orders to cut to **pieces** all who were found in these places of resort; whilst the rest, going through the streets of the city, massacred **all** who came in their way. He next ordered the city to **be** plundered and set on fire, pulled down all their stately buildings, **and** carried away

---

[1] Philosophy of Religion, at the **end.** [2] Rollin states the number at 80,000.

captive ten thousand of those who had escaped the slaughter. Not yet satisfied with the blood of the **Jews**, Antiochus resolved, either totally to abolish their religion, or to destroy their whole race. He issued a decree that all nations within his dominions should forsake their old religion and gods, and worship those of the king, under the most severe penalties. He dedicated the temple at Jerusalem to Jupiter Olympus, and set up his own statue on the altar of burnt-offering; and all who refused to come and worship this idol were either massacred or put to some cruel tortures, till they either complied or expired under the hands of the executioners. He put to death Eleazar, one of the most illustrious of the Jews, a venerable old man, ninety years of age, and a doctor of the law, " whose life had been one continued series of spotless innocence," and his execution was accompanied with the most cruel torments. He seized the *seven brothers*, commonly called the *Maccabees*, along with their mother, and caused them to be scourged in a most inhuman manner, in order to compel them to swallow swine's flesh, which their law forbade, and, when they refused, he was so exasperated that he ordered brazen pans and cauldrons to be heated; and, when they were red, he caused the tongue of the eldest to be cut off, had the skin torn from his head, and the extremity of his hands and feet cut off, before his mother and his brethren. After being mutilated, he was brought close to the fire, and fried in the pan. The second brother was then taken, and after the hair of his head with the skin was torn away, he was tortured in the same manner as his elder brother; and in like manner were the other five brethren put to death; the last of whom, who was the youngest, he caused to be tortured more grievously than the rest. Last of all, the mother also suffered death.[1]

Hearing, some time afterwards, that the Jews had revolted, he assembled all his troops, which formed a mighty army, and determined to destroy the whole Jewish nation, and to settle other people in their country. He commanded Lysias, one of his generals, to extirpate them root and branch, so as not to

---

[1] The details of these shocking cruelties may be seen in Rollin's Ancient History, vol. vii.

leave one Hebrew in the country. When in Persia, advice was brought him of the defeat of Lysias, and that the Jews had retaken the temple, thrown down the altars and idols which he had set up, and re-established their ancient worship. At this news his fury rose to madness. In the violence of his rage, he set out with **all possible expedition, like** an infernal fiend, breathing nothing but menaces on his march, and venting only final ruin and destruction to every inhabitant of Judea, and to all that appertained to them. He commanded his coachman **to drive with the** utmost speed, that no **time** might **be** lost for **fully** satiating his vengeance, threatening, at **the** same time, with horrid imprecations, to make Jerusalem the **burying** place of the whole Jewish nation, and not to leave one single **inhabi**tant within its confines. But the Almighty, against **whose** providence he was raging, interposed, and stopped him in his wild career. "He was seized," says Rollin, "with incredible pains in his bowels, and the most excessive pangs of the cholic." Still, his pride and fury **were not** abated: he suffered himself to be hurried away **by** the wild transport of his rage, and breathing nothing but vengeance against the land of Judea and its inabitants, he gave orders to proceed with still greater celerity in his journey. But, as his horses were running forward impetuously, he fell from his chariot, and bruised every part of his body in so dreadful a manner, that he suffered inexpressible torments; and soon after finished **an** impious life by a miserable death.

The Turks, in their wars with neighbouring States, both in **former and** present times, have been proverbial for the male**volence** they have displayed, and the cruelties they have exercised towards their enemies. The following is only one instance out **of a** thousand, which might be produced, of the desperate length to **which** human beings will proceed in treachery, and in the infliction of torment, when under the influence of a principle of malignity.

In the war with Turkey **and** the States of Venice, about the **year 1571,** the Venetians were besieged by the Turks in the city **of** Famagosta in **the** island of Cyprus. Through famine and want of ammunition, the Venetian garrison was compelled to enter upon terms of capitulation. A treaty was accordingly set on foot, and hostages exchanged. The following terms were agreed to by both parties: That the officers and soldiers should march out with all the honours of war, drums beating, colours flying, five pieces of cannon, all their baggage, and be conveyed in safety to Candia, under an escort of three Turkish galleys; and that the inhabitants should remain in the free use of their religion, untouched in their property, and in full possession of their freedom. Next day, Bragadino, the Venetian commander, went to pay his compliments to Mustapha, the Turkish general, attended by some of his chief officers. At first they met with a civil reception, Mustapha ordering a seat to be placed for Bragadino on his own right hand. They soon entered into discourse about the prisoners, and Mustapha taxing Bragadino with some violences committed by the garrison during the suspension granted for settling a capitulation, Bragadino, with a generous disdain, denied the charge. Upon which Mustapha, rising up in a fury, ordered him to be bound hand and foot, and the others to be massacred before his face, without regard to hospitality, their bravery, the treaty subsisting, or their being unarmed.

Bragadino was reserved for a more cruel treatment: after being insulted with the most vilifying and opprobrious language, after undergoing the most excruciating tortures, after having his ears, nose, and lips slit, his neck was stretched upon a block, and trampled upon by the dastardly Mustapha, who asked him, where was now that *Christ* whom he worshipped, and why he did not deliver him out of his hands? At the same time, the soldiers on board the fleet were despoiled of every thing, and lashed to the oars. This day's work being finished, Mustapha entered the city, where he gave immediate orders that Tiepolo, a person of high rank and authority, should be hanged upon a gibbet. A few days after, before Bragadino had recovered from the wounds he had received, he was carried in derision to all the breaches made in the walls, loaded with buckets filled with earth and mortar, and ordered to kiss the ground as often as he passed by Mustapha; a spectacle that raised pangs of pity in the callous hearts of the meanest Turkish soldiers, but could not raise compassion in the obdurate breast of Mustapha. Afterwards, the brave Bragadino was cooped up in a cage, and ignominiously hung to a sail-yard in one of the galleys, where his intrepid soldiers were chained to the oars. This sight rendered them almost furious: they exclaimed against the baseness, the treachery of Mustapha; they called aloud for revenge, and desired to be set at liberty, that they might, even without arms, rescue their brave general, and inflict the deserved punishment upon their mean, dastardly, and cowardly foes. Their request was answered with cruel lashes; Bragadino was taken down, conducted to the market-place, amidst the din of trumpets, drums, and other war-like instruments, where *he was flayed alive*, and a period put to his glorious life. His skin was hung, by way of trophy, to the sail-yard of a galley sent round all the coasts to insult the Venetians. His head, with that of Andrea Bragadino, his brother, Lodovico Martinenga, and the brave Quirino, were sent as presents to Selim, the Turkish emperor.[1]

Could an infernal fiend have devised more excruciating tortures, or have acted with greater baseness and malignity, than this treacherous and cruel monster? What a horrible thing would it be to be subjected to the caprice, and under the control, of such a proud and vindictive spirit every day, only for a year, much more for hundreds and thousands of years! A group of such spirits, giving vent to their malevolent passions without control, are sufficient to produce a degree of misery among surrounding intelligences, surpassing every thing that the human mind, in the present state, can possibly conceive.

When the Norman barons and chevaliers, under William the Conqueror, had obtained possession of England, they displayed the most cruel and malignant dispositions towards the native inhabitants. They afflicted and harassed them in every shape, forcing them to work at the building of their castles; and when the castles were finished, they placed on them a garrison of wicked and diabolical men. They seized all whom they thought to possess any thing, men **and** women, by day and night; they carried them off; imprisoned them; and, to obtain from them gold or silver, inflicted on them tortures such as no martyrs ever underwent. Some they suspended by their feet, with **their** heads hang-

---

[1] See " Modern Universal History," vol. **xxvii**, pp. 405, 406.

ing in smoke; others were hung by the thumb, with fire under their feet. They pressed the heads of some by a leathern thong, so as to break the bones, and crush the brain; others were thrown into ditches full of snakes, toads, and other reptiles; others were put in the *chambre a crucit.* This was the name given in the Norman tongue to a sort of chest, short, strait, and shallow, lined with sharp stones, into which the sufferer was crammed to the dislocation of his limbs. In most of the castles was a horrible and frightful engine used for putting to the torture. This was a bundle of chains, so heavy that two or three men could hardly lift them. The unfortunate person upon whom they were laid, was kept on his feet by an iron collar fixed to a post, and could neither sit nor lie, nor sleep. They made many thousands die of hunger. They laid tribute upon tribute in the towns and villages. When the towns-people had no longer any thing to give, they plundered and burned the town. You might have travelled a whole day without finding one soul in the towns, or in the country one cultivated field. The poor died of hunger, and they who had formerly possessed something, now begged their bread from door to door. Never were more griefs and woes poured upon any land: nay, the Pagans in their invasions caused fewer than the men of whom I now speak. They spared neither the churchyards nor the churches; they took all that could be taken, and then set fire to the church. To till the ground had been as vain as to till the ground on the sea-shore.[1]

What scenes of wretchedness do such proud and malignant demons produce even in the present world! Can such spirits be supposed qualified for joining the general assembly of the Church of the first-born, and for taking a part in the beneficent operations of heaven? If they exist at all in a future world, they must exist in misery; and so long as such diabolical passions continue to rage, they must produce "lamentation and woe" among all the associates with which they are surrounded. Even within the confines of mortality, the man who is under the despotic sway of pride, ambition, and similar malevolent passions embitters every enjoyment he might

[1] Thierry's "History of the Norman Conquest," 3 vols. 1825.

otherwise possess, produces pain in the minds of others, and experiences in his own soul pangs similar in kind to those which are felt in the place of punishment. I shall illustrate this position by the spirit and temper displayed by two illustrious individuals; the one renowned in the political, the other in the literary world.

The first character to which I allude is that of *Napoleon Buonaparte*. This extraordinary man, who, for nearly twenty years, dazzled the whole eastern hemisphere, like a blazing meteor, appears to have been actuated by the most extravagant and restless *ambition*. Though he exercised many cruelties in the midst of his career, as at Jaffa and other places, yet delight in deeds of atrocity formed no part of his ruling passion, and were only occasionally resorted to, in order to accomplish his ambitious projects. The agitated state of mind into which he was thrown by his love of conquest, and the daring enterprises in which he embarked, is strikingly depicted by M. Segur, in his "History of Napoleon's Expedition to Russia." When at Vitepsk, on his way to Moscow, M. Segur says: "He at first hardly appeared bold enough to confess to himself a project of such great temerity as the marching against Moscow. But, by degrees, he assumed courage to look it in the face. He then began to deliberate, and the state of great irresolution which tormented his mind affected his whole frame. He was observed to wander about his apartments, as if pursued by some dangerous temptation: nothing could rivet his attention; he every moment began, quitted, and resumed his labour; he walked about without any object; enquired the hour, and looked at his watch: completely absorbed, he stopped, hummed a tune with an absent air, and again began walking about. In the midst of his perplexity, he occasionally addressed the persons whom he met with such half sentences as, "Well! What shall we do? Shall we stay where we are, or advance? How is it possible to stop short in the midst of so glorious a career!" He did not wait for their reply, but still kept wandering about, as if he was looking for something, or somebody, to terminate his indecision. At length, quite overwhelmed with the weight of such an important consideration, and oppressed with so great an uncertainty, he would throw himself on one of the beds which he had caused to be laid on the floor of his apartments. His frame, exhausted by the heat and the struggles of his mind, could only bear a covering of the slightest texture. It was in that state that he passed a portion of the day at Vitepsk."

The same restless agitations seemed to have accompanied him at every step in this daring expedition. "At Borodino," says the same writer, "his anxiety was so great as to prevent him from sleeping. He kept calling incessantly to know the hour, inquiring if any noise was heard, and sending persons to ascertain if the enemy was still before him. Tranquillized for a few moments, anxiety of an opposite description again seized him. He became frightened at the destitute state of the soldiers, etc. He sent for Bessieres, that one of his marshals in whom he had the greatest confidence: he called him back several times, and repeated his pressing questions, etc. Dreading that his orders had not been obeyed, he got up once more, and questioned the grenadiers on guard at the entrance of his tent, if they had received their provisions. Satisfied with the answer, he went in, and soon fell into a doze. Shortly after he called once more. His aide-de-camp found him now supporting his head with both his hands; he seemed by what was overheard, to be meditating on the *vanities of glory:* '*What is war? A trade of barbarians, the whole art of which consists in being the strongest on a given point.*' He then complained of the fickleness of fortune, which he now began to experience. He again tried to take some rest. But the marches he had just made with the army, the fatigues of the preceding days and nights, so many cares, and his intense and anxious expectations, had worn him out. An irritating fever, a dry cough, and excessive thirst, consumed him. During the remainder of the night, he made vain attempts to quench the burning thirst that consumed him."

What man, that ever enjoyed the pleasures of tranquillity, would envy such a state of mind as that which has now been described, although the individual were surrounded with every earthly glory? Such mad ambition as that which raged in the breast of this singular personage, must be a perpetual torment to its possessor, in whatever region of the universe he exists, and must produce baleful effects on every one within the sphere of its influence. The coolness with which such characters calculate on the destruction of human life, and the miseries which their lawless passions produce on their fellow-creatures, appear in the following extract:

"He asked Rapp, if he thought we should gain the victory. 'No doubt,' was the reply, 'but it will be sanguinary.' 'I know it,' resumed Napoleon, 'but I have 80,000 men; I shall lose 20,000; I shall enter Moscow with 60,000; the stragglers will then rejoin us, and afterwards the battalions on the march; and we shall be stronger than we were before the battle.'"

The other personage to whom I alluded is Lord Byron. The following sketches of his character are taken from "Recollections of the life of Lord Byron, from the year 1808, to the year 1818. Taken from authentic documents," etc. by R. C. Dallas, Esq.

"He reduced his palate," says Mr. Dallas, "to a diet the most simple and abstemious, but the passions of his heart were too mighty; nor did it ever enter his mind to overcome *them*. Resentment, anger, and hatred, held full sway over him; and his greatest gratification at that time, was in overcharging his pen with gall, which flowed in every direction, against individuals, his country, the world, the universe, creation, and the Creator. Misanthropy, disgust of life, leading to scepticism and impiety, prevailed in his heart and embittered his existence. Unaccustomed to female society, he at once dreaded and abhorred it. As for domestic happiness he had no idea of it. 'A large family,' he said, 'appeared like opposite ingredients, mixed *per* force in the same salad, and I never relished the composition.' He was so completely disgusted with his relations, especially the female part of them, that he completely avoided them. 'I consider,' said he, 'collateral ties as the work of prejudice, and not the bond of the heart, which must choose for itself, unshackled.' In correspondence with such dispositions and sentiments, he talked of his relation, the Earl of Carlisle, with indignation. Having received from him a frigid letter, he 'determined to lash his relation with all the gall he could throw into satire.' He declaimed against the ties of consanguinity, and abjured even the society of his sister, from which he entirely withdrew himself, until after the publication of 'Childe Harold,' when at length he yielded to my persuasions, and made advances to a friendly correspondence."

Here we have a picture of an individual, in whom "resentment, anger, and hatred," reigned without control; who could vent his rage even against the Creator, and the universe he had formed; who hated his fellow-creatures, and even his own existence; who spurned at the ties of relationship, and "abjured even the society of his sister." What horrible mischiefs and miseries would a character of this description produce, were such malevolent passions to rage with unbounded violence, without being checked by those restraints which human laws impose in the present state!

I shall state only another example of this description, taken from Captain Cochrane's "Travels in Russia." "On arriving at the Prussian frontiers," says the captain, "My passport demanded, myself interrogated by a set of whiskered ruffians, obliged to move from one guard to another, the object of sarcasm and official tyranny, I wanted no inducement, fatigued as I was, to proceed on my journey, but even this was not permitted me. A large public room, full of military rubbish, and two long benches serving as chairs to an equally long table, were the place and furniture allotted me. I asked the landlord for supper, he laughed at me; and to my demand of a bed, *grinningly* pointed to the floor, and refused me even a portion of the straw which he had brought in for the soldiers. Of all the demons that ever existed, or have been imagined in human shape, I thought the landlord of the inn the blackest. The figure of Gil Peres occurred to me; but it sunk in the comparison with the wretch then before me, for ill nature, malignity, and personal hideousness. His face half covered with a black beard and large bristly whiskers, his stature below the common, his head sunk between the shoulders to make room for the protuberance of his back, his eyes buried in the ragged locks of his lank grisly hair; add to this a club foot, and a voice which, on every attempt to speak, was like the shrieking of a screechowl, and you have some faint idea of this mockery of a man." Here we have presented to view a human being, who, in the malignity of his mind, and in the conformation of his body, bears a certain resemblance to those wretched beings in whose breast benevolence never glows, and in whose dwellings nothing is seen but the most haggard and deformed objects, and nothing heard but horrid imprecations, and the sounds of woe.

Let us now suppose, for a moment, a vast assemblage of beings, of the description to which I have adverted, collected in a dark and dreary region. Let us suppose many thousands of millions of such characters as *Nero*, who set fire to Rome, that he might amuse himself with the wailings and lamentations which this calamity inspired, and insulted heaven by offering thanksgivings to the gods, after murdering his wife and his mother: *Tiberius*, who delighted in torturing his subjects, and massacring them in the most tormenting and cruel manner: *Caligula*, celebrated in the annals of folly, cruelty, and impiety, who murdered many of his subjects with his own hand, and caused thousands who were guilty of no crimes to be cruelly butchered: *Antiochus Epiphanes*, who butchered forty thousands of the inhabitants of Jerusalem in cold blood, and rushed forward, like an infernal demon, with the intention of destroying every inhabitant of Judea: *Hamilcar*, who threw all the prisoners that came into his hand to be devoured by wild beasts: *Asdrubal*, who put out the eyes of all the Roman captives he had taken during two years, cut off their noses, fingers, legs, and arms, tore their skin to pieces with iron rakes and harrows, and threw them headlong from the top of his battlements: *Jenghiz Khan*, who caused seventy chiefs to be thrown into as many cauldrons of boiling water, and took pleasure in beholding his army beheading a hundred thousand prisoners at once: *Tamerlane*, who displayed his sportive cruelty in pounding three or four thousand people in large mortars, or building them among bricks and mortar into a wall: *Mustapha*, who treacherously murdered the Venetian officers, after having entered into a treaty with them, and who beheld with delight the noble-minded Bragadino, whom he had cruelly tortured, flayed alive: *Buonaparte*, whose mad ambition sacrificed so many millions of human beings: and *Lord Byron*,[1] in

---

The Author trusts, that none of his readers will for a moment sup-

whose breast "resentment, anger, and hatred," raged with violence, and who made his gall flow out "against individuals, his country, the world, the universe, creation, and the Creator:" let us suppose such characters associated together, in a world where no pleasing objects meet the eye, or cheer the heart and imagination; and let us likewise suppose, that the malignant principles and boisterous passions which reigned in their minds during the present state, still continue to rage with uncontrolled and perpetual violence against all surrounding associates: it is evident, that, in such a case, a scene of misery would be produced, beyond the power of the human mind either to conceive or to describe. If so dreadful effects have been produced by such diabolical passions even in the present world, where Providence "sets restraining bounds to the wrath of man," and where benignant dispositions are blended with the evil principles which so generally prevail, what must be the effects where *pure malignity*, without any mixture of benevolent feelings, reigns *universally*, is perpetually tormenting its objects, is ever increasing in its fury, and is never controlled by physical obstructions or by moral considerations! This is the society of hell; this is the essence of future misery; this is "the worm that never dies, and the fire that is never quenched;" and the natural effects produced by it are universal anguish and despair, "weeping, and wailing, and gnashing of teeth." If such be the end of the ungodly, and the malignant despisers of God's law, and the riches of his mercy as manifested in Christ Jesus, how careful should we be to counteract every evil propensity and passion, and how fervently ought we to join in the prayer of the Psalmist, and in the resolution of Jacob: "Gather not my soul with sinners, nor my life with bloody men." "O, my soul, come not thou into their secret; unto their assembly, mine honour, be not thou united!"

pose, that in bringing forward the above-mentioned characters as examples of malignity, he presumes to decide on their eternal destiny. His object merely is to show, that such malignant principles and passions as they displayed in the general tenor of their conduct, *if resolutely persisted in*, necessarily lead to misery. With regard to Napoleon and Lord Byron, he is disposed to indulge a hope, that their malevolent dispositions were in some measure counteracted, before they passed into the eternal world. The grounds of his hope, on this point, are stated in the Appendix.

Let none imagine, because I have selected some of the more atrocious characters recorded in history, as illustrations of the effects of depravity, that only such are " vessels of wrath, fitted for destruction. The principle of malevolence is substantially the same in every heart where it is predominant, however much it may be varnished over by hypocrisy, dissimulation, and the various forms of politeness which prevail in the world; and it requires only a certain stimulus to excite it to action, and full scope to exert its energies, in order to produce the most horrible and extensive effects. Several of the atrocious characters to which I have alluded, appeared, in the commencement of their career, to be possessed of a certain portion of benevolence, and of other amiable qualities. Nero, in the beginning of his reign, showed several marks of the greatest kindness and condescension, affability, complaisance, and popularity. When he was desired to sign his name to a list of malefactors that were to be executed, he exclaimed, " *Would to Heaven I could not write!*" Caligula began his reign with every promising appearance of becoming the real father of his people. Tiberius at first concealed his thoughts under the mask of an impenetrable dissimulation. He governed with moderation, and even appeared to excel in modesty. But afterwards, when these individuals became intoxicated with power, and had thrown aside all considerations of morality and decorum, the latent principles of malignity burst forth in all their violence, till they became a scourge and an execration to mankind. So it will happen with those who now harbour malicious and vindictive passions, under a cloak of dissimulation and fashionable politeness, when they enter the invisible world under the dominion of such affections. When the restraints of society, of common decorum, and of human laws, are completely removed; when they have lost all hopes of the Divine mercy; when they find themselves surrounded by none but malignant associates, and when they feel the effects of their infernal malice and revenge; those passions which sometimes lay dormant in this life, will be roused into action, and rage with ungovernable fury against every one around, against themselves, "against the universe, and against the Creator."

Nor let it be imagined, that God will interpose at the hour

of death, and, by an exertion of his power and benevolence, destroy the principles of sin, and prepare such characters for the joys of heaven. Such an interference, in every individual case, would imply a continued miracle, and would be inconsistent with the established order of the Divine government; as it would supersede the use of all those instructions, admonitions, and moral preparations, which God hath appointed for rendering his people "*meet* for the inheritance of the saints in light;" and would prevent the moral renovation of the world, which is now gradually effecting by the exertions of those who are "renewed in the spirit of their minds." It is true, indeed, that the mercy of God is infinite, and that so long as there is life there is hope; so that the most abandoned sinner has no reason to despair, while he remains within the confines of the present state. But as for those who pass from time into eternity, evidently under the power of revengeful and depraved passions, we have but slender grounds on which to hope that they shall ever afterwards be prepared for the felicity of heaven.

From the whole of what I have stated in this department of my subject, it is evident that there are *two different states* in the future world; or, in other words, *a heaven* and *a hell;* a state of happiness, and a state of misery. If human beings are to exist at all in another region of creation, and throughout an unlimited duration, it is necessary that there be a separation effected, on the ground of their leading dispositions and characters. The nature of things, the moral constitution of the universe, and the happiness of the intelligent creation, as well as the decree of the Creator, require that such an arrangement should take place. For it is altogether incompatible with the laws of moral order, that pride, hatred, malignity, and revenge, should dwell in the same abode with humility, benevolence, friendship, and love; or that beings, actuated by principles and affections, diametrically opposite to each other, could engage with harmony in the same employments, and relish the same pleasures. Were such an incongruous asssociation permitted, the moral universe would soon become a scene of universal anarchy, and happiness banished from all worlds. So that the two states of immortality revealed in Scripture, are equally accordant with the dictates of reason, and with the declaration of our Saviour, who has solemnly assured us, that "the wicked shall depart into everlasting punishment, and the righteous into life eternal."

APPENDIX.

THE following facts and documents in relation to Lord Byron, lead us to indulge the hope, that, prior, to his dissolution, he was actuated by sentiments and dispositions different from those which are stated at pages 290, 291.

The lady of Mr. John Sheppard of Frome having died some time ago, leaving amongst her papers a prayer, which her husband believed to have been composed on behalf of the noble Poet. Mr. Sheppard addressed it to his Lordship, which called forth the reply which is here subjoined.

Frome, Somerset, November 21*st*, 1821.

To the Right Honourable Lord Byron, Pisa.

MY LORD,—More than two years since, a lovely and beloved wife was taken from me by a lingering disease, after a very short union. She possessed unvarying gentleness and fortitude, and a piety so retiring, as rarely to disclose itself in words; but so influential, as to produce uniform benevolence of conduct. In the last hour of life, after a farewell look on a lately born and only infant, for whom she had evinced inexpressible affection, her last whispers were "God's happiness! God's happiness!" Since the second anniversary of her decease, I have read some papers which no one had seen during her life, and which contained her most secret thoughts. I am induced to communicate to your Lordship a passage from these papers, which, there is no doubt, refers to yourself; as I have more than once heard the writer mention your agility on the rocks at Hastings:

"O, my God! I take encouragement from the assurance of thy word, to pray to Thee in behalf of one for whom I have lately been much interested. May the person to whom I allude (and who is now, we fear, as much distinguished for his neglect of Thee, as for the transcendent talents Thou hast bestowed on him,) be awakened to a sense of his own danger, and led to seek that peace of mind, in a proper sense of religion, which he has found this world's enjoyments unable to procure. Do thou grant that his future example may be productive of far more extensive benefit, than his past conduct and writings have been of evil; and may the Sun of Righteousness, which, we trust, will, at some future period, arise upon him, be bright in proportion to the darkness of those clouds which guilt has raised, and soothing in proportion to the keenness of that agony which the punishment of his vices has inflicted on him! May the hope that the sincerity of my own efforts for the attainment of holiness, and the approval of my own love to the great Author of religion, will render this prayer, and every other for the welfare of mankind, more efficacious, and cheer me in the path of duty; but, let me not forget, that, while we are permitted to animate ourselves to exertion by every innocent motive, these are but the lesser streams which may serve to increase the current, but which, deprived of the grand Fountain of good, (a deep conviction of inborn sin, and firm belief in the efficacy of Christ's death, for the salvation of those who trust in him, and really seek to serve him,) would soon dry up, and leave us as barren of every virtue as before.

Hastings, July 31*st*, 1814."

There is nothing, my lord, in this extract, which, in a literary sense, can at all interest you; but it may, perhaps, appear to you worthy of reflection, how deep and expansive a concern for the happiness of others, a Christian faith can awaken in the midst of youth and prosperity. Here is nothing poetical and splendid, as in the expostulatory homage of M. Delamartine; but here is the *sublime,* my lord; for this intercession was offered on your account, to the supreme Source of happiness. It sprang from a faith more confirmed than that of the French poet, and from a charity, which, in combination with faith, showed its power unimpaired amidst the languors and pains of approaching dissolution. I will hope, that a prayer, which, I am sure, was deeply sincere, may not be always unavailing.

It would add nothing, my lord, to the fame with which your genius has surrounded you, for an unknown and obscure individual to express his admiration of it. I had rather be numbered with those who wish and pray, that "wisdom from above," and "peace," and "joy," may enter such a mind.

THE ANSWER.

Pisa, Dec. 8th, 1821.

Sir,—I have received your letter. I need not say that the extract which it contains has affected me, because it would imply a want of all feeling to have read it with indifference. Though I am not quite sure that it was intended by the writer for me, yet the date, the place where it was written, with some other circumstances, which you mention, render the allusion probable. But, for whomsoever it was meant, I have read it with all the pleasure which can arise from so melancholy a topic. I say *pleasure*, because your brief and simple picture of the life and demeanour of the excellent person, whom I trust that you will again meet, cannot be contemplated without the admiration due to her virtues, and her pure and unpretending piety. Her last moments were particularly striking; and I do not know that, in the course of reading the story of mankind, and still less in my observations upon the existing portion, I ever met with any thing so unostentatiously beautiful. Indisputably, the firm believers in the Gospel have a great advantage over all others: for this simple reason, that, if true, they will have their reward hereafter; and if there be no hereafter, they can be but with the infidel in his eternal sleep, having had the assistance of an exalted hope through life, without subsequent disappointment, since (at the worst of them) "out of nothing, nothing can arise," not even sorrow. But a man's creed does not depend upon *himself;* **who** can say, I *will* believe this, that, or the other; and, least of all, that which he least can comprehend? I have however observed, that those who have begun with extreme faith, have, in the end, greatly narrowed it, as Chillingworth, Clarke, (who ended as an Arian,) and some others; while, on the other hand, nothing is more common, than for the early sceptic to end in a firm belief, like Maupertius and Henry Kirke White. But my business is to acknowledge **your letter, and not to** make a dissertation. I **am** obliged to you **for your good** wishes, and more obliged by **the** extract from **the papers** of the beloved object whose qualities **you have so** well described **in a few** words. I can assure you, that **all the fame which ever cheated** humanity **into** higher **notions of its own** importance, would never weigh **on my** mind against the pure **and pious** interest **which a virtuous** being may be pleased to take **in my** welfare. **In this** point of view, I would not exchange the prayer of the deceased in my behalf, for the united glory of Homer, Cæsar, and Napoleon, could such be accumulated upon a living **head. Do** me the justice to suppose, that "video meliora proboque," however the "deteriora sequor" may have been applied to my conduct. I have the honour to be, your obliged and **obedient servant,**

BYRON.

P.S.—I do not know that I am addressing a clergyman; but I presume that you will not be affronted by the mistake (if it is one) on the address of this letter. One who has so well explained, and deeply felt, the doctrines of religion, will excuse the error which led me to believe him its minister.

This letter, every one will admit, exhibits Lord Byron in a much more amiable point of view than the traits of his character sketched by Mr. Dallas, prior to the year 1818. The following account of his death-bed sentiments is extracted from "Last Days of Lord Byron."

A very few days before his Lordship's death, Mr. Parry relates: " It was seven o'clock in the evening when I saw him, and then I took a chair at his request, and sat down by his bedside, and remained till ten o'clock. He sat up in his bed, and was then calm and collected. He talked with me on a variety of subjects, connected with himself and his family. He spake of death also with great composure, and though he did not believe his end was so very near, there was something about him so serious and so firm, so resigned and composed, so different from any thing I had ever before seen in him, that my mind misgave, and at times foreboded his speedy dissolution. 'Parry,' he said, when I first went to him, 'I have much wished to see you to-day. I have had most strange feelings, but my head is now better. I have no gloomy thoughts, and no idea but I shall recover. I am perfectly collected; I am sure I am in my senses; but a melancholy will creep over me at times.' The mention of the subject brought the melancholy topics back, and a few exclamations showed what occupied Lord Byron's mind when he was left in silence and solitude. 'My wife! my Ada! my country! the situation of this place, my removal impossible, and perhaps death, all combine to make me sad. I am convinced of the happiness of domestic life. No man on earth respects a virtuous woman more than I do; and the prospect of retirement in England, with my wife and Ada, gives me an idea of happiness I have never experienced before. Retirement will be every thing to me, for heretofore to me life has been like the ocean in a storm. You have no conception of the unaccountable thoughts which come into my mind when the fever attacks me. Eternity and space are before me, but on this subject, thank God, I am happy and at ease. The thought of living eternally, of again reviving, is a great pleasure. Christianity is the purest and most liberal religion in the world; but the numerous teachers who are continually worrying mankind with their denunciations and their doctrines, are the greatest enemies of religion. I have read with more attention than half of them the Book of Christianity, and I admire the liberal and truly charitable principles which Christ has laid down. There are questions connected with this subject which none but Almighty God can solve.

Time and space who can conceive? None but God; on him I rely.'"

Who knows but the prayer of the amiable young lady inserted above, was the mean of leading his lordship to indulge such sentiments, and of ultimately securing his eternal happiness! "The effectual fervent prayer of a righteous man availeth much." This consideration should not only excite us to offer up intercessions in behalf of particular individuals, but also to use every prudent and delicate mean, by conversation, epistolary correspondence, or otherwise, to rouse the attention of those, especially in the higher circles of life, who appear unconcerned about "the things that relate to their everlasting peace."

The following lines, written by Lord Byron, are said to have been found in his Bible:

> "Within this awful Volume lies
> The mystery of mysteries.
> Oh! happiest they of human race,
> To whom our God has given grace,
> To hear, to read, to watch, to pray,
> To lift the latch, and force the way;
> But better had they ne'er been born,
> Who read to doubt, or read to scorn."

With regard to *Buonaparte*, we have nothing so satisfactory as in the case of Byron, that might lead us to conclude that his moral and religious sentiments were changed for the better. In his solitude of St. Helena, however, it appears that the subject of religion occasionally occupied his attention. The following anecdote, extracted from La Casas' Journal, will show the opinion which he entertained of the morality of the New Testament:

In a conversation on the subject of religion, which he had with his friends at St. Helena, he said, among many other things, "'How is it possible that conviction can find its way to our hearts, when we hear the absurd language, and witness the acts of iniquity, of the greatest number of those whose business it is to preach to us? I am surrounded with priests who preach incessantly that their reign is not of this world, and yet they lay hands upon every thing they can get. The

Pope is the head of that religion from heaven, and he thinks only of this world,' etc. The Emperor ended the conversation by desiring my son to bring him the New Testament, and taking it from the beginning, he read as far as the conclusion of the speech of Jesus on the mountain. *He expressed himself struck with the highest admiration at the purity, the sublimity, the beauty of the morality it contained,* and we all experienced the same feeling."

www.ingramcontent.com/pod-product-compliance
Lightning Source LLC
Chambersburg PA
CBHW022117230426
43672CB00008B/1409